EDWARD THOMAS
THE LAST FOUR YEARS

EDWARD THOMAS 1913

EDWARD THOMAS

THE LAST FOUR YEARS

Book One of
The Memoirs of
Eleanor Farjeon

LONDON
OXFORD UNIVERSITY PRESS
1958

Oxford University Press, Amen House, London E.C.4

GLASGOW NEW YORK TORONTO MELBOURNE WELLINGTON
BOMBAY CALCUTTA MADRAS KARACHI KUALA LUMPUR
CAPE TOWN IBADAN NAIROBI ACCRA

Printed in Great Britain by Richard Clay and Company, Ltd.,
Bungay, Suffolk

48,688

A Preface to the
Memoir as a Whole

Tomorrow? Why, Tomorrow I may be
Myself with Yesterday's Seven Thousand Years
(*The Rubaiyat of Omar Khayyam*)

WHEN my Mother died in 1933 I wrote a memoir of our family
childhood against a background of the early lives of our
parents.[1] The record ended in 1903, the year of my Father's
death. I have often been asked if I would not go on with the
story, and always supposed that at some time or other I might
pick up the threads, but not immediately. Although the thirty
years between those two deaths held some of my deepest experiences, I was not ready to write about them. Now in my
old age I want to do so, before my own time comes to be with
Yesterday's Seven Thousand Years. Entry into Omar's rather
limited idea of the Past takes less than a split second, and his
few millions of Yesterdays may, in my eighth decade, lie
around any corner. I must harvest my last half-century while
I can.

As I look over its medley of crops, I see that to try to cram
them into one big basket is asking for trouble. If I attempted
a steadily consecutive journey from the nursery days onwards,
I would lose my direction among the highways and byways of
the spreading years, crowded with their variety of simultaneous
experience. Instead of writing one swollen heterogeneous book
I hope to write four, and pursue a mainroad of my life in each
of them.

This first book covers the years of my friendship with

[1] *A Nursery in the Nineties.*

Edward Thomas, from the end of 1912 to the spring of 1917.

The second, after stepping back to pick up the threads of our family story, will move forward to my professional years in the publishing and theatre worlds, and particularly to the collaborations with my brother Bertie. I see him as the central person of this book; it will end with his death in 1945, five days before V-Day.

The third, very personal, book will cover the years from 1920 to 1949, which enclose an unbroken experience. This, like the two others, and the Nursery book, ends with a death.

When the people in whom we are deepest rooted die, death seems to end a chapter in our lives. Given up to grief, we may feel this is the end of the book itself. Not till our own unimaginable death can the book be closed, and an astonishment undreamed of may be reserved for our own last chapter. The fourth book of my memoir will be this chapter, or will try to be. I may find it the most difficult to write; and I have a long road to go before I come to it. If I do not live to write it I shall carry it gratefully and with joy to the Life it has made me sure of.

For Helen

A Foreword

My friendship with Edward Thomas began in the late autumn of 1912. It was a friendship death could not end when, in April 1917, he died.

These years live for me, not only in my heart, but in the many letters Edward wrote to me during them, only a few of which have been published; they will appear in this book with Helen Thomas's loving consent. It is because of them that I have chosen to make Edward's the first book of my memoirs, beginning in midstream before going back to an earlier part of my life. Edward Thomas has his sure place now among our most English poets, and anything connected with him has an importance outside myself. The letters, printed in full without omissions, form a running record of his last four years. Their sequence has much more than a reference value; to lovers of his work it will help to reveal something more of one of the least self-revealing of men: a man whose 'central evil' was self-consciousness, 'carried as far beyond selfishness as selfishness is beyond self-denial'. He could write this of himself in 1913, only two years before the torturing self-consciousness was transformed into the poet's self-expression, and two years later still into the self-denial of the soldier's death in France. He could have been safe, if he had chosen to be.

So this first book is, in a sense, a double memoir. The continuity of his letters enables me to follow closely the course of those years in my life, with annotations and descriptions of things we did, and friends we had, in common. Many of these friends will reappear in my other books, as they connect themselves with the central object. The object here is Edward.

When I met him I was thirty-one, and only just emerging from a fantasy-life into one of natural human relationships. The strange game of TAR which my brother Harry initiated when I was four years old, and which I have described in the book of our childhood, had continued its powerful influence for far too long. I had indulged myself, night and day, in prolonged states of self-hypnosis of which I did not know the danger, and at twenty-nine was as emotionally immature as a girl of eighteen. My undisciplined delight in writing had developed eagerly through poetry and music, instead of through life, and I had written scarcely anything worth keeping.

I wonder now how the sort of person I was could have become a companion to the sort of person Edward was. No one was quicker than he to distinguish what was genuine from what was sham; and to a quarter-century spent in unreal dreams I added a lamentable ignorance of the realities he loved best. I couldn't tell a sycamore from an ash, and was apt to write of trees as temples of Pan. But I could walk and carry a knapsack, and thanks to my father had been brought up on nothing second-rate in poetry. Since 1910 my brother Bertie and I had found our way together into an exciting group of new friends. When among them, I still had to struggle against my childhood's legacy of abnormal shyness, and I was only at ease with those who could dispel it. The reserves peculiar to Edward often made it necessary for his friends to meet him more than half-way; with my want of self-confidence I found this difficult. By some means the difficulty was overcome. He counted on me for friendship; and I loved him with all my heart. He was far too penetrating not to know this, but only by two words, in one of his last letters from France, did he allow himself to show me that he knew. Our four years were undemonstrative, and unfailing.

It is important that this should be made clear, and accepted. Surmise and conjecture may sometimes unravel a truth, but oftener lead away from it. A misconception of the nature of our friendship would make Edward Thomas appear to be what he was not. Helen, my brother Bertie, and one or two close friends, had my confidence; Edward trusted me never to give it to him. If I had, our friendship must have come to an end.

Contents

List of Plates

Acknowledgments

THREE portions of this memoir, describing a holiday with Robert Frost, a walk with D. H. Lawrence, and Edward Thomas's last weeks in France, have appeared in *The London Magazine*. The section on James Guthrie was written for *The Sussex County Magazine* after his death in 1953. To the editors of both periodicals I offer my thanks for their sympathetic help and interest.

The letters from Gordon Bottomley are printed by permission of Professor Claude Colleer Abbott, and those from D. H. Lawrence by permission of Lawrence Pollinger and Messrs. Heinemann. Messrs. Faber and Faber, publishers of the *Collected Poems*, have readily added their approval to Helen's.

I wish also to express my gratitude to Miss Clare Nicholl who volunteered to save my eyes from overstrain by typing the major part of the letters before I began to write the book; and to Mrs. Joyce Maxwell, whose close co-operation in typing and re-typing the long manuscript while I was writing it, must have shortened my labour by a year. Without these friends I doubt if it would be finished yet.

1912–1913

ONE day towards the close of 1912, my brother Bertie said to me, 'Edward Thomas is coming to town tomorrow and wants me and Godwin to have tea with him. He has asked if you and Rosalind would come too.'

Bertie and I had drawn very close together since my brother Joe's marriage in 1910, to Frances Wood from Boston. Fan was an intimate friend of our American relatives; for years we had heard of 'Woodsie' from our visiting Jefferson aunts and uncles. In 1909, when she came to London for the first time, she stayed with us as a matter of course, and she and Joe fell in love with each other. Their marriage made the first break in the continuity of our home life.

Bertie and Joe had been knit together from childhood in something of the same indescribable bond that had always knit Harry, the eldest of us, and me. Now Joe was gone from Fellows Road, and Harry, absorbed in his teaching at the Royal Academy of Music, had sharply cut the Gordian knot of the mystical game we called TAR which had held me spellbound into my late twenties. He did so without any warning, in a strange and silent way of his own. I am sure now that he had determined, rightly, that it was bad for me to pursue an illusionary life any longer; but the suddenness with which the life came unexplained to an end was a shock. For awhile the bottom fell out of my existence. Then Bertie and I mended our disintegrated worlds together, and caused some uneasiness in

B   I

our placid home by our advanced ideas on Socialism, Art, the Woman's Vote, and Sex. For about three years now we had become part of a circle of young people who met regularly on the tennis-court and in the garden-studio of Frederick Corder's house in Albion Road. Corder was Harry's last professor at the R.A.M., and his children, Dolly and Paul, were our close friends. The brilliant group with whom, several times a week, we played games, invented entertainments, discussed life, and thronged the theatre galleries to drink in Wagner, dote on the Russian dancers, and adore the Irish players, included promising beginners like Arnold Bax, Myra Hess, Gertrude and Stacy Aumonier, the Antonietti family, and little Harriet Cohen: and in chief, Arnold's greatest friend, Godwin Baynes.

Godwin was a young doctor, preparing to specialize in nervous diseases; long afterwards he became Jung's friend and translator in England. This giant rowing-blue from Cambridge (six-foot-four in his socks), with a heart and brain to match his physical prowess, was the most popular man I have ever known. When he was talking to you he compelled you to feel that you were more interesting to him than any other person in the room, and I still think that at the given moment this was almost true. He was the sun-god of a dozen circles besides ours, and we found our firmament enlarged from other spheres with Thornycrofts and Radfords, Oliviers, Stracheys, and Meynells. College and medical friends, Fabian, literary, and musical friends, revolved in his orbit; the party began to glow when Godwin appeared. Maitland Radford, a young man of keen wit and shrewd judgement, assayed his values with a detachment not possible to most of us, and for 'Tiny' Baynes's empire invented the name 'Godwinia'. One of Godwin's solar systems could never be completely included in another, but the circles frequently overlapped; a Stephens, a Marillier, a Wells, a Rupert Brooke, would shoot like a star from the periphery of this one into that. Some of them, Radfords, Meynells, Thornycrofts, came to stay. Godwin was engaged to Rosalind Thornycroft.

§2

That spring we began to notice that our gatherings saw less and less of Godwin. Rumour got about that he had acquired 'a Patient'. 'Where's Godwin?' somebody might ask at a party. 'Gone to see his Patient.' 'Isn't Godwin coming to-night'—to Covent Garden, Drury Lane, the Court Theatre? 'He's treating his Patient.' Olive Hockin, artist, ski-ing champion, and our most positive suffragette, whose home in the Berkshire woods was not far from that of Godwin's family in Mortimer, arranged a Whitsun week-end for several of us; on Theale platform we learned that Godwin had deserted us again. Cursing the Patient roundly, why, we demanded, could not our sun-god shine on us for at least one day, or even half a day? It transpired that the Patient lived on a hilltop in Hampshire. The picnic on the Berkshire wild-rose common, the evening swim in the woodland bathing-pool, lost their savour. Why didn't this Patient of Godwin's recover or die? What was his name? Nobody knew. Bunny Garnett, from one of Godwinia's other dominions, could have told us. It was he who actually brought Godwin Baynes and Edward Thomas together, in the hope that the vigorous optimism of the one might help to cure the melancholia of the other. This writer of exquisite prose, this fine critic of poetry, was one of the literary coterie of which Bunny's father, Edward Garnett, was himself the centre. Godwin was as much at home in it as he was on the Cam, or in the wards of Bart's. And I think it was he who persuaded Edward Thomas, an unenthusiastic cricketer, to join Clifford Bax's Wiltshire cricket team that summer.

In his Elizabethan manor at Broughton Gifford, Clifford loved every year to re-create the Periclean Golden Age with a group of gifted young men. The Cricket Week was the high-spot of their year; Bertie, Lynn Hartley, Arnold, Stacy Aumonier, J. C. Snaith, and especially the crack bat, Major by name, counted the days to it. Sport, though the paramount object, was far from the only qualification for that Eleven; you need not be a Jessop or a Rhodes, as long as you had wit or charm or intellect, love of music and poetry, an interest in chess and indiscreet paper-games, a speculative mind, an eloquent tongue to discourse, could score a boundary in dialectics, or stump a sophistry outside its crease: such delights ruled the grey-stone manor morning and night during the golden week when colonnades of Madonna lilies, that toiled not nor span, led youth to the ancient door. Heraclitus, bowled for a blob in every innings, would have been welcome in that team at close of play, when the sun was talked down the sky. Francis Colmer, the most erratic cricketer of them all, was as essential to it as Major's double figures. He had been Arnold's and Clifford's private tutor, a scholar of a dry and ribald humour. He scored few runs, and was safe to drop a catch— but once in the long field he made an impossible one when he wasn't looking. No incident in Clifford's carefully-kept annals was more famed, or oftener quoted. I can almost persuade myself that I *saw* Colmer astounded when he found a ball stuck hard against his palm, and the nonchalance with which, the next moment, he tossed it in the air, the merest nothing, to the hilarious cheers of his fellow-fieldsmen.

In this gay company Edward that summer stood hunched reluctantly (in the long field too), on a different village green every day, and every evening took part in the *bout-rimés*, the chess-tourney planned to cover the whole period, and the symposia of talk far into the night. Edward was prized and delighted in for his quality. He and Bertie became attached to each other; they shared the same undercurrent of humour, the same passions for Shakespeare and fishing, sneaking away before breakfast to catch trout. In the autumn Edward included Bertie regularly among the friends whom he arranged to meet at lunch or tea whenever business brought him up to London. Before one such visit he suggested that Godwin's fiancée and Bertie's sister should join them at the Cottage Tea-rooms in the Strand.

Rosalind was almost as shy as I was, but supporting each other we met Edward with Bertie in Trafalgar Square. My first impressions were of his tall easy figure, his tawny colour, the grave pleasant tones of his voice, and a swift sidelong glance

PLATE I

EDWARD AT BROUGHTON GIFFORD

from his keen eyes when Bertie introduced us. Talk was rather diffident till we reached the tea-rooms, where Godwin's presence glowed on and put us at ease. I don't remember anything that was said, but to look at and listen to Edward was enough; he had a higher degree of beauty of person, voice, and mind than I had ever known combined in anybody, or have known since. When we parted I hoped I should see him again. Clifford Bax himself arranged this after Christmas, inviting me and my mother to Broughton Gifford in late February, when Edward would be on his way home to Hampshire towards the end of one of the long solitary walks on which he gathered material for his next book. He liked making his friends' homes houses of call whenever possible; Jack Haines's in Hucclecote, Gordon Bottomley's 'Sheiling' in Westmorland, and Clifford's Wiltshire manor were among those he loved best to stay in.

§3

At the New Year I sent Edward a card expressing my good wishes for 1913, and the hope that it might bring him happiness with Godwin's help, whose warmth made life happy for so many of us. The card depicted a galley in full sail. His reply, my first sight of his writing, came on a postcard, marked Jan. 10, 1913:

Wick Green
Petersfield

Thank you very much for your card which I take to imply an offer of lessons in navigation (higher) at Broughton Gifford in February. I hope it does, for I am still at sea. If Bertie could be at St. George's at 3.30 on Wednesday the 15th I should be glad.

Edward Thomas.

In Wiltshire I did not give, but received from Edward lessons in navigation (lower), when we had our first walks together; it was my beginner's experience of large-scale map-walking that took us everywhere except the highroads. In the

5

middle of fields which cows and thawing snow had churned into bog, he paused, clay pipe between his teeth, hazel-stick up-ended under his arm, intent on the map spread open on both hands. Re-folding it, he ploughed across the width of the morass, aware of some completely invisible track. I laboured after him, the mud sucking my boots deeper at each step. Edward, his long legs keeping up the negligent lope, half-stride half-lounge, which carried him faster, while he seemed to walk more leisurely than anybody else, glanced over his shoulder at my plight and said, 'Tread as if you were walking in a dream'. I tried, and it answered.

After supper we sat by the enormous fireplace where, if talk wilted, Clifford cast a fly to lure a topic. 'Tell us, Edward, what we are to think of Longfellow.' Edward called this Clifford's Ceremonial. Clifford, he knew, had no need whatever to be told what to think of Longfellow, but any poet is a stepping-stone to all others, and by bedtime the talk was ranging from Plato to Yeats. In one of his books, Clifford has said how much he had to learn from Edward, who was ten years ahead of him among the poets; especially the moderns, to appraise whom as they appeared was part of Edward's living. Of the old ones he loved none so much as Shelley; the one poet, he declared, of whose imperfections he could not be critical. I have only heard one other lover of English whose tongue, when poetry was loosed on the air, matched Edward's; I was there during the one unforgettable hour when they met. That will come in its place, some four years later.

Edward could not afford a whole week of holiday free of writing, preparing his next book or reviewing others. He read me and Clifford the beginnings of a collection of odd little fables he was inventing, fragments of mock folk-lore based on homely proverbs. We enjoyed and praised them; and when they came to be published (under the title of *Four-and-Twenty Blackbirds*) they were dedicated to me and Clifford jointly.

Before Mother and I left Broughton Gifford, Edward was on his way home. In sending him some 'notes' he must have asked me for I seem to have pursued the theme of the Higher

6

Navigation by including another picture of ships. In his acknowledgement from Wick Green on March 13 his second postcard says:

Greetings and thank you for your notes and the three happy ships. I got to Rudge and found an old house, a chapel connected with Fulke Greville and with a nice living inmate. I am home now and glad of your good wishes and good news and hopeful of another meeting.

E. T.

§4

After this, when he came to London, I found myself included in his appointments, for tea at the Cottage Tea-rooms, a fruit-lunch at Shearn's, or a call at Fellows Road, where Mother was glad to see him again. She was a woman of delicate charm and humour, and Edward appreciated and was easy with her. In April he told me that he and his family would be away at Easter; they at the sea in Norfolk, and he walking somewhere, filling his notebooks as usual. The Wick Green house would be vacant, and he offered it to Bertie and me for the Easter week-end, or as long as we pleased. It stood, with his little study in the garden, on the ridge above the Leg o' Mutton Hill where the Sarsen stone stands now that is his monument.

'May we ask some friends?' we inquired.

'Ask whom you like and do what you like in the house,' said Edward, and then in his gravest tone, 'only be careful not to dance the floors down.'

We did not know him well enough then to suspect his gravity; and visualizing some sort of jerry-built cottage, we promised to be particularly careful.

Bertie and I had never had such a chance to make free before, to invite a party to a house of our own. We had no idea of its size, but we knew that the Thomas family numbered five, and that many of our friends were hardened campers. We immediately inaugurated a comprehensive house-party: the

Corders, the Baxes, the Antoniettis, Myra, Godwin and Rosalind, and her sister Joan Thornycroft, whom we knew less
well than Rosalind, were among the invited, and others I
can't remember. They were asked indiscriminately for the
whole Easter week-end, or as much of it as they could manage.
We had no time to get replies from everybody, but before I
and Paul Corder (the vanguard) took train for Petersfield, we
knew that only Olga of the Antoniettis would presently join
us, and that Clifford and Dolly Corder had fallen out of the
party. Our knapsacks heavy with food, we began the long trek
from the station to Steep, and thence to the top of Stoner Hill,
ignorant of how many were coming, or for how long, or how
many beds there were to accommodate them. The country
was entirely unknown to us. Leaving Steep behind we began
to mount, and the beechen beauty of Stoner hanger took our
breath away; so, when we reached the summit, did the house.
It had been built for the Thomases by the craftsman Geoffrey
Lupton, an Old Bedalian (the Thomas children were young
Bedalians). I can't better Robert Eckert's description of the
place in his life of Edward. Lupton, a disciple of William
Morris, had 'planned to build the house almost entirely by
hand, from the oak, to be seasoned, sawed, and planed near
by, to the bricks, and the great nails, hinges, and hasps to be
forged in the village. Native oak planks were to be used for
the floor, native stone for the thresholds. He suggested the
house should be long and low, facing south, with the living-
room to the east, and with windows on all sides except the
north.' The house was built on ground owned by Lupton,
not far from his own house 'at the edge of a plateau, over-
looking a deep and densely wooded coomb, reached by a
path that wound beside a stream up through the hanger. On
top, 400 feet above the sea, was a wide view of the South
Downs.' How many times I was to climb that glorious hanger,
with Baba shuffling her feet among the beechmast, and hear
Edward's 'Coo-ee!', at the end of his day's work, ring across
the coomb from his study, while ours rang back less lustily, I
could not foresee. Dazed with delight, I wound upwards for
the first time under the young beech-leaves, to the house at

the top which Paul might have built himself. For he, a musician like his father, was also a disciple of the Morris way of life, a splendid carpenter, a metal-worker, and a weaver of stuffs. Dance the floors down indeed! We had our first laugh, unpacked our provisions, took stock of the beds, and waited for Bertie, Myra, and Olga to join us in the evening. We three girls shared the biggest bedroom, the boys took the children's rooms; in the five succeeding days these became dormitories. Friends appeared and disappeared, some for the whole time, some for a night or two. Lovely Joan Thornycroft, on a walking-tour with a friend, arrived one evening, and next day vanished again. When beds gave out newcomers slept on couches or the floor. It was soon plain that our food-stocks wouldn't last; on Saturday we raided the local shop for its entire supplies of bread and fruit and groceries. We cooked in shifts, and ate at random. Edith, Helen Thomas's daily help from the village, washed up and made beds in a state of continuous giggle. We fell in love with the painting of a charming little girl—one of Edward's children, we presumed. We walked and talked, and ransacked the bookshelves for indiscriminate reading . . . Godwin and Rosalind have joined us. Arnold has come. . . .

Myra has retired to a sunny nook outside with a volume of Lafcadio Hearn, and is heard wailing, 'I can't bear it, I can't bear it!' We rush to her aid, and find her in semi-hysteria— 'No! if it happens again I can't *bear* it!' Bertie snatches the book from her limp hand and insists on reading aloud a ghastly incident about a lonely valley inhabited by evil things with faces as bald as eggs.[1] At the denouement we are *all* hysterical, and Myra completely collapsed . . . .

---

[1] A timid traveller, crossing the haunted valley by night, sees a woman weeping with her face in her hands. He entreats her to tell him what her trouble is, she removes her hands from her face, and it is featureless—as bald as an egg. Shrieking with fear he flies, trying to find a way out of the horrible place—he meets a travelling tinker who asks him roughly what's the matter with him— he babbles the story—'and, oh sir! the woman's face was as bald as an egg!' 'Hey! Was it anything like *this*?' The tinker wipes his face with his hand from forehead to chin, and presents to the gibbering traveller a face as bald as . . .

Stop! I can't bear it, wails Myra.

For some time afterwards—'Hey! was it anything like *this*?' was a password among us.

Paul storms in from a walk, announcing indignantly that high on the tallest pine-tree in the Stoner gorge hangs a signboard warning trespassers of prosecution. His indignation takes fire, sentence is pronounced on the notice-board—after lunch it shall be cut down! We flock to the turn on the road from which it is visible, high out of reach. Bertie, Paul, and Godwin scramble down to the base of the tree in the coomb. Thirty foot of bare pine-trunk challenges them. Paul makes the first attempt, slides down defeated after a very few feet, and is followed by Bertie, who gets only a little higher. Last, Godwin clasps the trunk with his mighty arms and knees, scales the tree-trunk like a giant monkey on a stick, panting heavily as he nears the goal, cheered by the girls looking down from the upper road—he arrives, hangs on by one arm in mid-air, wrenches off the offending board, and slides down again! We bear the trophy home triumphantly, chop it up, and after tea make a bonfire of it. May the fumes suffocate Squire Trevor-Battye, arch-enemy of ancient Rights of Way. . . .

Godwin—all of us inert in the afternoon (why do I remember this pointless moment so distinctly?)—stirs, stretches, and yawns amiably, 'Let's go to the end of the ridge and sneer at Harry Roberts's horses'. We troop obediently after him, from some high point stare across some distant valley, sneer at the unseen horses of a man we don't know, troop back again, and relapse into inertia. . . .

Arnold Bax, one of our earliest comers and longest stayers, had arrived straight from Majorca, where he and Clifford with Gustav Holst and Balfour Gardiner had been holiday-making. He brought with him a jet-black cigar of great length and girth, resembling a lumpy stick of liquorice. Installed on the mantelpiece, it became our aim to get it smoked before we left. The men took turns at it several times a day. When Paul paled and succumbed, when Bertie, Arnold, and even Godwin had cried enough, Olga and I weighed in with a few puffs; but the cigar from Majorca defeated us in the end. I think it was left on the mantelpiece as a memento.

One by one the visitors faded away. With Edith's help we

left things orderly, and in May Edward wrote from Wick Green the only letter beginning 'My dear Miss Farjeon'.

Wick Green
7 V 13

My dear Miss Farjeon
    I have just got home after a rather tiring time of work in London, and feel I must write and say what a pleasant feeling you have left here. My wife and I are grateful for it, and so is Edith. We all 3 want you to come again. Our cottage may be ready for us late in June but before we leave here I hope you will come. But I am not certain if there is any time free this month. Shall I let you know? I am sorry I did not arrange to see you in town, but it was not easy. There will be other times. Please remember me to Bertie and Godwin and Rosalind and ask Godwin if he mentioned me to Clifford Sharp of the 'New Statesman'.
    My book grows and I decline.

Yours ever
Edward Thomas.

The next time I saw Edward in town I confessed to our destruction of the sign board. He was amused, and said the squire, who was trying to deprive the villagers of their rights, had descended angrily on him, accusing Mervyn, who had frequently defied the sign, and trespassed deliberately. But Mervyn had his alibi in Norfolk, where the family was on holiday; and the house-party on Wick Green was never suspected.

§5

During the next two months we continued to meet in London for lunch or tea, and corresponded in between. When I ceased to be 'Miss Farjeon' Edward laid aside some of his reticences, revealing a little of himself and Helen in casual remarks. Of her he said: 'During the nine months before her baby is born, her face is one perpetual smile. My wife could be the happiest woman on earth—and I won't let her.' He said she wrote better letters than any woman he knew—'only it is a different letter each time you read it'. I knew what he meant

11

when she and I began to write to one another. For someone like Helen, who lived the lives of several women in full, everything she did must be done with rapidity, and her writing is more like a housefly's idea of shorthand than anything else I can think of. Her letters have to be read first by guesswork, then by inspiration, and finally by sheer knowledge of her dear self: *this* undecipherable sentence *must* be *thus*, for *those* are the only words that would express her. But I hadn't yet had my first letter from her.

Of himself, when we had been talking about Shakespeare, Edward once said, 'I suppose every man thinks that Hamlet was written for him, but I *know* he was written for me.'

I found more and more truth in this as I knew him more. His world of brooding thoughts and tormented sensibilities—and the fineness of the thought and the sensibility—must have brought his self-communings very near Hamlet's. And he had Hamlet's gift of grappling to his soul with hoops of steel the friends with whom his affections had been tried.

His confidences increased my longing to help him. I noticed that he was seeing much less of Godwin, and asked him why. He said, 'Godwin can't really help me. When he first came to see me he made me feel that I was the most important person in the world to him. As I came to know his world I found he gave the same impression to everybody—and I don't like being one of a crowd.'

One day I took my pen and my courage in hand, and dared to touch on his psychological problems. His reply is a rare instance of his unburdening himself against his will. It was enclosed with a copy of *Foliage* ('Davies' last book'). At this time he was reviewing poetry for two papers, and this must have been one of my earliest presents of his second review copy. The reference to postcards isn't clear; perhaps I had offered not to trouble him with letters.

Undated; postmark illegible

My dear Eleanor Are you better now? I hope you are. If not and in any case you may find something in Davies' last book—not nearly so much as usual, though—to like. Can you choose your time at the week end? Could you come on Monday afternoon and stay the night? My Mother will be here on Sunday and things always go a little stiffly with her—she is diffident and sad and not clever.

I don't want postcards from you, except that they would put me at my ease, especially in these days when to write more than a page means attempting the impossible and wearying myself and uselessly afflicting others with some part of my little yet endless tale. It has got to its dullest and its worst page now. The point is I have got to help myself and have been steadily spoiling myself for the job for I don't know how long. I am very incontinent to say these things. If I had never said them to anyone I should have been someone else and somewhere else. You see the central evil is self-consciousness carried as far beyond selfishness as selfishness is beyond self denial, (not very scientific comparison) and now amounting to a disease and all I have got to fight it with is the knowledge that in truth I am not the isolated selfconsidering brain which I have come to seem—the *knowledge* that I am something more, but not the belief that I can reopen the connection between the brain and the rest.

I think perhaps having said that much I ought to say Don't speak to me about it, because it is endless and no good is to be done by talking or writing about it. And yet I am letting this go. Well, all my thoughts are of myself, alas, except the scraps I can give to my 8 novels, now almost done with. And I keep afflicting myself by imagining all the distasteful work as if it were a great impossible mountain just ahead. Please forgive me and try not to give any thought to this flat grey shore which surprises the tide by being inaccessible to it.

I haven't even read Hodgson's poem yet, tho it is by me.

Tell me when you are coming to talk about Keats not me—did I tell you I had accepted rotten terms to do a rotten little book on Keats. I am rather thinking of going away to work and be alone and not inflict 5 persons at once.

Goodbye.
Edward Thomas.

§6

I had to miss the chance of spending a night at Wick Green before he and Helen moved down to Steep, but from this time my coming to stay with them was always in view, only delayed by the unfinished state of the new house. It was one of a group of semi-detached cottages that were being built on a raw plot of ground near Bedales, where Mervyn and Bronwen were day-scholars. They were intended for workmen, but when the rents, though fairly moderate, made them hang fire, the Thomases decided to put in for one, for economy and convenience, sacrificing their glorious position on the ridge. Summer ambled on, and so did the building.

Postmark June 16 1913
Wick Green

Dear Eleanor   I haven't forgotten your letter for a month, but I have been finishing, then typing, a book and have only spent half a day in London. Nor has it been possible to ask you here, nor is it possible now as our move is not fixed and there are arrangements and destructions and distributions going on. But I am to be in London on Wednesday. Now is the afternoon *free in any case*? That is to say will you write to me at 13 Rusham Rd, Balham, and tell me if you could meet me at 3.30 or 4 at the Cottage Tea Rooms, Strand, and I will at once write back?

The point is I may have to go back early in the afternoon, but I don't think I shall, and if you could meet me, I should have another argument against. I suppose it is impossible to produce Dr. Baynes. Please remind Bertie that I continue or remain, and that my remains are here. They feel extraordinarily unlike cricket though if they go on shrinking they might be equal to grasshopper eventually. This is however a beautiful day.

Yours ever
Edward Thomas.

And again, in June, with three more of the Proverb stories for *Four-and-Twenty Blackbirds*. I had suggested that it might be possible to get Rosalind Thornycroft to illustrate them. (She had brilliant gifts, but idled with them. Twenty years later Bertie and I had almost to force her to collaborate with us in *Kings and Queens*.)

Wick Green   Petersfield

Dear Eleanor   I am sending you 3 stories. Heinemann hasn't decided yet, I hear, but in any case I think it would be well to let nobody but yourselves know the scheme as it would be very easy for somebody to get before me. But if they should please Rosalind and she should be inclined to adorn them I hope she will and hope Heinemann may feel inclined to publish my tales and her drawings. It might however be indiscreet to publish one as we were thinking of doing because somebody else might be inspired to do likewise and get before me.

It now seems possible we may move very soon. If possible I may ask you to come, but it mayn't be possible. Tomorrow I hope to travel towards Broughton Gifford.

Yours and Bertie's
Edward Thomas

P.S. Will Bertie address this letter to 'Vanity Fair'? Please.

In July summer-holiday plans began to be discussed. Our family always spent part of the time at the White Horse Hotel, a simple inn in Overstrand. The previous year Bertie and I had arranged with Gertrude and Stacy Aumonier to extend our Norfolk holiday from the sea to the Broads. Stacy shared Bertie's ardour for fishing, and I loved fresh water better than salt, and grass better than sand. We chartered a two-cabin houseboat for a week in mid-August, from Hart's Boathouse in Wroxham. Then came the disastrous Norfolk rains and floods of 1912, which ruined East Anglian farmers and land-ladies. Hart's agreed, for cash down, to postpone the contract till next summer. So 1913 found us with a houseboat to the good and a berth to spare, as Bertie had to fall out. When I suggested that Edward should make our fourth the Aumoniers jumped at it. Gertrude had not met him, but Stacy could assure her that he would be congenial. I sent him an invitation for August 16th from all three of us.

Postmark June 1913

Friday   'The Star' Weyhill
beyond Andover

Dear Eleanor,   Tidy or not this is a very attractive suggestion. But the difficulty is my wife is to be away during that time and I shall be responsible for my boy and should normally have had him away walking or cycling with me. Now I cannot possibly say at once whether I should be free. I would suggest bringing him with me. He is $13\frac{1}{2}$, would love it, and would not be in the way (I

15

believe). But,—well in fact, I *do* at the moment suggest it. He could
sleep with me or anywhere. Please tell me if this is impossible.
If it is I will see what can be done, because I should very much like
it. I shall quite understand that the most beatific creature of 13½
might be a difficulty. About the 9th there is no uncertainty. I will
come if you will tell me in time when and where to meet you. It is
now near the end of an easy day's cycling through Winchester and
Andover. I expect to culminate at Broughton Gifford tomorrow.
With my true thanks to host and hostesses,

Yours ever
Edward Thomas.

We agreed, of course, to include Mervyn in the party; he
could sleep on the floor of Edward's and Stacy's cabin.

A last abortive effort was made to get me to Wick Green in
July.

Postmark June 1913
Friday   Wick Green   Petersfield

Dear Eleanor, We are all sorry you can't come. However,
Mervyn and I at any rate will see you before so very long. He would
like a tent as well as any bed, I think. When you can come our way,
will you? I think there's certain to be room near by. Thank you
for what you say about the Proverbs. I am specially glad you
didn't exclude the *Gift Horse* as Heinemann's reader does. There is
no further news of them as a book. If Rosalind finds a solution I
shall be delighted. Clifford says she is very good. I should think
better of her of course if she had turned up last week. We are now
stirring things up. We may move next week. I got back on
Wednesday after a pleasant day with Clifford, three bathes in the
Avon, and four quite excellent days cycling and walking, in which
I rediscovered the town of Stockbridge and the village of Chitterne.
I shall see you the week after next then. You will tell me where.

Yours ever
Edward Thomas

Our next letters were concerned with the whereabouts of
the houseboat, and dovetailing dates. Among these country
matters, a literary one cropped up. Batsford was consulting
Clifford Bax about a series of Belles-Lettres, choice little books
on subjects chosen by their authors; Clifford was contributing

one on 'Friendship', and he suggested my name and Edward's among others as contributors to the series. I think we were paid ten pounds each; it was my first paid-for book, and how I dared to choose 'Trees' for my title I cannot think—perhaps because I knew almost nothing about them. But hadn't Edward equal temerity in choosing 'Ecstasy' for his subject?

17 vii 13   Wick Green for some time to come

Dear Eleanor Thank you for the book and the letter. Would you—could you—have been more severe had you known I introduced the subject of Ecstasy to Batsford in a fit of curiosity and daring. It is most probable I shall never be able to begin it. In any case I feel sure you need not anticipate any serious harm.

I see that Hickling Green which has an inn is under half a mile from the N. corner of Hickling Broad and that Catfield Station is two miles from either. Catfield village is half a mile from the station and under two miles from the Broad by a road that takes you over Catfield Common which looks possible for a tent. The nearest station to the Broad is Potter Heigham, $1\frac{1}{2}$ miles from the S. end, parts of the village being only $\frac{1}{2}$ a mile from the water. Apparently you go via Great Yarmouth or North Walsham.

Yours and Bertie's
Edward Thomas

Postmark July 21   Steep on Tuesday, and for
all I know for ever after

Sunday   Wick Green (*scored through*)
Petersfield

Dear Eleanor Thank you. I shan't compete for the Dunce's Stool. I couldn't smile in it. However, something may happen when we have moved and we get a fine day again and I don't make faces at it.—Ranworth looks charming on the map and the $5\frac{1}{2}$ miles further from the station should be all to the good. I suppose we might arrange all to go down together and drive together, unless Mervyn and I bicycle. I forgot to tell you about food. The more *green* vegetables, fruit, fat, grease, butter etc. of all kinds, I have the better. I try never to touch sugar. No alcohol. Brown bread if it is to be had without revolution. But it is likely that new conditions will make us rather less portentously serious about these perfectly futile, because perfectly and exclusively physical, laws.

I didn't go to Godwin's after all. It was a rotten day for me, not very much improved at the end by Maitland.

Yours ever
Edward Thomas.

Ranworth Broad was eventually settled on (and *was* charming). I promised Edward an alliterative diet.

28th July 1913   (*Stamped heading of* Wick Green, Petersfield,
                                crossed out and Steep *substituted*
                                                                in ink.)

Dear Eleanor   Very well. Lettuce & Lard is just the thing. I couldn't write before. We have moved & I have been . . . It would not do to describe. Now perhaps the strong warm tide which you tell me of is beginning to reach me. I wish it would—I was going to say with all my heart, but that is or was the difficulty. If it were not I should not hesitate to do so much about Ecstasy. However I am really quartering the ground now & shall at least be able to put a bell or two in my Dunce's cap. We look forward to the Fawn or whatever it has grown to. Mervyn eats lettuce but not lard. He likes brown bread hard (not muslin) as much as I do. He has a way of doing what he is told & will be useful I think. We shall discover a stable for our cycles I expect. If I am in town before the 17th I shall see you; if not then on the 16th. Will you tell me your train? It is now rather doubtful when if at all I can get to Broughton next month. Is it possible you could come down for the week end before the 16th? I think we can put you up. Mervyn sleeps out. Also there is a bed to be had not far off.

Yours ever
Edward Thomas.

At last the date of my meeting Helen was fixed. I was to go to Steep on the 9th, by which time Edward would be returning from Broughton Gifford, he having decided after all to join the Cricket Week for the last few days.

2nd August 1913

Dear Eleanor   I hope your back will be fit for its load but if it isn't let me carry it up here for you on the 9th. From Romsey you train to Fratton, & change there for Petersfield, usually having at least an hour's wait at Fratton. From Fareham you couldn't get nearer to us than Privett which is 6 miles off. Let us know the time of the train you come by. But I hope you will be fit for Dartmoor.

I'll send on a blanket, towels to you c/o Hart's later on & look forward to travelling down with you—don't forget to tell me the train when all is settled & you know where the Fawn is to lie.

I expect to set out towards Broughton tomorrow afternoon & reach it on Monday.

Yours ever
Edward Thomas.

§7

From Edward's roundabout directions of the route to Petersfield by way of Romsey, it appears that I might have been coming to Hampshire from Devon. Tramping and camping on Dartmoor were in vogue then. I was a good tramper, but could only carry a moderate load, was prone to sore throats and chest-colds, and still rather timid of unknown conditions; so though it was often mooted that I should join Bertie and Paul, Godwin and Rosalind, among the moorland mists and wild ponies, sing folk-songs round a primus stove at evening, and sleep in a bag under a tent at night, I never did. On August 9th I made an uncomplicated journey to Petersfield from London.

Early in the week I had my first letter from Helen. It was short, and warm and touchingly humble. She hoped I would not be disappointed in her, she wasn't intellectual, but 'very primitive'. I wondered, with a slight pang, what sort of woman she imagined me to be. I soon came to know how little at ease her simple nature felt itself among Edward's more sophisticated friends. Helen's happiest setting was a cottage in the country. She had grown up among books in the library of her father, James Ashcroft Noble, and her home-making would always breathe of them, but the vigorous prejudices as well as the generous affections of her deeply-wise humanity came from life, not from literature; the wisdom was in her hands when they were making bread, or sewing, or digging, and in her voice when she was comforting her baby. I tried to answer the letter reassuringly. I had no picture of the woman who wrote it, and who was to meet my late afternoon train on Petersfield platform, but when I got out of the carriage nobody was there who could be mistaken for her.

Helen had always too much to do to be punctual; for her, a coming guest meant breathless preparation, a bedroom full of flowers, an oven full of cakes, everything shining that could be made to shine. I hitched on my knapsack, and as I crossed the line saw a quick energetic figure scurrying towards me on the Bell Hill road. I waved my stick, called 'Helen!'—she called back 'Eleanor!'—we met laughing, and embraced, and after that looked at each other. She has described this meeting in *World Without End*, getting only a few details out of season. In essence it is true; we met, not in April, but in August without an instant of acquaintanceship. Edward, she told me, was not yet back from Wiltshire. Before we reached Steep he appeared from some cross-country walking-point and joined us. He was not in a good mood. To cover it I chattered about cricket, asking for news of Clifford, Arnold, Stacy—and what was Bertie's average? I was delighted to hear that he had scored over fifty in his last innings. But the talk was still constrained; and that evening at supper I saw the first sign of the irritability Edward could not control. Some nothing Helen said or did, or hadn't done, caused it. It took me by surprise. She speaks in her book of the flash of astonishment on my face when it occurred. But it passed, without spoiling the evening. At other times it did not. As my visits became more intimate, I saw how he was the greatest sufferer when he could not help 'inflicting five persons at once'. Bronwen, a child of eleven who adored her father and was adored by him, seemed to know by instinct that the way to help irritability is not to be hurt by it. She was the child of the portrait we had fallen in love with at Easter, and looked like a small princess in a story-book, in a frock as pretty as Helen's needle could make it, and a pink snood in her hair. Her nature was gay; to a sharp accent from her father she answered airily—'Very well, very well, my dear sir!' and did what he wanted smilingly.

The baby Myfanwy, who for years was only called Baba, was asleep. She was a critical baby, not very easy to win, and deeply prejudiced, said Helen anxiously, against spectacle-wearers. I told her to bring Baba in to me early while I was still in bed, and in the morning a chubby three-year-old was plumped beside my pillow and left there. I introduced myself to her as Cocky-Peacock, and called her Polly-Parrot. She responded in the soft serious voice that was one of her charms. We sang a song together. Then she reached for a picture-book on a shelf by the bed.

'What does it say?'

'Wait till I put some more eyes on, Polly-Parrot.'

She watched me with immense solemnity as I put on my glasses. Was it touch-and-go? '*Now* what does it say, Cocky-Peacock?' I came down to breakfast accepted.

The week-end went successfully, indoors and out. It was of a pattern I was to spend at all seasons and in all weathers in the Steep cottage during the next three years. Meals were leisurely, because of Edward's indigestion; we sat long over them, talking—and sat long after them, still talking. Edward and Helen did their morning chores, the washing-up together, then Helen to the bedrooms and Edward to the garden. As term-time was over, Bronwen and Mervyn also had chores to do, and if Mervyn was rather slow in setting about cleaning the family shoes, Edward showed signs of impatience. Mervyn was a pleasant, friendly boy; he was looking forward to our holiday on the Broads, and we liked each other. I wasn't allowed to do much besides shake the table-cloth and make my bed.

During my visits Edward slackened work a little. On most days he went in the morning or afternoon to his study in the garden on the ridge; for when he left Wick Green the Luptons allowed him to keep this privacy for his writing. Half an hour before meal-time I walked up the hanger with the children to call him; at the last bend our 'Coo-ees!' rang across the coomb, and his rang back like an echo. We went to meet him at the top of the road, then all walked down together under the beeches, green, red, or barren according to the season. Baba

liked to run, taller than we were, on the raised bank that
bordered the dip down to the valley. In autumn she ruffled
the fallen leaves as she ran.

But if the day was irresistibly fine, housework and writing
were thrown to the winds, Helen packed a sudden picnic, and
Edward led us a few miles to some special haunt he loved. On
the way home we sang songs to lighten the road for Baba's small
tired legs. When she grew fretful we took her one by each hand
and covered several yards of the way with running swings
which she called 'Flying Angels'. Once on a stretch of road
where horses had passed—'Give me a Flying Angel over all
that dung,' she demanded, to Edward's glee. And when even
this celestial transit palled, he mounted her on his shoulders,
grasping her ankles while she clasped his forehead, and towered
above us from her tall safe perch. Meanwhile Bronwen, loiter-
ing behind, had to be fetched again and again out of some
green ditch where she was picking speedwell or herb-robert.

Bronwen was Edward's most eager sharer of wild-flower
lore; she knew as many as he did, had an eye almost as quick,
and on any ramble hunted the hedges with rapturous little
sighs, intent on making a posy, just a *little* posy, *all* pink, *all*
yellow, *all* white-and-blue. But when it was made exactly to
her fancy, she spied an interloper she could not resist, scabious
or viper's bugloss joined the campions, and instead of a posy
she came home with a bunch. In his happiest poem ('If I
should ever by chance grow rich') Edward offers to bestow
on his elder daughter half a dozen sweet-named places:

> Codham, Cockridden, and Childerditch,
> Roses, Pyrgo, and Lapwater;

provided she finds the first white violet of the year before he
does. Every spring it was a race between them.

My ignorance of wild-flowers horrified Bronwen. After our
first walk she gathered a hundred of them, taught me their
names, and next day sat me down to a neatly-ruled examination
paper, with the numbered specimens laid out in precise order
on the table. I was given an hour to do my paper in: 60 for a
Pass, 70 for Honours. Edward, looking in to propose a walk,

found me knitting my brows over agrimony, mouse-eared-hawkweed, and birdfoot-trefoil, and went off laughing to dig potatoes till my hour was up. I had a memory like wax for names, and I topped 90. Bronwen was proud of me. But wax hardens with time. I should be sorry to have to pass that paper now.

I think I like best to remember the hour before our supper, while Helen was busy in the little kitchen, and Edward gave Baba her bath before the fire, singing Welsh songs while he dried her, till Helen came and carried her up to bed. And after supper, the washing-up done, Helen threaded her darning-needle and Edward filled his clay, and read to us in his beautiful grave unemphatic voice. One might I asked him to fill a clay for me; he had a store of them in different states of foulness, the foulest sweetening in whisky or baking in the ashes on the hearth. He found one not too black and not too new, packed it lightly, and went on reading—Hodgson's 'Eve' perhaps—with an occasional sidelong glance. But I didn't disgrace my father, who had sucked his cutty over a fire in the Australian Bush in his gold-digging days. Presently the book of poetry was laid down, there was another hour of talk, Helen rolled up a pair of socks, Edward knocked out our pipes, the fire was raked out, the cinders were sifted, and we went up to bed.

I left on August 12th. Helen urged me to come again soon, and Edward carried my knapsack to the station.

§8

Lettercard dated 13th August 1913.   *From* Steep, Petersfield.

Dear Eleanor, I forgot to ask if you know where letters had better be addressed, or shan't we know till we get there? Also I forgot to say there's one rule for Mervyn I should like to keep—that he shall have his last meal at tea time & never a meal just before bed, & this tea need include nothing extraordinarily solid—just bread & butter & salad or fruit or anything cold & handy or nothing if need be. And will you tell me if you think it will be practicable and

decent for me (not necessarily alone) to make an expedition or two
to Norwich, Oulton, or Lowestoft? I hope your back and your
soul did not suffer here.

Yours ever
Edward Thomas.

The houseboat holiday was another happy time. We met at
Wroxham and were towed to Ranworth Broad. The weather
was fine. Gertrude was cook-in-chief and I and the men washed
dishes and tidied up. Sometimes we ate on deck, and often
on the bank, in the meadow alongside, where Gertrude did
not altogether approve of Edward's camping method of
washing-up the knives by thrusting them into the earth and
wiping the blades on the grass.

I don't think Edward made any of the special expeditions he
had suggested, but while Stacy wandered away to paint exquisite water-colours, he and I walked somewhere or other
every day, and I saw how natural he was with country-folk, an
old carrier who gave us a lift in his cart, an old woman who let
him fill his pockets with early apples for a few pence. He
stuffed his pockets so full that when he went back for more she
doubled the price, grumbling a little, and he paid up with a
sheepish smile, like a little boy caught stealing. The amazing
keenness of Edward's sight was brought home to me on these
walks; he would remark on some bird in a distant tree when
to me the tree was only a blur on the landscape. (Once when
we were riding on an open bus-top in town, he pointed out to
me the curious difference in the two eyes of a dog sitting in a
window. I took his word for it.) On several mornings Edward
and Stacy punted with their tackle to mid-Broad, where they
moored themselves for an absorbed hour or two, and punted
back again with empty creels. I don't think either of them
caught a single fish for Gertrude to fry. Once Mervyn and I
were allowed to sit moored with them, but as we weren't fishing ourselves and mustn't talk, we didn't ask to go twice.
With a rod of our own in our hands and a bob to watch, we
would at least have shared the pleasures of hope in which our
taciturn companions were immersed.

I still have one or two snapshots of this holiday: Mervyn

PLATE II

'SAINTS' ON *THE FAWN*

EDWARD WASHING UP

ELEANOR ON THE
DOWNS

smiling against a leafy background, and another which he
took from the bank of the four of us standing on the houseboat after a meal. At the last moment Edward cried, 'Let us
be Saints!' and he and Stacy held white cardboard plates halo-
like behind their heads.

By the sixth day I fancy Gertrude had had her fill of the
camping life, for she and Stacy returned to town a day ahead of
us. This gave me a cabin to myself, and Mervyn was promoted
from the floor to Stacy's bunk. Next day we waited till the
man from Hart's came to take the houseboat in tow; then the
carrier carted the three of us to the nearest station.

Helen had gone with friends to Switzerland, and Edward
extended the children's holiday, staying with them near James
Guthrie in Flansham. I also extended mine among friends in
Milford-on-Sea, and from there planned a trek across the
counties to Viola Meynell. This would be my first visit to
'Humphreys', the Meynell homestead in Greatham, which for
the next seven years was often mine. Maitland Radford was to
join us, and he and I and Viola were going to ramble over the
Downs to Lewes and Berwick. Before I set out Edward suggested that on my way to Greatham we might meet somewhere
in Sussex for a walk.

Postmark August 28th, 1913.   *From* Flansham, Thursday.

In a room all over photographs, vases, texts, certificates,
geraniums, oleographs of a boy (showing left cheek) & girl (showing right cheek) praying etc. But nevertheless Dear Eleanor, if
you can come do. The only thing is we shall most likely leave
here on Thursday next week. Bronwen then goes to an aunt at
Chiswick with Myfanwy. I take her up to town & may stay that
night with Godwin, while Mervyn walks to Selsfield House, East
Grinstead (Selsfield hamlet is near Turner's Hill, Rowfant, Worth
Forest, Crabbit Park etc.), where he and I are to stay with Vivian
Locke Ellis till about the 15th. Now as Mrs Ellis is not very well I
can't positively invite you there, & Ellis is too shy for a simple
short meeting. But if you are nearby I should like to see you & will
meet you at any place in the neighbourhood, such as Worth church
or West Hoathly Church, & walk an hour or two with you, morning or afternoon or evening, & for that purpose put myself in your

hands to be done with as you would be done by. For in spite of my imperfect Collins that week was a great & good week for me & shall be the fountain of many others such, praise or no praise. And it is very much worth for me to know that you thought the same. Therefore there's no need to sully Ben Nevis with ceremony.

Thank you again for the comments on my Proverbs. I shall revise the [?] [1] when I next get at them. But as to the last sentence in 'A Cat may look at a king' I think I meant to imply that other countries had already discovered not the proverb but the fact (in natural history). Perhaps I left it too obscurely.

I will see to the Mares & Mehetable & the surviving confusion in 'A Bird in the Hand' & the repetition (which I think the children also objected to.)

We arrived here yesterday afternoon and bathed. We bathed again before breakfast. The sun is hot, the sky pale and bright, there is a wind. The sea is warm & quiet & all colours between white & purple. The children have gone to Bognor about nothing in particular. I have been reading some unnecessary books. I have the thin edge of a wedge of anxiety penetrating me, but (especially with fine weather) we shall do very well for a week I hope. I want to work & feel I ought to work.

Now Mervyn's back & we shall bathe again.

With our love to you & mine to Bertie.

Yours ever
Edward Thomas.

I gave Edward a train-time at some point where he and the children could join me.

Postcard dated August 30th

That is very good. So we will meet you at 2.37 & hope to have found a room for you. Here are the letters for the letter game. It is raining a little. Is it possible to bathe to excess? I incline to believe it.

If you don't start till Wednesday you may reappear near East Grinstead perhaps? Helen writes more than cheerfully from Switzerland. The children have found friends here & don't mind me. I fill up with reviews. Don't fail.

E. T.

---

[1] I can't make out this word.

The children's friends were the three sons of James Guthrie ('Totch', Robin, and John), who lived in the White House in Flansham—not the house from which Edward had written his previous letter (for nothing could be less like the Guthrie interior than 'texts, certificates, and oleographs'). James Guthrie, artist, poet, printer, and craftsman, was one of Edward's staunchest friends. Robin tells me that when he stayed at Flansham Edward was a tireless and passionate swimmer, 'bathing to excess' with the boys, playing with them near shore, then suddenly leaving them to swim far out to sea till his head was a speck in the distance.

I met Edward with the children somewhere, we walked somewhere, and parted somewhere. Mervyn trudged on to the Locke Ellises in East Grinstead, I trudged on to Greatham, and Edward took Bronwen to Helen's sister, Mary Valon, in Chiswick. Bronwen was not a sturdy walker, and when we separated I was responsible for a charabanc ride to the railway station.

I realized on this walk how far Edward's mood had shifted from the happy one on the Broads to a very grey one; it weighed him down till the end of the year. I sent a gay telegram after him to London, thanking him for the walk and signing it 'Eleanor Collins', to match his 'imperfect Collins' of thanks for the Norfolk holiday. He acknowledged it from Godwin's and Rosalind's new home in Bethnal Green, where Godwin was now practising among the poorest of the poor. The practice was a section of a big combine controlled by Dr. Harry Roberts, at whose horses we had sneered from Wick Green at Easter. Bethnal Green was far afield from most of Godwin's friends, but nothing kept them from flocking after him to the shabby old-fashioned scantily-furnished house warmed by his presence. Rosalind dispensed prescriptions (quite illicitly surely, but who cares now?) in the dispensary on the street-level, and hunted the Caledonian Market for cheap attractive crockery to help out the bits given them by their families. I chiefly remember a lovely old shawl which she got for half a crown, a curious trestle-bed apt to let its occupant down, and two lovable jerboas, who became dear to us all.

Sept. 5th

Godwins.

Dear Eleanor thank you for your letter & for your telegram with witty signature. I wish I could say at once I will come to Berwick, Lewes but it would mean leaving Mervyn to the Ellises for a longer time than I think I ought to. But this is 9 a.m. on Friday & before breakfast & there is time for considering. I will consider. Maitland saying last night on the telephone that he certainly was going to Lewes on Saturday. Godwin apparently cannot, Bertie as you now know I expect, is intending to go to Italy with Clifford on that day. So I will not desert you if I can avoid it.

The motor charabanc was really a blessing as Bronwen would have been unhappy over anything of a walk, while she enjoyed the ride. We got to town together yesterday morning & I saw a thousand people Arnold and Hodgson & then Bertie & David Garnett here—It would have been better walking. You have a good day today. I hope it will be good. And if we can't meet on Sunday let it be another day soon. God keep you.

Now (in the train) I cannot see how I can arrange for Lewes, especially as it has turned wet & on a wet day Mervyn is a burden I must undertake myself. But if it does turn out possible I will take the only possible Sunday morning train from East Grinstead to Lewes. But this I should telegraph to you tomorrow evening at Lewes, or by a letter reaching the P.O. by 8.30 on Sunday morning. Have you had a wet week? and a good one?

I'm sick of talking & writing about books & I am trying to hit on a subject—an itinerary or a fiction—I can't yet do an autobiography—which will enable me to put my material in a continuous and united form instead of my usual patchwork. Can you help? If you can—

Yours ever
Edward Thomas.

I had lunch with Clifford & Arnold & Bertie was added unto us afterwards, but I was an elderly literary outsider. The landscape as I write is rain clay Beecham & Heinz.

Clifford's sudden invitation to introduce Bertie to the Venice he loved came as news to me.

The ramble to Lewes and Berwick never took place. I arrived at Greatham, a day before Maitland, shy, and a little

28

overwhelmed [by] the bevies of Meynells at supper. Afterwards Viola took me to a cottage on the far edge of the estate,
where her five-year-old niece, Sylvia Lucas, was ill in bed.
The previous week she had cut her knee on a rusty scythe; the
wound had had medical attention, and not at first been taken
seriously. But now it became apparent that something was
wrong. The child, very white and fragile, very big-eyed,
welcomed her favourite aunt with a lovely smile, and almost at
once asked 'Prudie' to play her a tune. What tune would Sylvia
like? In a frail voice she began to sing a queer little air:

> Manners make Ladies but not such as these,
> Manners make Ladies but not such as these . . .

Viola played the tune on a piano with one finger. Sylvia
demanded it again and again, and made us sing it with her.
When we left the cottage to walk back in the dark, we were
both crying quietly. The little girl was very ill—so ill, that I
believe but for our projected walking-tour which never came
off, she would have died.

On Sunday Maitland arrived, full of gaiety, knapsack on
back. Viola told him about Sylvia, and he asked to be allowed
to see her. When he came back from the cottage to the big
house his face was no longer gay. He talked to Wilfrid Meynell
and then took things in hand. For hours he seemed to be tele-
phoning urgently to London, trying to get hold of Mr. Trotter;
when he succeeded, he convinced the great surgeon that the
child was in danger. Mr. Trotter arrived that afternoon,
examined Sylvia, who was now in a fever, and instant arrangements were made to take her to London. In the Hospital of
St. John and St. Elizabeth her life was saved. Her mother
of course went with her, steeling herself to help the child
through the long agonizing treatment without which she must
lose her leg. The five-year-old child steeled herself too. There
was a day when Dimpling Lucas arrived while the treatment
was in process, and Sylvia was screaming with pain. The
moment she saw her mother in the doorway she smiled
brightly, and, her face streaming with tears, asked, 'Did you
hear me pretending to cry?'

Maitland accompanied the Lucases to London, and our trek over the Downs was abandoned. I sent Edward word in time to prevent his going fruitlessly to Lewes, and suggested that we might meet elsewhere for a walk on my way home.

Postmark September 6th
Saturday 10 a.m.   Selsfield House
                                                   East Grinstead.

Dear Eleanor   I posted a letter to you (addressed to Lewes P.O.) at 6 yesterday & then arriving here got your telegram & this morning your letter. At any rate I will be in Worth churchyard at 12 (not midnight) on Tuesday, but Sunday at Greatham is as difficult as at Lewes. It would mean leaving Mervyn with a re-sourceless man (from Mervyn's point of view) in a childless large house: probably for a rainy day. So I don't think I can. If I can I will. But the rain makes a slight problem even for me because it makes Ellis greyer & I haven't work that justifies my going up to the attic where I wrote a book in May. So it means smoking & waiting for chance thoughts out of the rain and grey & considering the 35 years that have certainly passed, the 35 that may conceivably be to come. Today I shall most likely escape this for a few hours with de la Mare & Newbolt and some others. I hope you haven't the same difficulties or any worse ones.

Mervyn is fidgetting with the terrestrial globe, with the type-writer, etc., & I cannot write more.
                                                   Yours ever
                                                   Edward Thomas.

Edward brought Mervyn along with him to Worth. The grey mood had now thoroughly set in. Everything Mervyn said and did seemed to irk him. We spent some time in Worth churchyard, where Edward dug curiosities of names and epi-taphs out of old stones; then we bought fruit for a picnic. After it, when Mervyn had made himself scarce, I said, 'Don't you think you are unnecessarily hard on Mervyn?' He an-swered wearily, 'Perhaps I am—but I dare say it gives him something to kick against.' They saw me off in the late after-noon at Three Bridges.

Postmark Sept. 15th.

Monday.   London.

My dear Eleanor,   I have not been neglecting your letter as a
demi-Collins. But I thought I might have found a part of a day that
you also could spare. And I didn't, especially as I am returning
earlier tomorrow with the children while Helen is up at an Eye
Hospital & just catches (or misses) the train at Waterloo which
we mean to get at Clapham junction. And I can think of nothing
much except the chances of doing work when there is none that is
wanted. I must try to hit upon something unprofitable if there's
nothing of the other kind. I must work or I shall consume myself
with dissatisfaction & various envy. So that I shall be particularly
glad if you do invent that compost you have nobly attempted.—I
have about 3 weeks of my study to do something with. After that
I hope I shall *see* you. I am very glad they appreciated you at 3
Bridges. It would have been wretched to zig-zag through dripping
junctions in twilight.

Mervyn & I had such a good walk townwards on Saturday
through Lingfield & Crowhurst. The sun shone & we didn't annoy
one another.
Yours ever
Edward Thomas.

Who was that Sussex ghost? There are so many & so many kinds.
Don't let his (or her) brains be too much for me, nor yet too little,
though that is not likely. When you come down to Steep ask me for a
really good clay.

I was home again. Bertie and Clifford were already in
Venice, where they seemed to be spending most of the day in
their lodgings, playing an interminable game of paper-cricket;
it involved the throwing of dice with plus-and-minus chances
of making runs and being caught or bowled, according to
whether the cup was rattled for the redoubtable Major or the
unpredictable Colmer. They also amused themselves with
writing, turn and turn about, two lines at a time, impromptu
parodies of Masefield and Francis Thompson, addressed to
their friends. I received a scintillating 'Corymbus' in the latter
vein that bristled with incredible adjectives.

Edward stayed immersed in his study on the ridge, and
wrestled with *Ecstasy*, while he himself was never further from
it. I sent him some plan for a book that he might compile.

31

Letter dated Sept. 18th.

Steep,
Petersfield.

My dear Eleanor, Thank you. Thank you. And I have been
revising the stories by gaslight. Only 'A Cat may look at a King' is
missing & one other. But I expect the complete set back from
Heinemann & can finish the revision then; after which I am going
to let an agent see what he can do. If it won't bother you will you
look at this extra one which I had rejected & tell me if it can anyhow be amended? I doubt it & don't expect it.

I like your scheme for the book of books: so does Helen. Granted
an impulse on top of this hill I shall use it. Probably I shall modify it.
For example I think I cannot make it an allegory or parable with a
cheerful significance. If it has one it will be accidental or as the gods
provide. We and you shall see. These first days are rather barren.
I read most of the time—bad verses, other men's, Frederick Tennyson's, for example. And there is no swing yet here or up there.
'Three weeks' by the way, referred to the time I have clear before I
come to town again. That is all. At present I don't expect to be
turned out of my study. I shall just go on doing dull things till
something turns up.—Helen's eyes are only having new spectacles
fitted to them.—This morning came a postcard from Bertie. If he
does come down here after Venice I shall be glad.

I feel cured of the ambition to do Ecstasy & must seek for something more profane & more suitable for a material if insubstantial
pen. My halo even is material and substantial too. The photographs are excellent & Mervyn's envy. I think you score over
Gertrude, who seems to realise it. This letter is a fake, you per-
ceive, but the heart is in the right place notwithstanding.

We send our love to you to leaven the mess.

Yours ever,
Edward Thomas.

As I could not go down to claim my 'really good clay' till
he was less beset, I spent a few days in the Berkshire woods
with Godwin's friend and neighbour Olive Hockin. She was
a very strong, sturdily-built woman, with deeply-planted
muscle-bound emotions which she did not believe could be
reciprocated. She was the staunchest of friends to those who
convinced her of their liking for her. On a winter-sports

holiday in Switzerland, where she had outclassed the male ski-
ing champions, Godwin was taken too ill to return home.
Olive stayed behind to nurse him, became passionately
attached to him, and for years endured deep suffering inarticu-
lately. She found her outlet in painting. Her richly-coloured
pictures were lush in the Rossettian fashion; in reading she
loved mediæval legend, Butcher and Lang's Odyssey, Burne-
Jones's memoirs, Morris's tapestried romances, and the
Utopia of 'News from Nowhere'. She lived a plain hard life,
not from poverty but because it appealed to her nature and her
principles. She fought for the Suffrage with dogged loyalty
and went to prison for it for three months. Prison hardships
as such meant nothing to her, but she was a vigorous animal
caged, and broke down from sheer loss of her liberty. We all
liked this taciturn, utterly honest, utterly fearless woman, who
loved luxuriance in art and scorned luxurious living, but only
a few of us made headway with her. Paul Corder, honest and
taciturn as herself, was one; I was another, for quite opposite
reasons. I lacked her dominant qualities of courage and
endurance, but went forward to human beings as she longed to
do, and could not. Now and then I shared her hermit-life in
the woods, where she spent hours with her paints and brushes
among the burning colours of the autumn trees and skies
reflected in an inland lake she loved. Sometimes she carried
her outfit to the top of a pine-tree, painting the sunset waters
and the red trunks far below her, as fearless of heights as an
eagle in its eyrie.

   She knew how wanting I was in physical courage, and tried
to make me as fearless as she was. One evening she loaded
herself with rugs and sleeping-bags, and we went through
the glowing trees to the water's edge. The forest rides were
thick with fantastic fungus, with every spotted red and orange
shape seen by the poet who showed us the puckish glades of his
English midlands, and called them a wood near Athens. The
Berkshire woods are the woods of midsummer dream, and
this was one of the enchanted evenings, so clear, so coloured,
so very still that anything might come to pass in it. The ground
shelved steeply under the trees to the lake. Olive spread our

bags and rugs at the top, and we ate and talked or sat silent while the reflections changed colour, and stars came into them. Very small sounds—a pine-cone crickling or an acorn falling, or a little creature moving among the fern—made listening more important than talking. After awhile we crept into our sleeping-bags. Olive showed me how to hollow a place in the ground for my hip. It was my first night in the open. I did not sleep much, and did not want to. Every sleeping moment was a waste of this difference from all I had been used to. In the early morning Olive stripped and plunged into the lake; I did too, but slipped more timorously into the water's brink, and when I found it shelving out of reach I took my morning bath under the trees. In the middle of the lake, quite far away, a flat stone rose from a hidden base, like a little altar. 'There's something on it,' called Olive; 'someone has been here.' She swam out, and presently came back smiling. 'It's a crown of wild parsley, Godwin has been sacrificing to the deity. Swim out and see.' But I could only manage a few strokes in salt water, and in fresh water none. Olive tried to persuade me to let her carry me on her back, assuring me that she was strong enough to bear me, but I feared my own fear if I lost confidence and clutched her. These were the days when I dreamed of becoming a poet, but not by playing Arion to Olive's dolphin. She laughed and swam out again to the crowned altar, and I was alone among the reeds.

From the far side of the lake rang hoarse shouts and the baying of hounds, and through the trees opposite came the hunting-pack. The rout raced savagely in my direction. If it followed the path above the bank right round, it must soon reach me. Filled with wild fear I crouched in the rushes, hoping I was hidden. I felt terror, not of the men, but of the hounds. Now I knew how Actaeon felt when the goddess set her pack on him, and also how Artemis felt exposed to Actaeon. Three quarters of the way round the pack found a new scent, and pursued it up and away into the forest. My terror left me with a feeling of elation, as though for one moment I had taken part in one of the Greek legends dear to me since I was eight years old. A wood near Athens, Diana's bathing-pool, a crown of parsley dedicated by an absent hero to a presiding God. I've always been more grateful to Olive for that memory of fear than for all the courage she tried to instil in me.

Sept. 25th. Steep, Petersfield.

My dear Eleanor, I have got on so far today that I am sorry I wrote yesterday & perhaps put you off. If I didn't could you come down on Sunday evening by the 5.25 from Waterloo? I want to know where it was you had the lake & the wood & Diana in Berkshire. I should like to be there some time.

This morning came, with a refusal, a rejected M.S. & the statement that 2 books had earned 5/- in 6 months & a very fine poem by Bertie & Clifford entitled 'Walking Tom' which might have provided Masefield with the ideas of 'The Everlasting Mercy' & 'The Widow in the Bye Street' if it had preceded them. We have been reading it with admiration & delight, the thought of those 2 in Venice writing it is a thing to add permanently to the associations of Venice. I want to tell them so. Will you forward the note? I received this poem for Sunday Night, & with it a tabulated statement of everyone's scores (yours & mine etc.) at wit fancy humour fun irony & sarcasm.

I want to give you de la Mare's 'Peacock Pie'. Will you ask for it when you come?

It will not be too late for additions in Ecstasy on Sunday.

Helen sends her love.

Yours ever
Edward Thomas.

I wrote to say I would come down on the Sunday to claim the book, the pipe, and to hear the poem, and knowing at what low ebb things were for him in many ways, I took my courage in my hands again to ask if he would let me help to tide over at least his material crisis. I wasn't yet earning anything much myself, but I had about two hundred pounds in the Post Office, a legacy from my grandfather, kept untouched for about eight years.

Friday   Steep
                                                        Petersfield

My dear Eleanor,   I knew already. I knew as soon as you hinted.
Which is unusual for me & I think will tell you much that I could
not easily say. This being so you will know that I should have no
qualms in accepting. And yet I think very likely I shall refuse,
because I am not yet badly off. I owe nothing, & for some time
need owe nothing. And I don't like to borrow, raise my standard
for a year & then go down with a greater bump. If the difficulty
were temporary I would say yes at once, but I fear it isn't. If I had
something in mind which the money would make possible I would
say yes. Perhaps there is something. But I write instantly & therefore even more shortly than I should have done. I hope more than
ever you will come on Sunday evening. It is now 4 & I must go
up to the study.
    I stayed up the hill not coming home to dinner or you would
have had this tonight.
                                                      Yours ever
                                                    Edward Thomas.

    The Sunday must have been my second visit to Steep.
Edward gave me the 'really good clay' he had broken in for me,
and handed me a book bound in dark blue cloth saying, 'Read
this, and if you are worthy of it, keep it.' I was, of course,
found worthy of his second review copy of *Peacock Pie*. It is
the only edition of it I have ever owned or wanted, though
many lovely illustrated ones have succeeded it. For Edward
Peacock Pie was one of the two pure-gold nuggets he dug out
of his reviewing of poetry; he would have parted with it to
no one who did not love it as he did. The second, given me a
year later with same formula, was Robert Frost's *North of
Boston*. This was Edward's most precious find of all. He gave
me lesser books without conditions; I could like them or not
as I pleased.
    After supper we sat in the small room behind the kitchen-
scullery which he used as his study at home. It had no exit
except into the main room, and when, hemmed-in, he heard
through the wall a garrulous woman visitor chattering with
Helen at the door, he would make one long-legged stride over

the window-sill, and flee. That evening he read several poems from *Peacock Pie*, then Shelley's 'Question', and finally 'Walking Tom', Clifford-and-Bertie's parody of Masefield. It was dedicated to Edward, Tom's *alter ego*. The degradation of this lost soul was depicted, step by step, through every sin in the calendar. In each verse, as he drew nearer to damnation, he lost another friend. With one of them, Arthur Ransome, Tom added murder to his crime-sheet, bashing him over the head with

> His latest work, called 'Oscar Wilde, a Study',
> A bloody book his blood made still more bloody.

Finally, when he had but one friend left—

> Even Eleanor, disgusted but polite,
> Returned unclasped the shameful hand he proffered.

But the Masefield School never abandoned hope. Two angelical young men of infinite charm, one fair, one dark (easily recognizable as the creators of the poem), discovered Tom in the gutter, took him by the hands, and led him to the heights of Hampstead Heath—

> . . . where they with daisies crowned him,
> And chanted pious hymns and danced around him,
> And told him that the Lord at last had found him.

Edward read Tom's salvation aloud with reverential gravity, which Helen and I interrupted with laughter. I think it did a lot to dispel his grey mood.

§9

Oct. 5.   15 Rusham Rd.   Balham

My dear Eleanor,   Will you forgive me if I do not turn up tomorrow? I have an appointment of uncertain time with an American just before & may not be able to come. In any case it would be 4.30 I could come. So if it suits you you will wait there; if you dislike the uncertainty don't come but forgive me. You understand; I might not come at all . . .

Yours ever
Edward Thomas.

I am quite sure it suited me to wait from 4.30 onwards, most likely at the Cottage Tea-rooms; and I am pretty sure he presently arrived, very likely from St. George's, the restaurant in St. Martin's Lane where his literary coterie met for lunch. And he may have mentioned the names of some who were there: Hodgson, Locke Ellis, Bottomley, de la Mare, Monro, Davies, who were his friends of long standing. But he did not name the American who was to become the greatest friend of his life.

Of five more letters in October one only is dated, on the 25th; the others I place by the references in them: to the varying fortunes of *Four-and-Twenty Blackbirds* (accepted at last by Heinemann), and the struggle with, and abandonment of, *Ecstasy*.

I had had a few things published in *The Vineyard*, was on pleasant terms with Mrs. Joseph King, the editress, and suggested trying to serialize some of the Proverbs.

13 Rusham Rd.
Balham S.W.

Dear Eleanor   Thank you. Thank you. And here are the other proverbs returned by Hodgson. Don't hurry about them as you did over these others. I don't know about the Vineyard. They have refused everything I've sent & its the sort of show I don't like being refused by. But since Helen met the Proprietress I had thought of trying again. Not, I think, with the Proverbs. How can they be in low water. Aren't they as rich as rich?

I shall see you tonight almost certainly but send this in case I don't.

Yours ever
Edward Thomas.

Wednesday   Steep, Petersfield

My dear Eleanor,   Thank you for many things and yet I can't say Come, because today I began writing about Ecstasy and very badly and the only thing to do for my peace is to go on and on writing and see what happens. Now a great deal might happen in a few days—then if you were free you would come perhaps. Helen's sister Mary is coming for the day on Sunday and Marston is expected on

Wednesday night. Otherwise all days are good for you. But don't— you wouldn't—count on me more than you know you may. Meantime will you write?

Heinemann wants to have another look at the Proverbs, he says. In any case I don't think I shall bother with illustrations unless a heavendescended one drops and offers itself. Thank you above all for liking 2's Company, though what you like was stolen from some mediaeval source—the counting of the cheeses, I mean. I felt that nothing really happened; things were only 'said to have occurred'. I rather want you to agree.

Thank you (less) for the photograph. It is good of the more inanimate objects.

I hope you will be here soon, tho I have nothing from Clifford and Bertie yet. If you don't come then I think I could manage some time on the evening of Friday week or the morning of the Saturday (the 8th)—I am on my way then not very willingly to Monro's with Hodgson.

In the mad hurry between gardening and Ecstasy

Yours ever
Edward Thomas

I am so set on writing *Something* new (I mean on Ecstasy) that I am sure I am very objectionable except to my pen and paper, but I hope (though I couldn't *try*) that I haven't been more than inevitably so to you. At least I didn't wait.

'Thank you (less) for the photograph. It is good of the more inanimate objects.' A houseboat snapshot of Edward, bending over some crocks and cutlery, washing-up.

'Marston is coming.'

Marston ('Muffin' to his friends), plump, easy-going, and very amusing, had been the official artist to the Shackleton Expedition to the South Pole. After he came back he married Harry Roberts's daughter and now lived the simple life of the little community in the Hampshire valley not very far from Steep. He was one of the men who could make Edward roar with laughter. At the South Pole he discovered the gift for imitating penguins so truly that when he gave their call the birds flocked across the ice from all sides to waddle about him as one of themselves. The penguin tribe, he told us, is a

Matriarchy in which the males greatly outnumber the females.
In the mating-season each female has her pick of many suitors.
Muffin described one such courtship watched by the Shackleton
crew. It was conducted gregariously on a great ice-field, where
the ladies stationed themselves at suitable distances, and the
wooer made his overtures by presenting his love with a stone.
This, if she fancied him, became the cornerstone of her nest.
If she did not, she pecked him mercilessly. Dejected and bleed-
ing, he rolled his unwanted offering away, to be joined by the
rejected from the other queues. When all the females had
chosen their mates, a sorry flock of bachelors remained. But
one of them plucked up heart to try again, and pushing his
nest-stone across the ice, deposited it hopefully at Muffin's feet.
After this Muffin was known as Penguin.

One night this month, when I was staying in Steep, Edward
gave me a copy of *Light and Twilight* which he had picked up
secondhand in a bookshop in town. The price, 1/3, is still
pencilled on the fly-leaf, and opposite it in ink his inscription,
'Eleanor Farjeon from Edward Thomas, 1913'. It was the
first of his books that he had given me, the first of his prose
that I had ever read. That night in bed I read the exquisite
'Flower-Gatherer', and the two following it: 'A Group of
Statuary' and 'Home'—that haunting haunted tale of a young
soldier 'dying in a far land' with his brain full of 'the mists, the
mountains, the rivers, the fire in the fern, the castles, the
knights, the kings and queens, the mountain boys at cricket,
the old man with the foxes, the inn dogs lying in the sun . . .
the sun . . . the mist . . . his country . . . not the country he
had fought for . . . the country he was going to . . .': the
country his Welsh father had taken him to from London,
when he was a boy. 'Tomorrow,' the father had said, 'we will
take the train at midnight, and before noon we will be finding a curlew's nest on the moor just by where the old battle
was.'

'What battle, father?' said the boy.

'Why, one of the old battles when we beat the English, I
suppose,' said he . . .

Next morning I tried to tell him, shyly and inadequately,

something of what his writing had made me feel. Then I asked, 'Haven't you ever written poetry, Edward?'

'Me?' He uttered a short self-scornful laugh. 'I couldn't write a poem to save my life.'

How strange! this writer, capable of imaginative prose, whose secret self pined for beauty, who could evaluate the poetry of other men, and make or break a new poet with a review—'couldn't write a poem to save his life'. But only a few days before he said so, he had kept an appointment of uncertain time, with an American in London.

I read the rest of *Light and Twilight* at home, and wrote what I felt better than I could say it.

Steep.

My dear Eleanor,   I am reading two novels a day for the next few & last few days, every page of them, & can think of little else. But I do thank you for what you say about 'Light & Twilight'. Not time alone prevents me from quite facing the question how far the 'Stile' & others represent something which 3 years have shut a door on. But I don't think doors do shut—not quite fast. I remember how I used to think at 17 or so of games I had as it seemed accidentally given up but as it fell out, for ever, & of people I never meant to leave but whom I did leave for ever, & used to try to get back & thought I could, yet didn't. This new difficulty is the same. I don't think in either case I am the same person. If I have time I shall prove that I am a very similar one. But there have been noticeable vanishings, I was going to say not natural ones, which would be absurd, because it is my nature that allows uncongenial work, anxiety etc. to destroy or change so much and so fast, so that during the last few weeks I have been like a misty wet dull flat shore, like that at Flansham when the sea seemed to have gone away for ever, & I haven't believed in another tide. I know now that what I thought a new strength about 2 months ago was only the quiet of weakness consummated.

However, I have work for some time ahead & I suppose I shall do it. You will be glad to hear that Heinemann accepts the Proverbs & I shall soon be trying St. Nicholas etc. with them, as the book must wait till the Autumn of 1914. The illustrator is not yet chosen.

When I have a little leisure I will look up some of my unpublished papers & send them. Don't forget your story, tho at the moment I could not look at it or anything outside the novels I have to consider for a Times' article.

Yours ever,
Edward Thomas.

PS.   Don't mention this 'Times' article as it is a very trying test on which a lot may depend & I only accepted it in the hope of better things from there later. It has to be done at great pressure too.

So the struggle to place *Four-and-Twenty Blackbirds* was happily over; had prospects of work on *The Times*, he was pleased with what I could say about his work, and he was willing to read something of my own. I hadn't much to show him but my invention of a mock-Elizabethan poet, Nathaniel Downes, whose diary, with eleven poems from his *Shepheards Gyrlonde*, had appeared in *Blackwood's Magazine* (and been accepted as genuine by the literary reviews); and a long fanciful story, *The Soul of Kol Nikon*. It was written very much under the influence of the Celtic Twilight, and Arnold Bax had read it with enthusiasm, and introduced it to Joseph Plunkett in Dublin. It ran serially for several months in *The Irish Review*, and his Irish friends had echoed Arnold's praise. Years after, when I came to know James Stephens, he always referred to it as 'a work of janius'. These good opinions emboldened me to hope that Edward might like Kol too; and I had several copies bound up in cloth, through the generosity of Clifford Bax, who reserved fifty numbers of each issue of the magazine for the purpose. One of these I offered to send to Edward.

Undated letter from Steep.

My dear Eleanor,   I am just tearing away & returning this, asking for the printed 'Kol'—Please. I will write again when I am not tearing away. But I suddenly had to do a rotten article on Conrad. Thank you for your letter. I am going to write.

Yours ever
Edward Thomas.

Kol Nikon was posted and acknowledged at once.

Postmarked Petersfield.
Friday.

My dear Eleanor   I have not had a moment to spare for your book or anything, because I have been trying to get rid of all the reviews I have had to do before I leave on Monday—I think I shall do it. Also I meant to type 'Ecstasy'. I did a third, then soberly & finally decided it was mostly muck & so ill arranged that it could not be rewritten. That is the end & I am left with what consolation I can extract from knowing I can sometimes avoid both print & guineas. Perhaps I can find another subject for Batsford.

I am not sure if I can see you in town next week. My plans are not formed. And moreover since it is useless to speak of what is in my mind the less I see the better of anyone who can't ignore that there is something there—what it is even I, after exhausting study, don't really know. But if I can see you I will. I shall be mostly or entirely at 13 Rusham Rd till Wednesday; then presumably at Ellis'.

Meanwhile tell Bertie that I at least hope his play will not be excepted.

Yours ever
Edward Thomas.

Farewell to *Ecstasy*. Only too literally at the moment. He was settling in with Locke Ellis at Selsfield House till the end of the year.

Letter card dated Nov. 5th.

My dear Eleanor,   Thank you for the stationery. I know.—I am sorry I couldn't begin to use it sooner. But I have not found life any better tho it is simpler, & I have been working all day, really hard, as hard as one can in my state of mind, & this very day I have begun to write an abridgement of what I have been reading about Keats' life & character. It is difficult & slow & unrewarding & my head's thick with it & I am furthermore anxious as to whether I shall do anything but abridge—e.g. say something about the poems that I really think. However, it is begun. A thrush sings every hour of the daylight as I work, from 6.30 to 5 : also men hammer & saw, repairing Ellis' dilapidations. So you will agree that Keats is better off than I, though he couldn't buy Donald's photograph or even want to.—Mrs. Cox, mother of Theresa, Honor & Barbara Cox,

of Sizewell was here for the week-end.—What an absurd remark.
This is to say that I hope you are well & see Clifford & Godwin &
other blessed inhabitants of the earth.

> Yours ever
> Edward Thomas.

Mrs. Cox was the wife of Joan and Rosalind Thornycroft's
Uncle Oswald. Lady Thornycroft, when Miss Agatha Cox,
had been known as the Belle of Tunbridge Wells. She was the
outstanding beauty of a cluster of lovely sisters, one of whom
married Sir Sidney Olivier, and all of whom continued to
produce bevies of lovely girls. Oswald had his own share of
the family good looks, and his three daughters were not the
least lovely of these groups of cousins. Theresa was as sweet
as wild-roses, Barbara was a slim young Swan Princess, and
Honor, the youngest, was a glorious golden child out of Greek
legend. They, like the Thornycrofts, were pupils at King
Alfred's School in Hampstead, the famous co-educational day-
school under John Russell, whose second in command was
George Chester Earle. This master wakened their imagina-
tions to the glories of English literature in an inspired fashion
of his own. Long before I met him I heard that Mrs. Cox, a
woman of great intelligence, considered George Earle the
finest teacher she had ever known, adding, 'and perhaps the
only teacher'. The first appearance of his name in my memoirs
is not casual. I owe him thirty years of happiness.

Edward's next letter is in answer to news I sent him of
Clifford Bax and Olga Antonietti.

Nov. 12th.   Petersfield.

My dear Eleanor,   I am glad you began to like the book, & hope
others will do so. My next best appreciators are the Australians.
They have been ordering 2000 copies of my 'Celtic Stories' for their
schools. I didn't think they (the Colonials) had any virtues.

I hope Clifford & Olga will come through all right & get to peace.
I entirely agree with you without hesitation, because I know that
Daphne would be no better & Clifford the worse for making any
attempt to abide by the letter of their marriage, especially as there
is money enough to keep them separately, & as Clifford is called

away so decidedly. Please give Clifford my love & blessing. I may be in town on Monday next, & would like to go over there & see him, but not if he is still busy with his troubles. Could we both go there at tea-time?

You are used now to these skimming letters. I am still deep in Keats, & getting on as well as I could have hoped & better than I expected, but only by filling my days & latterly my nights with it, to the neglect of everything else.

My Times article is not to be printed. It overlapped with another already done, was not (they say through no fault of mine) what they wanted, so they got another man to do it in a hurry & have sent me another book, & I don't know yet if the review of that will please them any better.

I didn't complain of the thrush! He is a most noble bird, & sings in the wildest & darkest dawns eternally as if he were in a poem & not born for death at all like other thrushes & me.

Goodbye
Edward Thomas.

Undated letter.   at Selsfield House,
                                                   East Grinstead.

My dear Eleanor,   This must make up for lack of many things, including reading of your MS which lies untouched while I go on at Keats. I really have begun & am going on though I have this morning had my Proverbs returned by Heinemann—his evasions & my irritability together did it.

Rosalind thanked me this morning for The Icknield Way & I was told of a puff of 'Light and Twilight' which I think I ought to thank Joe for. Will you convey my sense of silence on a peak in Darien as I stood & looked over the greater world from the height of 'Answers'?

Yours ever
Edward Thomas.

I had given my brother Joe *Light and Twilight* to read, and the puff in *Answers*, the paper he was then writing for, was the result.

In his next letter Edward rejects *Kol Nikon*—but with what gentleness he tempers his honesty and judgement, rather than hurt the sensitiveness of a friend. 'The poisoner of Wilcox' could not have been kinder, but he had to be unswervingly true to his opinion.

5th December 1913   at Selsfield House
                                                     East Grinstead.

My dear Eleanor,   I have just been reading 'Kol Nikon' and have just got to 'The Little Grey Man' & am wondering if I ought to go on after the sentence where he 'sank his hand in the moon-ray and drew forth a silver horn & offered it to Kol.' For I find myself trying in vain to see or in some way to apprehend the action. Perhaps you will solve the difficulty as Clifford does with Arnold Bennett, say 'Materialist', more gently, perhaps less firmly. Speaking loosely, there are many kinds of reality—the reality of Tom Jones, of Don Quixote, of Venus & Adonis, of Lamia, of La Belle Dame sans Merci, & of 'I heard a horseman ride over the hill', & perhaps a hundred other kinds, & though I am incapable of most of them yet I recognise them. Only I cannot recognise the kind used in that sentence from 'Kol Nikon'. I am shooting in the dark. Honestly I hope I have shot myself, because the only other victim would be you, & I can afford to admit another inability in myself, but would not willingly be the one to prove an inability in you. Tell me what you think. Is the poisoner of Wilcox a scalp-hunter? [1] Or is he only a felo de se? Or has he really in these last few months taken leave of some of his senses as from time to time he believes? Well at least he has written a book on Keats & begun one on himself—no less than an autobiography, not a chronological & geographical history of E.T. but an attempt to put on paper what he sees when he thinks of himself from 1878 to about 1895. It is really done because he thinks he must do something other than reviewing & he can't face the novel concerning people unlike himself which he fancied on a fine rainy night walk he was going to attempt. So much about that writer of books.

  I am staying on here till the end of the year when my movements will depend on Ellis who may go to Italy & will in any case most likely leave this house with me somewhere outside of it. It's a pity because here I have found it possible to write & make a sort of cloistered tranquility so long as I hear no bad news from home. I went home for 2 days last week-end, thought things were worse than they were, & returned here all the worse for it myself anyhow. At Christmas Helen & the children are coming here for a week or

  [1] 'The poisoner of Wilcox' refers to his famous satirical review of Ella Wheeler's poetry, in which he placed her on a Shakespearian level by speaking of her throughout as Wilcox. For this devastating article her pleased publishers rewarded him with a complete set of her works which he evidently lacked as some of them hadn't been mentioned.

so. Meantime I shall do what work I get & wait for something to turn up & as you see think about myself, in spite of reading authors ancient & most modern who tell me its the devil. If I am up for more than a few hours before Christmas—about the Monday or Tuesday before—I shall see if you are in town & willing to try again in spite of the revelations over the page. In any case I am

Yours ever
Edward Thomas.

I don't remember how I answered this letter, but I must have done so in a way that enabled him to amplify his criticism without fearing to hurt a growing friendship. I wasn't badly hurt; but I must have been disappointed, and not as able then, as I am today, to appreciate the fineness of the surgeon's knife which divided the immaturities of fancy from the reality of imagination.

8th December 1913   at Selsfield House.

My dear Eleanor For two letters & for Hudson's book & for glimpses of a world far from mine, my thanks. There is rather more to say than I am giving myself a chance of saying. Davies has been here 5 days & we three have talked & smoked a lot & I have done mostly half-days of work, so that what with some reviewing & the autobiography I feel as if I were busy.

First about Kol Nikon. I did mean that my objection to that one phrase was one that had recurred not always so definitely from the page where I began to read about the Mild Berchta. At that passage I said to myself, either the writer has seen Her or not. If she has seen Her whom am I to judge? If not, then the passage is too long; it should have been as brief & clear as if Defoe had been writing of something not of his world. At the same time I should have drawn the conclusion—with hesitation—that you had not seen Her. In my callous reviewer's style I should have said She was an invention who stood (to you) for an infinity of things aspired after, guessed at, & deeply felt too, but not an artistic expression. Is this brutal? Much reviewing prevents me from seeing books as men walking. I hit them & get quite a shock when I find I have hit a man: yet go on hitting books all the same. However I know that you don't want me to tell lies even to save my own soul & it's doubtful if I could do so by being a polite saint in the matter of Kol

47

Nikon. I won't go on until I know if you want me to for the sake of truth & a perfect understanding.

As for handsome terms of apology I haven't a top or even a barrel. And writing about myself aged 6, 7, 8, 9 doesn't spontaneously generate handsome terms. The autobiography has begun by being the briefest quietest carefullest account of virtually everything I can remember up to the age of 8. I don't trust myself to build up the self of which these things were true. I scarcely allow myself any reflection or explanation. 20 pages of it don't seem fearfully dull, though all the material is as commonplace & unillumined as anything any of my hundreds of school-fellows could recall, I am sure. If it were clearlier written I would send it to you. Some day I shall type it & then I will. If there is anything it is more unlike than 'The Story of My Heart' it is 'Lavengro'. I am so glad you like 'Lavengro'. Borrow was a romantic, & whatever came into his head while he was looking backward in a creative imaginative mood he put down, adding also an element out of his favourite kind of fiction, the Rogue Novels, & particularly coincidences. It has no value as a record of facts. It is a picture of a man revealing himself by his attitude towards his childhood & youth. I should call it fiction with all 4 legs on the ground of fact but baying at the moon. Your criticism of the meeting with the apple woman's son is, as far as I know, new, & I think certainly true. I am trying to be true to the facts. There is no spirit (up to 9 years old) in connection with them. I extenuate nothing & set down naught in malice. But I quite see that this may turn out futile & will need a lot of cutting down unless I persuade myself to make an entirely different thing. I don't know what I was. I only know what I did & later on, sometimes, what I thought. I hardly expect it to be published. It is pure experiment so far.

Homes & Haunts I have got to Detest, & I believe I have been doing it intolerably ill through indifference & haste to be done with it, but in a soberer state of mind I see that I mustn't throw away £70 or so if I can possibly get it. For the present I am forgetting it.

After Xmas Mrs. Ellis goes to Switzerland & Italy. Ellis can't decide what to do. I don't think it will be Sizewell. I am waiting for him to decide. He may go to town but return here for week-ends; in which case I might stay here alone. If he keeps to town I also may stay in town, with my people, unless I can get very cheap country lodgings, which is doubtful. Italy is doubtful, especially for me. I can't run away from work & spend a lot of money into the bargain.

If you go to Rottingdean I might be able to see you & hear the creaking get fainter. I was sorry to hear you speak so badly of yourself & hope it really can be walked off in January. I hope this letter isn't going to add a twinge or take away a particle of the power to laugh at twinges.

Yes I do have to say 'Up with me!' 3 or 4 times but the sponge gets squeezed. It's queer but I *couldn't* shirk that ridiculous torture.

I do like Olga, decidedly.

Goodbye. I will let you know about the 22nd or 23rd., more likely the 22nd as Helen & the children are due here on the 23rd. If its fine Mervyn will cycle, putting up one night on the way.

> Ever yours,
> Edward Thomas.

'Yes, I do have to say "Up with me!" 3 or 4 times but the sponge gets squeezed.'

This magic formula was initiated by Godwin Baynes for the squeezing of an icy sponge down the spine in the winter-morning cold bath. The full invocation (a quotation, I think) ran:

> Up with me, up with me into the blue,
> For thy song, lark, is strong!

Then you squeezed the sponge. The intrepid cold-bathers of our circle stiffened their courage with it, shiveringly; but Godwin, splashing behind the bathroom door, chanted it with ecstasy. His sponge sounded like Niagara.

A last reference to *Kol Nikon* in Edward's next must be due to my exonerating him from finishing the story.

Postmark December 14th, 1913.

Selsfield House.

My dear Eleanor   I ought to have written before, so missed these bad days, bad I daresay chiefly because of 3 sleepless nights. I am writing foolish letters all round. But I will try to spare you, tho it means omitting everything.

At present it requires an effort to say I am going to read 'Kol'. I know nothing certain except that I shall eat lunch in a quarter of an hour's time. But when your letter came it would have been simple to say—'Of course I am going to read Kol.'

E   49

I have just walked over to see Gordon Bottomley and R C Trevelyan at Trevelyan's house on Leith Hill & back again; on Friday & Saturday, beautiful days, with a deadly night in between, a carrions corpse eaten up by wormy thoughts & halfdreams (including a curious beautiful group of young people, one a girl of 13 or so, with one arm round an elder youth's waist, looking at me— my part being to defend my own works; I forget the rest.) Today is Sunday, after another sleepless night and letterless Sunday.

Ellis' plans weave a gnatlike dance. But it does seem likely I shall go from here on Jan 15. In fact I feel inclined to profess firmness for that date & so give my hosts the chance of doing without me thereafter. They know well how this suits me, but I may quite likely have got softly onto their nerves, since I can be as presumptuous as I am half-piscatorially umble.

I am giving you more than a chance of filling up the gaps I leave. Laugh at *my* twinges, too. In my way I enjoy them. As to Mithridates, poison has become a simple diet to me. If only I were an aesthete I should try common things for a new sensation.

Monday morning.

I have just been looking over some letters I wrote yesterday & had to destroy one on account of its ridiculous invitation to an *editor* to look into my parlour & see the orrible sights. I won't destroy this. You could take it more cum grano than he could, & its no use patching it up.

I will let you know later about Monday.

I hope Bertie is all right by now.

My love to him & you.

Ever yours
Edward Thomas.

Postmark 16th December 1913.

at Selsfield House.

My dear Eleanor, Thank you. At any rate I have slept quite moderately well now for 3 nights. And I am very glad you could go to a theatre in spite of all, & Bertie too. So I conclude you will be able to have lunch with me somewhere on Monday. In writing to Clifford I asked if he was free. If so, perhaps we shall go there. Otherwise we might go to Shearns or Miles'—but Miles' is so crowded. Shearn's on the other hand is so desolate that it sucks one's blood perhaps. Or the Cottage. You decide. Only not the Savoyard. I expect Clifford will have written to you. At any rate I keep myself free for Monday from 1 to 3. In case you want to reach me on Monday morning I shall be at 13 Rusham Rd. Balham. I leave there on Sunday to walk Londonwards. The weather is often perfect for walking & this country provides innumerable walks—footpath walks—of all lengths, from the length required before breakfast upwards. I wish I could enjoy with something more than my senses & a sort of .00001 of my soul, the rest being either torpid or hunched up thinking long exhausted thoughts. However, something does enjoy all these little wet waste valleys with streamlets & alder & rough rocky sides & oakwoods & villages & ploughland on top. I always walk alone.

The autobiography grows, now a few pages on my father & mother, now on school work, now on play, now on pigeons, & so on. I don't know if it will turn out to have any continuity at all. My object at present is daily to focus on some period & get in all that relates to it, allowing one thing to follow the other that suggested it. It's very lean but I feel the shape of the sentences & alter continually with some unseen end in view. I have practically no other work. And as Ellis & Mrs. Ellis are away till Friday, & I hate forsaken houses (no *fear*, just a tendency to wretchedness), I am lucky to have this.

Yours ever
Edward Thomas.

Thursday.

Thank you for forwarding my letter to Clifford but this morning I've had a note *from him as if from Hammersmith*. But then I see it has been to Steep first.

§10

While Edward was staying indefinitely in East Grinstead, coming less often to town, I continued to go down to Steep to stay with Helen. It was during these days, and especially in the nights when we talked late, that the love between us came into full being.

'My wife could be the happiest woman on earth, if I would let her.' The truth is, Helen was oftener and more fully happy than any wife I knew. Her happiness was an inexhaustible well; its zest enhanced the good days, and was her source of power against the dark ones. If Edward knew that Hamlet was written for him, he knew too that Helen was no Ophelia, and whatever he was and did she would not drown.

The greatest gift which he and she gave me in common was in being their unreserved selves while I was with them, sharing with me both what was painful and what was happy in their lives. The three children and I were completely friends. While Bronwen continued my education out-of-doors, Helen inside the house taught me some principles of cottage cooking, at which she was superb. She loved defeating poverty by providing ample dishes out of nothing, she rejoiced in her strong health that could carry all loads. Being and doing were almost one thing to her. Now when I came for a night or a week-end the pattern was changed. There were still the rambles, the impulsive picnics because the day was too good to be wasted, the shared work of the house, the long sitting in talk over the good meals. I missed, and she how much more, the serene hour when Edward, pipe in mouth, knelt on the hearthrug by Baba in her warm bath, humming, it seemed, through the very stem of the clay, Welsh tunes with their native words, while he soaped the baby's chubby body and towelled it on his knee. We missed the after-supper hour when he read to us. Now, supper over, when the kitchen was 'redded up', instead of going to bed Helen made tea. She was avid for the friends she loved and could pour out her heart to, and we became midnight gossips, stirring our cups over the fire, and talking of people, of books, of our families, of our lives, of Edward. At one or two o'clock I might make a move—

'Oh *no*, Eleanor! not *yet*! I see you so *seldom*.'

More tea was made, we talked on till three or four.

One night when we had been talking only of Edward, of their first meeting, their early marriage, and his dark difficulties, I said, 'You know what I feel for him, don't you; you know I love him?'

'Yes, Eleanor, I do.'

'If it hurts you or him, if it ever could, I can go out of your lives now, rather than cause any pain.'

'Oh my darling! you mustn't *ever* go.' She put her arms

round me and said, 'If having you could make him any happier, I'd give him to you gladly.'

These words, said in utmost truth from one woman to another, I find hard even now to write down, but without them our story would be incomplete.

Christmas drew near. Helen prepared to join Edward at Selsfield House with the children. I went back to Fellows Road and our rich and multitudinous Christmas plans; and for the first time packed a huge and varied parcel for the five Thomases, crammed with nice presents and nonsense ones gaily-wrapped, and labelled against being opened till Christmas morning.

On Boxing Day Edward wrote me his last letter of the year.

at Selsfield House.

My dear Eleanor   Little did I think as I carried that parcel up from the station that it contained an electric flashlight for me. Sometimes I believe that you sent it just because it would be useful, sometimes that it is an earthly object with a heavenly meaning, sometimes that its purpose was to see what I should say about it. So that naturally it is hard to know which of the three possible letters I ought to write; harder still to write them all; quite easy not to write any one of them, I mean after Christmas day. But you should have seen that parcel opened. The surprise of the five people concerned was as great as when all the animals in Eden had names given them, & the pleasure as great as that of the couples who were chosen for the Ark. Mine being the most practised, indefatigable, undryable, pen, I suppose it ought to set about painting the picture which the Farjeons painted with the flesh of five Thomases upon the canvas of Christmas Day. But the fact is that I mulled the claret yesterday.

Goodbye. I hope I shall be able to arrange to come to Cliffords before long & see you there, having recovered from the drinking of the claret which I mulled yesterday. I hope it will not constantly reappear in my pen like this, in fact that I shall get it completely out of my system & tell you what a lot of cheerfulness we got out of everything else & especially that finely selected and masterfully packed box from Fellows Road. If only you could have included some of yourselves in the box! For excellent as the elements are—Ellises, Coxes & Thomases—still, somehow, I don't know. However.

Yours ever,
Edward Thomas.

1914

1914 must be the most important year in Edward's life. In it he discovered his deepest friendship in the American poet Robert Frost, and made in himself the even greater discovery of the English poet Edward Thomas.

When they began to meet in 1913, Frost was a poet unknown in his own country. He had chosen to bring his family to England, where he found a publisher for his first two books of poems. In the second of these, *North of Boston*, Edward made what he knew was the find of his lifetime, and his opinion, more than any other, brought Frost's worth to light in this country. Frost in his eighties is called 'the beloved poet' of America; but at forty he had already discovered what he had to say and how he wanted to say it, and what his poetry is now it was in 1914. Over the years he has filled and emptied and refilled his bucket with new water from the same living well. The draught is always fresh, and if Edward had lived to praise the books that followed the first two, he would have praised them no more and no less. He did live to read the third book, *Mountain Interval*, and ten weeks before he died wrote to me from France that the poems were 'very good, though never better or different from "North of Boston" '. He would have said the same of 'From Plane to Plane', in one of Frost's latest collections. He would have known that from first to last the poetry was inherent in the man who wrote it.

In the autumn of 1914 Edward's own living stream was

undammed. The undamming was Robert's doing when, after
reading his friend's prose, he told him he had been a poet all his
life, and with plain talk for his tools started the water flowing.
From October onwards the poetry came down in spate, and
produced in Edward's being the enharmonic change that made
him, not a different man, but the same man in another key.
Towards the end of the year the change from minor to major
begins to be felt in his letters.

§2

The first letter in 1914 still comes from Selsfield House,
early in January.

My dear Eleanor 'St. Nicholas' having returned the stories I have
chosen these for you to show to Rackham.

When do you go away & is it to Rottingdean? And shall I see
you in town if I come about the 15th? My plans are still in confusion.
After a brief hour of quite imaginary & blinking courage I rediscovered that I couldn't possibly lecture. Then sometimes I want
to be with the children more & to try my old study again. And of
course where one likes nothing choice is so very difficult. In any
case it seems pretty certain I shall not be here much after the 13th or
14th.

Helen hopes to go to my people with Baby tomorrow just for a
day or two, then to her sister's at Chiswick for another day or two.
Bronwen is there (Chiswick) already. Mervyn is with my people at
Balham wondering what to do. I don't know when they will all go
back to Steep but I suppose by the end of next week. Barbara &
Theresa leave here on Monday. They are very good indeed with
Baby who has been in bed all this week.

Yours ever
Edward Thomas

When I heard that Bronwen was already in London, and
Baba was coming, I wrote to Selsfield House asking Helen to
bring them both to the children's party we always gave in
January.

PLATE III

BRONWEN

HELEN

EDWARD

MERVYN

BABA

at Selsfield House
East Grinstead.

My dear Eleanor, I want to write at once, have had to discuss things with Helen too long to give me time for a letter. It is about the Party. Baby is out of sorts with a bad cold, also a boil. She could not possibly come to the Party. The question was, had Helen better travel with her at all: and she is not going to, but staying on here for a few days more. So I must bring Bronwen up to you on Saturday, and fetch her away. I will try to arrange with Clifford to spend the week end there, though Saturday night I must take Bronwen back to my people's. If I am at Clifford's, I shall see you and the catalogue of fruit trees. I feel unusually loth to plant trees now as I did in 1913.

If you have time I believe you will not mind looking at these proofs for me: and if you haven't you will say so.

On Saturday I shall just call at 4 and at 7. I don't want to feel like George Moore being introduced by Yeats to the Queen of the Fairies.

I hope Bertie is all right now.

Yours ever
Edward Thomas.

P.S. I have addressed Clifford at *11* Luxemburg Gardens. If that should be wrong, he is on the telephone. Would you tell him I want to come over to him on Sunday or even late on Saturday night? Please.

Gay children's parties were not Edward's *métier*, and I was prepared for him to do a vanishing act on our doorstep, but I hoped that at Clifford's we would have time to look through a catalogue and choose an apple-tree which I had promised him for a Christmas present.

Selsfield House
12 i 14

My dear Eleanor, Thank you for your letters. I have now arranged to go to Clifford's on Friday evening and to stay some time but probably I shall go down to Steep on Saturday to get some papers and perhaps move my books out of the study. Nothing else is settled; yet I can't start at once for the treasure of the Incas.

I only know I must work—if at nothing else then at the autobiography, tho it is now 15 years of age and so not an endless task
to finish. I want a subject to substitute for Ecstasy.

By this time you have probably heard from Helen. Baby is
apparently well, unless this new bout of frost has touched her somehow. Theresa and Barbara left today; and I was very sorry, chiefly
because I had *not* got into touch with them, tho I liked them. It is
rotten to be left with only one means of expression, and that my
prose. However, we did wave to one another. I find that at 15 I
was damnably like this and I ought to look forward and not back
obviously. Perhaps you will turn up on Friday? I am glad it is not
necessary for you to go away but hadn't you better? The moon and
the snow are very clean tonight.

> Yours ever
> Edward Thomas.

Clifford's home was now to become Edward's chief house of
call when he was in town, for Godwin and Rosalind had flitted
from Bethnal Green to Wisbech. Their going was a blow to us
all; and to them, I think. Why did they go? Godwin wanted
to 'find himself'. He told me that in London he was pulled
in too many directions, by too many interests, among too
many well-loved friends. He was running away from his
devastating popularity. The Wisbech practice was a favourable
one, under the aegis of the famous Misses Peckover of that
town, well out of reach of the distracting attractions of the
Russian Ballet (then at fever-heat), of Beecham Opera, of
multitudinous parties, arranged and impromptu. But what
then? Once more he had acquired a roomy old house, on the
market-square, with ample space for the friends he drew after
him. Radfords, Garnetts, Farjeons, and Baxes flocked north
when they could and would. Almost on arrival Godwin and
Ros planned a spring gathering, at the time of the Wisbech
Fair, when all their friends should be with them. They spoke
of it as The Millennium. Meanwhile we sallied to Cambridge-
shire in twos and threes, and Edward's next letter found me at
27, Old Market, where the Jerboas of Bethnal Green were no
more with us. I never knew what became of them.

11 Luxemburg Gardens
26.i.14.

My dear Eleanor, I am bowed but not bloody. Thank you for trying. The incident adds to the feeling that I am outside the world where work is done and money earned. It is worse in London where so many people are to be seen apparently of another kind. Clifford and Olga are very good, but I don't think I can stand London long, not much beyond the end of next week perhaps. So do come over when you can. Wisbech must have been a better place on Sunday, tho I was saved from tiddlywinks—Clifford said it wasn't so bad. I came in late and didn't get a word with Joe or anybody but S. North. Was it a good fat ham? If so why complain, especially if you (I mean Rosalind) were not in the car at all? But the young lady who expected Rosalind to challenge her to a duel must be a desperate character. I hope she is one of Godwin's patients, and that he won't bungle. But it all sounds very queer and if I am to go to foreign parts I may as well go to Wisbech and save fares. Bertie paying his fare was a distressing thought. Couldn't he get up early enough? I hope it was as fortunate a disability as when he didn't go to the Sheep Fair and scored 166, as they say and print.

I wish I had a good skeleton for a bad novel to while away the time. I am now 17 and the sands of life are fast running out—the thing is almost as long as a novel. But I have still your outline for a book.—Forgive me that I go on so slowly with 'Kol Nikon'. I have read positively nothing these 3 months that I have not had to read except this and the first chapter of 'Great Expectations'.

Is the jointing of this letter merely me in the hurry a letter puts me in or is it really a little insane?

With love to the core of Wisbech

Yours ever
Edward Thomas.

11 Luxemburg Gardens
30 1 14

My dear Eleanor, It is no use saying I am ashamed of saying so much and not all. Briefly, I just feel increasingly that I can't work and perhaps shan't work, and as I depend on work not only for a living but for my principal or sole enjoyment, you see . . . My enjoyment today is to tell a dirty publisher I won't have his 3 guineas and won't do the dirty job I said I would yesterday. In fact it is a pleasure, now that I can't get what I want, to refuse what others want. But it is absurd to tell you so.

Can you come round on Monday or Wednesday? I am booked for nearly all Tuesday. I am going away on the Friday to see some people at Northampton and Coventry, but I expect returning here on Monday or Tuesday, unless I shall have arranged to stay somewhere in the country. It is no use going home without plenty of work.

I hope you are not having too much of a good time at Wisbech.

Yours ever
Edward Thomas.

February is a rather blank month. He seems to have spent it largely at Clifford's in Hammersmith. On my birthday, a postcard:

Feb. 13th 1914

Yes; Monday.
Do you believe in fairies?

Why the query, and what my answer? Had he been taking Baba to *Peter Pan*?

Still in a sorry mood, he is looking for work; writing his autobiography, which I offer to type; somehow 'Kol' swims into the horizon again; and I accept an invitation to his birthday, on March 3rd, at Steep, when I shall present him with his apple-tree.

Going to Camberley.

My dear Eleanor   I suddenly had to do an article in the small hours this morning, then to copy it, and to write a long review, and to pack and to see people in town, and then was hauled away to Camberley by an unexpected telegram, or I would have written to you in sending back 'Kol'. But I hope you will send me the printed book or bring it when and if you come down for my birthday with that dwarf standard which is to cheer my declining years.

About my autobiography. It is a very tortuous M.S. full of corrections, and of directions backward and forward. I should be very glad of your opinion, but I will not expect you to do what you offer until you have seen the M.S., which I will send on that understanding when my luggage arrives at Steep—where I go on Friday evening. In any case it is noble and sweet of you to offer. Thank you very much.

Yours ever
Edward Thomas.

The next, from Steep, is altogether more hopeful in tone.

Steep
Petersfield

22 ii 14

My dear Eleanor, Thank you. You will now have two readers here, if not more, for Bronwen seems tempted. Do come on the 3rd if you can, and I will take a holiday. So far I have merely been racing through small jobs, but I hope to begin the long one this week. As for the autobiography, do not let either its dulness or its obscurities worry you, will you? You will see that there are many insertions to be made, I hope always provided for by cross references. I don't know if I have abbreviated, but I have a way of putting 'g' for 'ing',—'askg' for 'asking' &c. and cd for could, wd for would, and so on. There is a 4th volume (you will see that the pagination is continuous) which I need not send yet, especially as I have still something to add to it. Please tell me any things that occur to you in reading, whether they mean that you would rather stop or not.

I am glad to be back and to watch the plain and the downs from my study. We are all well and liking one another. By the way, you might come down for a Saturday to Tuesday next week end, except that I cannot take whole days off. Think it over, will you?

I have got a batch of books from the *Westminster* by de la Mare's intercession and quite a number of irons are in the fire. The Proverbs however are still homeless.

We send our love to you and Bertie—I hope he is not having more headaches.

Yours ever
Edward Thomas.

I did go down to Steep for his birthday, the first I spent with him and the family. I remember it as a very happy day; and what I chiefly remember is kissing both Helen and Edward good-night on my way up to bed. I thought it might be allowable on a birthday. I felt he was pleased, and Helen afterwards ran up to my room and hugged me as though I had made

61

her a beautiful present. It seems a tiny thing to record, but it took a little courage to slip through Edward's barriers, even on his birthday. One always had to go nine-tenths of the way to meet him.

I see from his next letter that we are on the eve of The Millennium in Wisbech.

My dear Eleanor   We are all sorry you will not be here on Friday and Saturday and twice sorry because you will not be able to do anything you want to except within a 3 mile radius. But as you say and as we say you must make up with an extra week end. Also I hope you will get to Wisbech all right. Should you still be in London and we have more than the inevitable night in town on our way to Wales I will let you know. Meantime we are most busy, gardening, writing, typewriting for me from morning till 1 a.m. and on the whole it suits me, tho I feel thin at times. The ground is almost just right and I have got all the roots in, and peas and beans (a first sowing). Now for potatoes and artichokes. Maitland disappeared the first fine day. He is a bit of a superman, I fancy, or else he was very well indeed.

I have looked through the typescript now, and it is very good (your part I mean). I almost wished you were wrong oftener than just to put Moonshers for Moonrakers: it would have suggested you enjoyed yourself between whiles. Of course I did laugh and I do not pretend not to, do I? I depict not what I *was* but what I see when I look back. I don't think I could do what I *was*.

There's a tune a lady has sent me for 'O'er the moor among the heather' and I wanted to hear from you what it sounds like.

Now I must try to clean my hands and have tea and get up to the study again and write about Meredith's Homes and Haunts. Work does not come tumbling in, not by any means. In fact if I were not so busy I should be seeing reasons for being pretty sick.

Goodbye and I hope you will get well and tell us so. This is the third blessed day and you ought to be out at any rate. All send our love to you.

Yours ever
Edward Thomas.

The Wisbech Millennium was a hurly-burly of gaudy nights and days: 27 Old Market faced on to the Market Place, and we stepped from the front door straight into the Fair at its thickest, into the hum and bustle of the booths and side-shows, and the pandemonium of the giant roundabouts. At night their coloured lights glared into the first-floor room where we assembled, when we were not spilling out into the streets to buy each other still more trumpery, gape at the sword-swallower, and bring home still more coconuts. Our party numbered too many crack shots to be popular with the gypsies who ran the shies. Nut after hairy nut succumbed to Bertie's deadliest Yorkers, and Godwin's balls slew seven at one blow. He returned half his spoils to the disgruntled showman before, laden with trophies, we piled into the cars of the most raucous roundabout, and started the switchback journey through nether Hell. When Bertie dropped a coconut into its bowels he sprang to his feet, demanding excitedly of the attendant demons as we whirled past that the machine be stopped instantly, and his property restored. The altercation waxed hotter at each round, but the *casus belli* never came to light.

Another memory of this garish week is of Bunny Garnett engaging to stand on his head while Bertie obliged with his star patriotic number: 'Thank God I am an Englishman'. Bunny adored this above all the nonsense-songs we invented to amuse our friends, but Bertie wasn't always in the mood. He accepted Bunny's bribe at its full value, drawing out the two verses mercilessly, till we feared Bunny would have an apoplexy. But at the finish he right-ended himself, and purple in the face blurted, 'THANK you, Bertie!'

On Sunday a paper-chase was organized. Joan, fleet as Atalanta, was one of the hares, and Godwin, who knew the district, was the other. After ten minutes we hounds were up and away. The trail led out of Wisbech, far afield into the private market-gardens cut across and across by a network of dykes. The pack cried havoc through a maze of apple-orchards. Godwin eluded it by leaping dyke after dyke, a feat beyond the rest of us. Presently I found myself within a stone's throw of Joan, inaccessible because of the ditch between. As we dodged back and forth, she seeking a way out and I a way round, our ears were assailed by angry shouts, two or three dykes away. One of our pack was in trouble: Bunny, dodging an irate fruit-farmer, also trying to find a way out or round. Hares and hounds turned tail and sneaked home, hoping that Godwin's scutcheon was not blotted. It would never do for the respected Misses Peckover to identify their new young doctor with a Sabbath-breaking rabble summonsed for trespassing. But the incident blew over without result, except that the Old Market house-party behaved circumspectly for the rest of the Millennium. From which I seem to have returned in some sort of 'a state'.

Steep
Friday

My dear Eleanor   I was expecting a letter although I owed you one really but you know I don't write letters, and now, crawling on at about 2 pages a day of the fiction and for 8 of Homes and Haunts which I can't refuse to do now with nothing else in prospect, except by the way that just as I am almost certainly dropping off from the D.C. the Daily News asks me to write about Christina Rossetti.

You are coming on the 4th then, which is the day of 'The Magic Chest'. We wish you could drop in on us these days of thunder and hail, snow and sleet, rain and wind. Coupled with my long slow work it is about all I can stand. However I do stand it.

I am sorry Wisbech sent you away in that state. But nobody could avoid bringing something away from that Fair I take it. Only you were unlucky. You should have had some of the twisty striped stuff instead. Or perhaps you did. On the whole Wisbech seems to be a microcosm rather than a paradise, though if it wasn't for the late hours I think I should go (upon being invited).

The news of Clifford is wretched enough, but one can imagine worse, and really one only wishes absolutely unbroken bliss for oneself—it makes others so intolerable. Now I have suggested I should go to Brook Green at 4 next Wednesday. But perhaps they are at Southwold. In case that is so shall we meet at the Cottage at 4? If they are at Brook Green you will come won't you? I may have another free time, and if so will let you know, but I have to go out of town during a very short visit and at an unsettled hour.

Don't let the Autobiography worry you whether you've a headache or not. If for example it becomes as unreadable as I can well believe, do something better than copy it please—only not destroy it.

Helen is out and I am writing with Baby on my arm—she is drawing Dead Men. I drew a bear that I saw in the sky yesterday after the thunder and now she must draw dead men that she saw in the sky. 'Down among the dead men' is a grisly delight to her. She sends her love with mine.

I have begun to read all sorts of things connected with Shelley now and shall probably do a book on his poetry before very long and whether anyone wants it or not.

> Yours ever
> Edward Thomas.

Postmark 24 March 1914   13 Rusham Rd.
Balham S.W.

My dear Eleanor, Evidently we did meet. That is what I should have done, at any rate. I was trying to be tolerable, you see, to a bard and I became intolerable to you. I am sorry, but glad you will see me on Wednesday notwithstanding. I expect to see Clifford and Olga tomorrow morning and will arrange about the next day and ask her to telephone to you decisively. She will not have gone by then I expect. Clifford wrote very sadly.

In case you want to write I shall be tomorrow night

> c/o Robert Frost
> The Bungalow
> Reynolds Rd
> Beaconsfield

What on earth can I have said for August 1st?
Then probably we meet at Brook Green on Wednesday.

> Yours ever
> Edward Thomas.

This is the first direct mention of Robert Frost among my letters. From now onward Edward began to talk about his friend, and was drawn after him as by a magnet, when Frost moved his family from Buckinghamshire to Herefordshire. *North of Boston* was in preparation, Frost had already shown Edward 'The Death of the Hired Man' in manuscript, and wherever they were together the great endless talk on poetry was pursued.

Postmark 30 March 1914

Steep

My dear Eleanor   Thank you ever so much and not one grumble,
except that I don't believe you would confess you had had enough.
I am glad you sent it in this way. The whole mass would be trying
now that I do the novel and 'Omes & 'Aunts daily, about 3 hours
each. At this moment I have Maitland to contend with, and very
glad I am, we all are. Without him we couldn't have stood this
return of the rain. He snatched a holiday and descended on the
Fordhams then on us.

The Christina article didn't go far enough. I was hurried and
anxious to do something. I ought to have done my best but
couldn't or I should not have forgotten Goblin Market. I hope it
wasn't very sluggish and dull. They haven't given me another
chance. But the Manchester Guardian has accepted some articles.

We expect to go to Wales on the 14th with no interval in town,
and to see you this very next Friday. When? And how do you do?
I think you looked better last Wednesday. We are all well. Goodbye, with my love.

E. T.

I talked to a Bedales master last night about the cricket match
and gave him Bertie's address.

That spring a friend offered me her old house in Kingham
for a fortnight. I asked Joan Thornycroft to spend the first
week there with me and Bertie, and invited Edward to make a
fourth. Bertie welcomed this, not only because of his affection
for his fellow-flyfisher, but because it would leave him more
freedom to fall in love with Joan. Edward scarcely knew her,
but I believe that from the moment he saw her she realized for
him the ideal of girlhood he had described in *Light and Twilight*.
Joan had a perfection of springtime loveliness, and, rarer still,
of movement; it was a delight to see her run, lightly and
gallantly, like a young stag. Edward loved grace of movement
even more than beauty of feature, and this is how he seems, in
'The End of a Day', to have seen Joan Thornycroft before he
set eyes on her. He is crossing a moor towards evening, after
a fatiguing day of storm, and as the sky begins to clear a girl
moves athwart his path 'in the slant rain': young and proud,

walking in a watery cold light that became more radiant every moment in the west.

> To me, losing all memory of the storm, it was as if the day had led up to this . . . I had emerged out of the darkness and mist into an immeasurable and wondrously open world, and across it moved the figure of the girl. . . . The girl was beautiful. . . . Had she leaped out of the earth or out of the sky to express in human shape the loveliness of the hour, she could not have been made otherwise by a sculptor god—solemn and joyous and proud with the pride of things that are perfect and know it not . . . I watched her plant her feet firmly and rise up lightly as one might do to whom these things were impossible and marvellous. . . . She could have run, she could have leapt and climbed, almost it seemed that she could have flown, yet she walked steadily across the moor.

This 'violet-eyed maid walking alone' evoked for him all the images of female love and loveliness sung of by poets.

> The unaccomplished hours hovered about her as she went. She might some day be a Helen, a Guinevere, a Persephone, an Electra, an Isoud, an Eurydice, an Antigone, a Nimue, an Alcestis, a Dido, a Lais, a Francesca, a Harriet. . . . And there were many more upon the grass under the western light . . . all drawn after her whithersoever she went, all praising her for her sweet lips, her long brown hair and its gloom and hidden smouldering fires, her eyes and her eyelids that were as the violet opened flower and the white closed bud, her breath sweet as the earth's, her height, whiteness, her swift limbs, and her rippling arms and wrists and hands, made for love and all fair service: her straightness, that was as the straightness of a tulip on the best day of spring.

I have quoted these passages rather fully because to me they are the key to one of Edward's dreams, to attain which would destroy it, the dream of 'things impossible and marvellous'. He wanted no more than to behold it at a distance; and I am not imagining, I am certain, that the girl he looked on as she crossed the moor he saw again in Joan Thornycroft, walking ahead of us on the Cotswold roads. Later in the year he was to write to me, 'There is no one like Joan'.

In my invitation to Kingham I held out a possible river as a lure. It reached him in Wales, where he had taken Mervyn and Bronwen for a holiday. The 'very nice Welsh youth', who played Welsh tunes to him on the viola in Laugharne, giving him a pleasure he remembered till he died, was Raymond Jeremy.

In the train on the way to
Little Iddens   c/o R. Frost
Ledington,
Ledbury
Herefordshire

My dear Eleanor,   I have been meaning to write every day since we came to Wales which we are now leaving for Herefordshire. There we expect to stay till the Friday or Saturday of next week. Then I had meant to go home on the following Tuesday. Now I should very much like to go to Kingham and think I could manage it if I spent the week end at home putting some notebooks together etc.—if I really could work there without being a nuisance. I have worked almost every day since I came away and I must continue to do so, partly to keep my conscience quiet partly because I have so much I want to get on with, especially after spending an awful lot on getting to Wales etc. Could I for instance work in the mornings and between 5 and 7.30? If so I am practically certain of coming. In any case I am very glad indeed to hear you can go away and enjoy yourself instead of having to retire for rest. If you could survive both reading and typing that autobiography I am sure you must be well again. You will like Kingham which I know a lot about, because a former subrector of my college lives there (and wrote a history of it later) Warde Fowler. The river positively exists.

We have had every possible pleasant condition of scenery weather lodging and company—at Laugharne we had a week of a very nice Welsh youth who plays the viola for Beecham and played Welsh airs for us all the evening; also a noble estuary between two high wooded precipices which admit two meeting rivers to Carmarthen Bay. I had a cold and I was mostly rather wretched, but the children enjoyed themselves and I contrived to get some of my kind of pleasure also. You ought to take one of the many empty cottages there. Cockles the only industry.

No news. Constables are looking at my Proverbs. Blackwood's

magazine wouldn't have a batch. The fiction crawls tediously towards the chief episode.

Helen has had a succession of visitors and says she is well and the peas coming up.

Well, I will come if I can, but if you want an immediate certainty, don't regard me.

With Mervyn's and Bronwen's love

Yours ever
Edward Thomas.

Three days later he is definite:

28   iv   14   c/o R. Frost
Little Iddens
Ledington
Ledbury

My dear Eleanor,   I think I will then, tho here is Muirhead Bone tempting me to Italy in half a dozen different ways. It could not be before Tuesday evening, however, as I must have Tuesday in town. Can you tell me what trains there are after 4? Its too early except for trout fishing, by the way.

The weather here makes me full of anxiety about next week's. It is perfectly warm and bright. However, perhaps it will take to raining at night which would be very pleasant and convenient.

Helen won't be up, I imagine, just at once. I am going there on Saturday (after a night in town) and staying till Monday or the Tuesday morning.

I must say cricket sounds absurd just now. But I hope Clifford likes it as much as ever and is fit for it. Its a long time since I heard of him and Olga.

Mrs. Radford invites me to a play and discussion about *politics*. This was reckoned a bait.

Yours ever
Edward Thomas.

§3

In Kingham Edward had all the time he needed for writing before breakfast and after tea. We carried our picnic luncheons into the open, in two packs, because although we four always

set out together we soon separated, without question or
explanation. It was becoming plain that however much
Edward might desire the unattainable to remain unattained,
Bertie did not; and then, Joan, whose easel he was carrying,
was looking out for a subject near at hand for a watercolour,
while Edward had some distant objective on his map. I could
walk twelve or fourteen miles without feeling tired, my rather
swift stride keeping abreast of his indolent one; and whenever
we came to a churchyard I sat on a tomb, while he did his
notebook prowl for oddities among the epitaphs. The weather
on the whole kept warm and bright; no trout-fishing was
attempted. We all came together again in the house before
supper-time. Joan and I had arranged a lazy commissariat,
and in addition to our tins and soup-packets there was a daily
supply of fresh vegetables, brought by the gardener of Basil
de Selincourt, who sold his market-garden produce locally;
we had unlimited asparagus, the best I remember. The
kitchen was next to the dining-room, with a hatch between;
and while Joan and I did the cooking, Bertie and Edward
stretched their legs, sucked their pipes, and chatted. Both had
quiet grave voices; they shared the same dry humour of under-
statement, and the murmurings that filtered through the hatch
were broken frequently by low-pitched laughter. One evening
before we left them Bertie broke out into heated protest against
brides' trousseaux.

'Why should they have all the fun?' demanded Bertie. 'Why
shouldn't men have trousseaux? If *they* start married life with
six dozen petticoats, why shouldn't *we* with six dozen white ties?'

'And three dozen dickies,' supplemented Edward.

'Four dozen,' Bertie amended. 'What about spats?'

We left them debating the correct quantities of these, of
braces and of Boston garters, and whether some should not be
hand-embroidered for Sundays. We lost what followed; but
while we stirred the soup ribald chuckles shook the serving-
hatch, increasing with each fresh proposal to shouts of pot-
house laughter.

'What do you suppose they can be suggesting *now*?' We
dared not surmise, and we were not informed.

PLATE IV

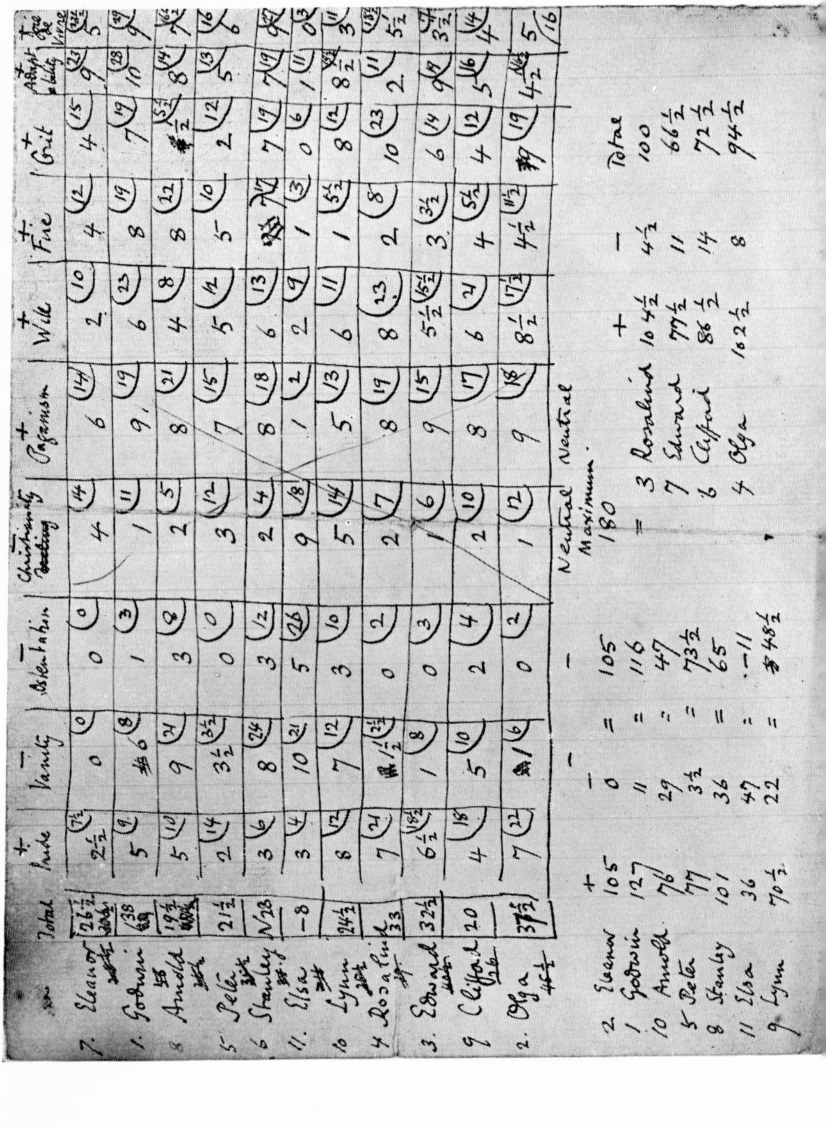

	Total	+ Pride	− Vanity	− Ostentation	Christianity ~~Feeling~~	+ Paganism	+ Will	+ Fire	+ Grit	+ Adaptability	+ Joie de Vivre
7. Eleanor ~~30½~~	26½	2½ (7½)	0 (0)	0 (0)	4 (14)	6 (14)	2 (10)	4 (12)	4 (15)	9 (23)	5 (32½)
1. Godwin	38	5 (9)	6 (8)	1 (3)	1 (11)	9 (19)	6 (23)	8 (19)	7 (19)	10 (28)	9 (29)
8 Arnold	19½	5 (10)	9 (21)	3 (8)	2 (5)	8 (21)	4 (8)	8 (22)	½ (5½)	8 (14)	7 (16½)
5 Peter	21½	2 (14)	3½ (3½)	0 (0)	3 (12)	7 (15)	5 (12)	5 (10)	2 (12)	5 (13)	6 (16)
6 Stanley	N 28	3 (6)	8 (24)	3 (12)	2 (4)	8 (18)	6 (13)	7 (17)	7 (19)	7 (19)	9 (27)
11. Elsa	−8	3 (4)	10 (21)	5 (26)	9 (18)	1 (2)	2 (9)	1 (3)	0 (6)	1 (11)	0 (3)
10 Lynn	24½	8 (12)	7 (12)	3 (10)	5 (14)	5 (13)	6 (11)	1 (5½)	8 (12)	8½ (13½)	3 (11)
4 Rosalind	33	7 (21)	1½ (2½)	0 (2)	2 (7)	8 (19)	8 (23)	2 (8)	10 (23)	2 (11)	5½ (18½)
3. Edward	32½	6½ (18½)	1 (8)	0 (3)	1 (6)	9 (15)	5½ (15½)	3 (3½)	6 (14)	9 (19)	3½ (17)
9 Clifford 26	20	4 (18)	5 (10)	2 (4)	2 (10)	8 (17)	6 (21)	4 (5½)	4 (12)	5 (16)	4 (14)
2. Olga 45½	37½	7 (22)	1 (6)	0 (2)	1 (12)	9 (18)	8½ (17½)	4½ (11½)	9 (19)	4½ (16½)	5 (16)

Neutral Neutral
Maximum 180

	+	−		
2 Eleanor	105	0	=	105
1 Godwin	127	11	=	116
10 Arnold	76	29	=	47
5 Peter	77	3½	=	73½
8 Stanley	101	36	=	65
11 Elsa	36	47	=	−11
9 Lynn	70½	22	=	48½

	+	−	Total
3 Rosalind	104½	4½	100
7 Edward	77½	11	66½
6 Clifford	86½	14	72½
4 Olga	102½	8	94½

After supper they took on the washing-up, lit their pipes again, and we played some of the paper-games which made invidious comparisons among our friends. We would write the chosen names down one side of the paper, and horizontally above the chosen subjects, Colours, Flowers, Beverages, Towns, to which we thought our friends best corresponded. I have an incompleted list of Edward's which throws a revealing light on what he thought of some of us: and of himself. Still more revealing is a table of Good and Bad qualities: Pride, Christianity, Adaptability, and so on: in which we were allotted points, maximum ten; after which, by some extremely complicated system, the Good Qualities were subtracted from the Bad, or the Bad ones added to the Good, and some plus-and-minus residue summed up our chances of heaven.

Then perhaps, at Edward's request, we carried a lamp into the long narrow drawing-room, where a piano stood on a dais at the far end. The room was dim, the whole house had a light-defying nature, its corners were cobwebbed with shadows. I was a sorry piano-player, but none of the other three could play at all. Edward hummed the airs he had heard lately from Raymond Jeremy, I fingered them out, Joan sang with us in her clear choir-boy tones, and Bertie was content to look and listen. The sweet Welsh tunes tumbled among the piano-keys, and nobody was critical. Presently we returned to the other room for a tray of tea before bedtime; and one might say, 'The door has been left open', and another might rise and shut it. A little later—'Didn't you shut the door?' Someone closed it again; and then again, and again. We drank our tea. The stairs creaked, the door swung slowly back. We looked at each other. Edward knocked out his pipe. 'Oh yes,' he said, 'I've known it all along. Haven't you?' We had; and although this is the mildest possible ghost-story, not one of us would have subscribed to a reasonable explanation of ancient floor-joints and door-latches. The house was strange, but it was not unhappy; and we were happy in it.

On one of our last walks, as Bertie and Joan drew away from us, I thought of the man far away to whom she was engaged, and sighed, 'Oh I wish he would fall in love with somebody in

India and marry her.' And Edward, his eyes praising Joan's swift limbs, her 'straightness of the tulip on the best day of spring', said quietly, 'It isn't very likely.'

§4

This was one of the great musical summers when Sir Joseph Beecham was challenging Wagner, Puccini, and Caruso at Covent Garden with a Grand Season of Mozart, Chaliapine, and Russian Ballet at Drury Lane. To Mr. Thomas Beecham, the conductor, German Opera then meant not 'The Ring' but 'The Magic Flute'. I had been hearing Grand Opera at Covent Garden for twenty years, from the time when my brother Harry began to study music and Augustus Harris sent us stalls and boxes lavishly throughout the Season. We had heard French and Italian opera sung by all the finest singers of the nineties, and later on the great Wagner seasons with Van Rooy and Ternina; but Mozart was still unfashionable among the tiaras. In 1914 London flocked to Drury Lane to rediscover him and to pursue the new passion for Russian Ballet with Karsavina and Nijinsky, and Russian Opera with Chaliapine. Edward himself began to catch the fever.

16 May 1914
  Monday   Steep

My dear Eleanor Thank you for the cards. You have had a splendid week. But has it cleared your cold away? I really forgot you were an invalid, but I think it was partly your fault. However, I hope you are not.

I am diabolically busy finishing those Welsh sketches and getting through some arrears, and as usual I see the fine weather glide by and merely know it is fine. So I am not sure when I shall be up next unless it is for a day next week. I wish I were going to the Magic Flute on Thursday.

(May I have my razor? I am so sorry to have left it for you to trouble over.) Bronwen is staying in town for the summer and I have no doubt enjoying it. We think of all going to Herefordshire in August, if we can let our cottage. If you should hear of anybody

72

who could do with such quarters (for about 25/- a week) would you tell us?

I shall let Clifford know about the Earlsfield match. Will he have moved by then I wonder.

Ever yours
Edward Thomas.

He had told me that 'The Magic Flute' was his favourite opera, and I invited him and Helen to its last performance before the Ballet Season set in.

On a postcard postmarked 24 May 1914

Steep
Petersfield

There was some advantage then in leaving Kingham early . . . I have just altered my plans and am coming up on Tuesday and will meet you on *Wednesday* to hear the Magic Flute if you will tell me what time suits. I shall be at 13 Rusham Rd. Balham Tuesday night. I am simply entangled in work or I would not have left your letter unanswered.

E. T.

P.S. I am so sorry I did not send that John Palmer; I have put your thanks to the credit of your deposit account.

When I met him and Helen at the Drury Lane they both looked strained. I put him in charge by handing him the tickets, and he said, smiling faintly, 'It's obvious Eleanor isn't a feminist'. As we made the climb to the amphitheatre I glanced at Helen inquiringly, and she shook her head. Edward's mood was waning again. He sat between us, adapting his long legs uncomfortably to the space between the rows; much of the time he leaned forward with his elbows on his knees and his chin in his hands. It was very hot in the roof of the theatre; in the intervals we fanned ourselves, drank lemonade, and talked without ease. This was my first hearing of the opera, and because of Edward's disenchanted mood I had to wait twenty-one years to feel its full enchantment at Glyndebourne. The next letter may not have been cryptic when it was written, but I can't make sense of the beginning now.

Postmark 2 June 1914

Steep

My dear Eleanor,   It is delicate and on the whole perhaps only I ought to ask for them, since if I can't ask for them I can have no right to read them. If I get them secondhand it looks too much perhaps like detached and critical curiosity. And really I am so hideously busy I oughtnt to handle such things. I shall be up not before Monday and then only for one night which I shall spend with Clifford I believe if he is ready so soon. But I don't know his address. If you see him will you ask him to send it to me and tell me if I shall arrive there about 8 on Monday? I shan't see you on Saturday because I shall be here writing prose duller than *The Doves* but possibly not worse. I suppose if I write 10000 there may be one or two good ones. (The figures remind me of what we didn't win on Durbar II. Have we still any chances whatever?) I didn't persist with Ellis's piece and suspect I should agree with you.

I don't know if Helen has written, but she will be up on Saturday week and begin to be free-ish on the Monday.

Ever yours

E. T.

In June Bertie came down badly with chickenpox, which was first suspected as being scarlet fever. I was soon able to write that this was 'a hoax' and I hoped the Thomases would go to the Ballet with me when I was out of quarantine. Edward was still gathering material for *Homes and Haunts*: a piece of book-making about literary notables, very little to his heart. Up north, on Mrs. Gaskell's track, he took the opportunity to stay with Gordon Bottomley at The Sheiling, a house he loved for its owner and for itself:

> It stands alone
> Up in a land of stone
> All worn like ancient stairs,
> A land of rocks and trees
> Nourished on wind and stone.

On his return he wrote to me from his parents' house in Balham, where Helen was joining him for a few days' walking in the Midlands. The postmark is June 22.

Saturday

13 Rusham Rd
Balham

My dear Eleanor   I am so glad it is a hoax but sorry you also are a victim. I think something can be arranged for the 29th or 30th. Helen and I may stay at Coventry till the 30th but return in time for the ballet—I've left my diary of the performances behind.

Now I have just had 3 whole days talking with Gordon Bottomley who lies in bed or on a chair and wishes it were a little cooler but otherwise is one of the happiest people in the world. He sometimes writes poetry and always has a varicose vein in one of his lungs. So you can imagine how unlike writing I am. After talking like that I can scarcely even write for money. But I did have to write on Midsummer for T.P. yesterday nevertheless.

I was in a house built by Mrs. Gaskell's daughter about the time that nice lady died—she used to stay and work near. A really lovely house in position (on a stoney hill all alone, with rabbits on the doorstep) and in furniture etc. No not *lovely* inside, but choice and convenient too. It was always as hot as I like it and I had a tarn to bathe in before breakfast two miles off, a tarn with a shore of white sand consisting of tiny shells. The sea a mile off; Helvellyn and Ingleborough always either visible or imaginable.

Please tell me some poems for a flower anthology. Its to be delivered in 3 weeks, so I shall have to work when I get back.

And I want to know if Bertie is part of the hoax also, or is he really ill?

You see this letter is very much like what I imagine the parody of me was. So I will add that I am well but blistered on one foot so as to hate pavements and that I shall be glad to see you at Drury Lane or anywhere else after you are freed.

Yours ever
Edward Thomas.

I could not send him a good account of Bertie, who was in a sad state because Joan might be on the verge of leaving England.

Helen and Edward snatched an evening at the Ballet before they left for their days of walking, which were to begin in Herefordshire, perhaps with a view to finding some holiday quarters for themselves near the Frosts.

13 Rusham Rd.
Balham

My dear Eleanor   We are just starting for Ledbury and are in a real hurry. Last night by the way we were at the ballet and one of the nicest things in that hot air was Joan Thorneycroft who transpired. Also Thamar, Papillons and Joseph which I liked in that order. Now we will go on Tuesday next if you will. Mrs. Radford wants us to assemble and have an early supper there and wants you too. Can it be done and will it?

Don't count this letter against me. The hurry is real not Thomassinine. And I hope Bertie is more resigned now. Give him my love and I hope you get well out of this very long dull joke on the 29th. Helen and I are

Yours ever
Edward Thomas.

Postcard postmarked
28 June 1914

Ledington,
Ledbury

Saturday

I am glad you can come on Tuesday. We meet for supper or tupper or whatever it is at 6 at Well Walk. I am glad to think that I am better than Kitchener as a mascot. It is splendid here, every day hot and bright. We are off to Coventry in the afternoon but returning to London on Monday.

E. T.

I suppose a big party of us were going together from the Radfords'. We were all Ballet-addicts, the original Balletomanes whom Bertie satirized more than twenty years later in one of his most famous Revue numbers: 'When Bolonsky danced Balushka in September Nineteen-Ten': all very well, dear Bertie, but when Nijinsky danced Petroushka in those prewar days, you had the disease as badly as any of us. I had forgotten till I came to re-read Edward's letters how badly he had it too.

§5

Then at last *North of Boston* was published. Edward passed on to me his second review copy, with his formula: 'If you are worthy of it'. I took it with me to Overstrand, our Norfolk holiday-place, where I was spending part of July with some of my family. I read and wrote to Edward about it before his reviews were published; I still have the column I cut out of the *Daily News*, and I am quoting a part of it here, not only because it reveals Edward's mind through Frost's, or because many things he says might be said of his own poems, but because for those who know little of his fine and influential work as a critic it is an example of his power 'to make or break a poet' in a single article. I don't recall how *North of Boston* was welcomed by other critics, but none of them carried as much weight as Edward; and the dailies he wrote for allowed him (unthinkable to-day!) eighteen inches for his praise or censure. He begins:

This is one of the most revolutionary books of modern times, but one of the quietest and least aggressive. It speaks, and it is poetry. It consists of fifteen poems, from fifty to three hundred lines long, depicting scenes from life, chiefly in the country, in New Hampshire. Two neighbour farmers go along opposite sides of their boundary wall, mending it and speaking of walls and of boundaries. A husband and wife discuss an old vagabond farm servant, who has come home to them, as it falls out, to die. Two travellers sit outside a deserted cottage, talking of those who once lived in it, talking until bees in the wall boards drive them away. A man who has lost his feet in a saw-mill talks to a friend, a child, and the lawyer comes from Boston about compensation. The poet himself describes the dreams of his eyes after a long day on a ladder picking apples, and the impression left on him by a neglected wood-pile in the snow on an evening walk. All but these last two are dialogue mainly: nearly all are in blank verse.

These poems are revolutionary because they lack the exaggeration of rhetoric, and even at first sight appear to lack the poetic intensity of which rhetoric is an imitation. Their language is free from the poetical words and forms that are the chief material of secondary poets. The metre avoids not only the old-fashioned pomp and sweetness, but the later fashion also of discord and fuss. In fact, the medium is common speech and common decasyllables, and Mr. Frost is at no pains to exclude blank verse lines resembling those employed, I think, by Andrew Lang in a leading article printed as prose. Yet almost all these poems are beautiful. They depend not at all on objects commonly admitted to be beautiful: neither have they merely a homely beauty, but are often grand, sometimes magical. Many, if not most, of the separate lines and separate sentences are plain and, in themselves, nothing. But they are bound together and made elements of beauty by a calm eagerness of emotion.

The review then goes on, for more than half its length, to copious quotations from the poems, with E. T.'s comments. It ends with this summing up:

The book is not without failures. Mystery falls into obscurity. In some lines I cannot hit upon the required accents. But his successes, like 'The Death of the Hired Man', put Mr. Frost above all other writers of verse in America. He will be accused of keeping monotonously at a low level, because his characters are quiet people, and he has chosen the unresisting medium of blank verse. I will only remark that he would lose far less than most modern writers by being printed as prose. If his work were so printed, it would have little in common with the kind of prose that runs to blank verse: in fact, it would turn out to be closer knit and more intimate than the finest prose is except in its finest passages. It is poetry because it is better than prose.

This review, as I have said, was written, but had not yet appeared when Edward addressed a letter to me at 'The White Horse', Overstrand, in answer to the one in which I had proved my right to keep my copy of these 'revolutionary' poems.

17 vii 14   Steep

My dear Eleanor   I am so glad you liked Frost. I wanted you to keep him and thought you would and you say just what I hoped you would. Your selection is just; only I would add 'The Death of the Hired Man', and the slighter ones, like 'Mending Wall' and 'Blueberries' are good too. I haven't seen any of my notices. Well, I should have written before, but I have been utterly abandoned to covering 20 sheets of this rotten paper day after day and still haven't finished. There have been intervals but all sorry ones. I feel that it can't go on much longer. I hate it all and find it more than difficult to keep up. So I am beginning to think of New Hampshire as the only possibility though really not thinking of it as quite possible either. It will be so deliberate and there will be so much time to see the drawbacks. Frost is coming this week-end. His wanting me is some encouragement. But then he has kept himself clear and true and not anxious. We go there about the 4th. I don't know if I can see you before that. I am up next week for a hurried day. Then the remaining days will only just suffice to get rid of this horrid 'Homes and Haunts'. The Anthology's done. The cottage is not let.

I was glad about Welsh and indifferent about the others, but, as it turned out, sorry Carpentier was called the winner. I suspect people only hoped Carpentier would win out of respect for the man who'd beaten Wells.

Are there many 'White Horses' in Norfolk? It's only a name there, I imagine. But the very name is better than the thing Dumpling, isn't it?

> Yours with our love ever
> Edward Thomas.

Bracing sea-air has never agreed with me, and I was obliged to leave Overstrand sooner than I intended. The Thomases suggested that I might spend part of August in Ledington and meet the Frosts, if they could find me some suitable lodging near by.

Our time in Ledington is practically all August from the Wednesday or Thursday after Bank Holiday, and perhaps a few days in September; 4 weeks altogether. Let me know soon when you will come. Frost and I want to plan an excursion into Wales.
My D.N. article on Frost was not what I wanted to do, but it was easier reading perhaps than a closer review would have been.

The next letter, from Steep, was written at the end of the month, when I was back in London.

Steep

My dear Eleanor,   I should think your letter didn't 'bother' me, not even (you see) to the extent of compelling me to write back at once. At the same time I have had qualms. But this is a wretched time, hustled about from work to pleasure at quite a pace. Now it is

work, to clear off what can be cleared off before starting to cycle
north with Mervyn. That will be on Tuesday next probably. If
we get there you will find us when we get back from Wales

> c/o Mr Chandler
> Ledington
> nr Ledbury
> Herefordshire

Ledbury is the nearest station. If you let us know your train I will
show you the cheap place unless you prefer the Castle Inn or whatever it is.

We expect Bronwen back on Friday or so and I have never seen
a Thomas with more pleasure I believe. She has been winning
swimming races. I don't think she is a Thomas, though.

Well at present I feel as if I might as well try lecturing or doctor-
ing or seafaring as selling butter and eggs in New Hampshire.

Helen says you had to leave Overstrand. I hope you are better
again and your mother too. You didn't mention Bertie. I am really
very sorry he can't play cricket. But I suppose he can write poetry.
—I didn't get to Joan's exhibition. I would have done for liking
for Joan, but pictures bore me mostly.

Ever yours (still daily Oming and aunting)

Edward Thomas.

Bertie, unfit for cricket, was camping in Devon and Cornwall. He and Joan were both at the Oliviers' camp on the
Helford River estuary when war was declared, and Harry was
in France. Until Harry was home I could not leave Mother,
who was anxious about him and the uncertainties in the air;
so I fixed a date much later in the month for my going to
Ledbury. On August 2nd Edward mentions the war for the
first time.

2 viii 14   Steep

My dear Eleanor   We are all busy getting ready—Mervyn and I to
leave tomorrow for Basingstoke and Kingsclere—and talking
rubbish about War. The other thing for the moment is Helen's
chance of getting up to Herefordshire by Guildford, Oxford, and
Worcester on Wednesday. We imagine it is a good chance. She
may have Peter the Russian boy with her as he can't be got home—
was hurried back from his ship at Milwall yesterday and is now a

dismal inmate (dismal when he remembers to be) with us. I am a little at a loose end after sending off Homes and Haunts yesterday. Who will want the thing now? I may as well write poetry. Did anyone ever begin at 36 in the shade? Yet I would almost as soon be on Dartmoor with Bertie and David. I was so glad to hear that Bertie was fit for camping. I had pictured him an appendage to a bad leg. And may he catch trout too? I thought there were things he couldn't do.

I will come to the Ballet if I am in England, be sure.

Bronwen is back too, too late for Goodwood. She is well, but wants to be well dressed too. She won some swimming races at school, did I tell you? By the way I remembered too late that you might have come to Goodwood if we had asked you. Helen and I went on Wednesday and had a very fine day, the walk back to Midhurst best of all, up over the Downs through Charlton Forest—did you know there were 8 or 9 miles by one or two of Forest there, running east and west along the south slope of the Downs? You would have known if you had come to East Dean or Charlton or Singleton.

But it is no use trying to write. I think about Alton Basingstoke Newbury Hungerford Aldbourne Swindon Cricklade Cirencester Gloucester Ledbury all the time except when I think of this wonderful summer, today, for example, which began dirtily enough and then turned to dark trees and the loveliest wild white cloud that never shed a drop and the wind blowing a sort of dark and white on you all day. This isn't a sketch for a minor poem in prose. Goodbye. We shall see you on the 20th I do hope. Meantime apples and walks and (I trust) some reviews to write.

Yours ever
Edward Thomas.

No, not a sketch for a minor poem in prose—yet perhaps the seed of a major one in verse. Whoever began 'at 36 in the shade' indeed! Edward had been writing poems in prose from boyhood; and his poetry, when he came at last to write it, was only poetry 'because it was better than prose'.

§6

Bertie returned from Dartmoor and enlisted. Joan's reasons for leaving England had come to a head, and she was preparing to go to India, as it seemed, for good. I don't think Bertie cared what became of him, and the varicose trouble in his legs which had developed after his recent illness was not bad enough to stand in his way.

Harry too had at last come back from France, where the patriotic fervour for war was spectacular. In the holiday hotel where he was held up he had become friendly with a young girl, who was particularly exalted when the brilliantly-uniformed French soldiers marched through the town. She poured scorn on the British Army, which, since the Boer War, had abandoned scarlet for sand-colour. Harry explained that on the battlefield khaki is less conspicuous than scarlet. 'Your soldiers wish to avoid being seen? What cowardice!' Harry suggested that cowardice is not the same thing as prudence. 'Prudence!' she scoffed. *'Et la Gloire?'*

I was now free to leave London, but was still waiting to hear what plans the Thomases had been able to make for my coming. When Edward did write (after I had done so twice, the second time perhaps rather drily), his letter made it clear that the Herefordshire holiday had not begun too happily. Helen was unwell, and anxious about Baba. The War filled not only the newspapers, but people's mouths and thoughts and hearts with the conventional clichés with which Edward had no patience. He had not yet written, but already felt: 'This is no case of petty right and wrong': and long before he enlisted he talked scornfully of the jingoism of profiteers and politicians, when some particularly vamped-up sentiment coloured the headlines. But the War was still only ten days old when Edward wrote from Ledington, where walking and talking with Frost was absorbing his time and his thoughts.

14 viii 14   c/o Mrs. Chandler
Ledington, Ledbury

My dear Eleanor   Thank you for two letters and a postscript. At anyrate the p.s. was deserved. But talk is worse for letters than writing is. It is bad for writing too. At least its *immediate* effect is bad on *mine*. And talk and strolling and odd games of cricket fill most days; or I might have written—you know if I should. Things are quietly disturbing away here where there are few papers, those late. Mr. Chandler is a soldier of 44 who saw 21 years' service and has this morning been sent for to Hereford. It may be that Frost and I will do some of the work he will leave behind. But if not, other things have postponed our Welsh trip. We can't go now in any case till after Baby's birthday. Abercrombie is to join us. It might be Tuesday. That would mean perhaps not returning till the 22nd. Would you like to know definitely, or would you come in any case on the 20th? We are doing rather moderately here. The boys are bored. Peter is here—he helps to raise the standard of what boys may do, I suppose. Bronwen is all right. Baby is, too, tho she had a very bad fall from a swing a few days ago and I thought she was going to lose a birthday. Helen is not up to very much, and I don't help. One thing and another leaves me very irritable indeed. The quarters are too close. I want to get away to Wales and should like a full week, but travelling has new inconveniences and things cost more than ever here, so I don't know what they'll be at inns. I haven't thought of serving my country, or of putting one leg round my neck and singing those songs that Clifford and Olga and Bertie and Joan like so much, but don't say so. I did think of turning plain reporter and giving unvarnished reports of country conversations about the war. But Frost discourages. In any case varnish is the thing. Do you read Harold Begbie for example? But this sounds as if I imagined myself a James Thomson or Richard Middleton who was going to die unrecognised and got some consolation from the imagining.

The one advantage of waiting a week to write to you is that Joan appears to have escaped the water bailiff. Of course if I could have done anything I would. But witty replies to water bailiffs are not my long suit.

Baby is grizzling upstairs. The Frosts are all over the house seeing Mr. Chandler off. Peter's chair creaks as he reads the Baroness Orczy and Mervyn sounds incompletely satisfied with the old Strand Magazines. But it is a very fine hot day. God is in *His* heaven all right, obviously and ostentatiously. Mr. Chandler will be in *his* in Hereford. Goodbye. I am sorry this letter turns out so. Please remember me to Clifford or is he serving our country?

Yours ever
Edward Thomas.

Peter was the Russian pupil from Bedales, for whom the Thomases assumed responsibility after he had been 'turned

back from his ship at Milwall' at the beginning of the
month.

Next, a postcard on the 17th.

Ledington

I have just heard I must write 10,000 words more to make my
book complete. It would be a blessing if you could lend me (bring
with you) Coleridge's 'Biographia Literaria' or his Letters or a good
life of him *or his* 'Anima Poetae'.

The place is a temperance hotel kept by one Maddox and is on the
left as you come down to the principal part of the town from the
station.

I may go to Wales for a day or two tomorrow, but it is not very
likely.

Baby had a good birthday.

Excuse this card in darkness.

I sent Baba a brightly-painted Russian farm for her birthday.
As a lodging for me in Ledington had still not been found, I
was to stay in Ledbury from my arrival on the 20th; I hoped,
only temporarily. A more detailed letter followed the postcard immediately.

Ledington
17 viii

My dear Eleanor,   I am sorry I sent off that horrid card written in
double darkness. Helen will do better. This is to say that Maddox's
temperance hotel is on your *right* coming down from Ledbury
station, and should you not be met you get here by leaving Ledbury
and the Ross Road and taking the first turning on the left hand road
at a fork in another mile, and then a rough lane in a quarter of a
mile on your right almost opposite a derelict smithy. The lane takes
you into a meadow like a green and we are at the one house on its
left side, 200 yards along.

Could you bring with you a folding unmounted Ordnance Map,
Sheet 81 (Hereford) in the large series? I have all other necessary
maps.

When you take your room at Ledbury don't arrange for more
than one night in case we find you a place near us here.

I expect now to go off to Wales on Wednesday or Thursday and
return about Sunday.

Baba liked her farmhouse which was set up at once, but has since concentrated on a doll's cradle. She now has spectacles, did you know? But she is recognisable.

If you have saved any war poems would you bring them with you?

Please remember me to Clifford and Olga.

Yours ever
Edward Thomas.

I was very glad when, just before I left London, the Thomases were able to find me rooms near them in Ledington, in an old-fashioned house kept by a Mr. and Mrs. Farmer. It stood on a rising lane between the 'meadow like a green' which contained the Chandlers' farm, and Little Iddens, the simple cottage higher up which was occupied by the Frosts. I had still not met them when I was delivered into the Farmers' hands.

Mr. Farmer was an elderly countryman with bad teeth and easy chuckling manners. Mrs. Farmer was a bulky dominant woman who did not invite intimacy; not so much unfriendly as stand-offish till she had got your measure. She stood no nonsense from anybody: I felt I should be sorry to incur her displeasure. She had stepped out of a chapter by George Eliot, her husband out of another by Thomas Hardy, and they had joined forces midway; it was obvious who was captain of the ship. They were the only inmates of the plain and solid house. It stood against the side of the lane, darkened by trees and thickly-growing shrubs. Its exterior was faintly forbidding, like that of its mistress, and inside it continued to exude the dingy character one might meet in a mid-Victorian novel. I was shown two rooms: a living-room, to the right of the entrance door, and a bedroom above it. They were large square chambers with windows facing the lane, and the lower room was so dimmed by the foliage outside that I seem only to remember it by lamplight. I wrote and took my meals there, at a long table pushed close against the wall opposite the windows. In the middle of the wall were double doors, which could not be opened while the table stood where it did. The doors gave into some room that ran at right angles to my dining-room along the side of the house, where the shrubs were too thick-set to allow you to peer in at the curtained windows; this room had also a door on to the passage inside the house, and the door was never ajar. The unlived-in room enhanced the literary atmosphere of my lodgings, as though it concealed some secret, not to be pried into till Chapter Twenty-three. The room I ate in had an old-fashioned fireplace at the far end opposite the door; my place was laid in the middle, so that I took my meals facing the mysterious double doors, with the windows behind me; the rest of the wall by the door was filled with a vast sideboard, dressed with the solid apparatus, cruets, dishes, tankards, used for breakfast and supper. Everything was on a Gargantuan scale. I had no doubt that this was the Farmers' usual dining-room, but Mrs. Farmer soon made it plain that they would be eating elsewhere, and that I was to consider the room as mine. She then introduced me to the bedroom upstairs, a much lighter chamber, spacious in spite of the enormous washstand and press. The double bed supported a mountainous feather mattress, stuffed by Mrs. Farmer with feathers from her own geese. It was so heavy that I could not have lugged it off the bed, but in the mornings Mrs. Farmer tossed it like a pancake, trounching and pummelling it as though she were kneading a gigantic mass of dough; the yeast worked under her fists as it billowed into shape again. This was the Farmers' own bedroom, ceded to me with their living-room. Although the house was not really a big one, I never quite mastered its geography; they ate in the kitchen, and for all I know slept there too. I felt that I was not expected to investigate whatever arrangements they had made that I might be comfortably accommodated. Nor did I penetrate into the cellars under the house, from the casks in which issued an unlimited supply of rough home-brewed cider. A big pewter jug of it was always kept filled on my sideboard, for me to pull at when I pleased. They disapproved of water as a drink. As the house was moderate in extent, so were the orchards they cultivated for their living, with help from an odd man. The fruit was all first-quality, grown for the expensive market; they specialized in the finest kinds of plums, pears, gages, nectarines, and dessert apples; the cider-apples were only for their cellar. They had chickens, of course; geese for their feather-beds, and pigs for their home-cured bacon. The thick coarse slices with bristles on the rind had a taste not to be bought in shops. As well as my two rooms I had three farm-house meals a day, all the fruit I cared to pick in the orchard at any time from any tree, and the constantly-replenished jug of cider. The charge for all this was one pound a week.

I don't know what Helen and Edward paid for their accommodation at the Chandlers' in the meadow; that small community seemed rather to have migrated to Ledington than to have been planted there, and I fancy Mrs. Chandler's larder included tins and packets unknown to Mrs. Farmer's. But the Chandlers were friendly, free-and-easy, and very likeable, especially the ex-sergeant Mr. Chandler, who seemed born for cockney humour in the trenches. He came to and from Hereford, preparing with great cheerfulness for France. Nobody was yet taking this very new war as a matter of long endurance. Many believed the slogan: 'Over by Christmas!' as they ran the gamut of the routine emotions, of which the most prevalent was suspicion of anything or anyone unaccountable: the chink of light between the curtains, the unfamiliar accent of a stranger. Edward told me that Frost's New Hampshire intonation had been suspect, and some of the natives had thrown stones at his windows, deciding that he must be a Hun. This suspicion was allayed before I came. Edward also told me that Frost's immediate reaction to the war was the feeling, common to many, that he must provide for the duration. He went into Ledbury to lay in stocks, and returned with a tin of mixed biscuits and a box of fancy soap.

In the evening, when I had settled in at the Farmers', I was taken to Robert's cottage up the lane.

It was a labourer's cottage, standing on a rough patch of land planted chiefly with potatoes, and its rent could only have been a few shillings weekly; it sufficed to accommodate Robert and Elinor and their four children. They were poor, and indifferent to the conditions of poverty. I think Robert had always taken life as it came where he found it. It had never succeeded in binding him to a routine job, and in the course of earning his education and his living he had done a number of different things, in classrooms, farms, and railway stations, where he cleaned the lamps. Whatever he did he made worth doing by the reality he carried within him, in his brains and in his hands. I remember his figure as middle-sized and compact, his manner friendly and undemonstrative; he looked at you directly, his talk was shrewd and speculative, withholding nothing and derived from nobody but himself. His New England speech came readily and leisurely, and of all the writers of worth whom I had met he spoke with the least sophistication. He was unhurried in all he said and did, an attitude reflected in his answer to my question of some plan ahead: 'Is there time for it?': 'There's all the time there is'. The Frosts did not live by the clock, their clock conformed to the Frosts. There was always time for the thing in hand. Meals (bedtimes too, I believe) were when you felt like them. Irregular hours for children meant an extension of experience for them; it was more important for a child to go for a walk in the dark than to have an unbroken night's rest. By day, walks and talks were not shortened for the sake of things less interesting. When the children were hungry enough to be more interested in eating than in what they were doing, they came indoors and helped themselves to food that was left available in the small pink-washed living-room: bread, fruit, cold rice in a bowl. I wonder if memory misleads me here; this is the general impression left on me after forty years. Elinor Frost, fragile and weariable, was not the naturally joyful housewife that Helen was, the home-maker who bustled from job to job on a breath of laughter, whose hearth glowed from her own warm centre; the centre of the Frosts was out-of-doors, and household standards mattered very little. If they had, Elinor struck me as too delicate to cope with them, indeed, none of the family seemed specially robust; but though they were pale-complexioned, they were lively and active, and too resourceful to be at a loose end. My dear Thomas children seemed lethargic by comparison, less easily interested and sooner bored. Time hung most heavily on the Russian boy's unenergetic hands, and his more adult outlook (as Edward had suggested in a letter) affected Mervyn. I could not imagine either of them betaking themselves, like Carol Frost, to pick Mrs. Farmer's fruit with tireless care from morning to night, for sheer love of doing it. Small wonder he was Mrs. Farmer's favourite. She entrusted to him her finest Pearmains and Jefferson Gages for the city markets, and gave him good snacks in her kitchen, so that he need not go home for his handful of cold rice. In his absorption Carol seemed to be the very embodiment of Robert's apple-picking poem. He came second to Lesley, a tall girl of noble promise, her mother's chief stand-by in the domestic chores. The two younger girls were generally occupied with something. Life, materially meagre, satisfied these children. The American strain inherited from my mother put me quickly at ease with them, and much of my day was spent in sharing their explorations, in the games we devised among us, the fruit-harvesting, and the picnic meals at one house or the other. Helen would bring Baba up to the Frosts, where the air was serenest, and over an al-fresco tea Robert and Edward pursued what seemed to be an endless duologue on the nature of poetry. Sometimes a communal job broke into it. Frost, glancing at his potato patch planted for winter provender, remarked that it was ready to be dug. Edward touched his forelock and agreed to tackle the job next day. In the morning we all turned up on the Frosts' 'lot' with potato-forks; the rows were divided among us. Even Carol deserted his pears and plums for awhile, and dug his potato-hill as indefatigably as he had gathered nectarines. The only indolent member of the outfit was Robert, who, smoking blandly, strolled up and down the patch, a self-appointed overseer of cheap labour; while with sleeves rolled up and sweat pouring down we forked our allotted rows. We stopped only for cups of tea in a corner of the ground, and as we finished, one by one downed forks. The mounds of earthy spuds lay exposed among the fallen haulms like a gold-digger's nuggets encrusted with quartz. To one side lay an irregular triangle that had been meted to nobody and was still undug. Edward leaned on his

fork, jerked his big earthy thumb, and, 'Wot abaht that little
bit, mister?' he mumbled.

Odd how indelible an impress can be made by the inflection
of half-a-dozen words. That blazing afternoon turning to
twilight in the potato-field, with the welcome drinks, the bodily
toil and ease of spirit, and Edward playing labourer to Robert's
boss, is a memory that quickens whenever I recall it. The
pleasure sprang from Edward's relaxation in Robert's company. The humour of the two friends was in perfect accord,
and the smile underlying Edward's voice never reached his
lips: '*Wot abaht that little bit, mister?*' Nor did Robert's smile,
bidding him finish the job.

And again after supper, potatoes left to dry on the upturned
furrows, hands washed clean of soil, sleeves let down over
tired arms, we gathered in the pink-distempered room where
the chairs were too few and some sat on the floor, and one
candle was lit; and the duet about poetry was resumed by the
two poets, one of whom still did not know he was one. Of all
Robert had to say then, and at other times, a particular incident sticks in my memory. He and Edward and I were
strolling along a lane, and Robert was talking of what he called
the 'cadence' in the human voice, which accompanied the
speech that came natural to it; as the speech native to his New
Englanders north of Boston followed the cadence which
changed it into the poetry Edward had described as 'better
than prose'. While we walked, we saw across two hedgerows
a man's figure standing against the skyline on top of a cart;
he had a fork in his hands with which he caught and attacked
some load, corn or manure, pitched from below. Frost
stopped and shouted a question across the fields—it might
have been, 'What are you doing there, this fine afternoon?' but
whatever the words the man could not have heard them. He
too shouted some answer that rang through the air, and it was
impossible for us to distinguish what he said. But the cadence
of the answer was as clear as that of the question. Robert
turned to Edward. 'That's what I mean,' he said.

I can't doubt that this was one of the revealing moments to
Edward, a moment in which his own cadence was made

clearer to himself; so that those who ever heard the movement of his beautiful reflective voice can hear it now in the simplest utterance of a small unforgettable poem.

> Yes, I remember Adlestrop——

The cadence is there, and out of the poet's lingering recollection a blackbird sings close by—

> . . . and round him mistier,
> Farther and farther, all the birds
> Of Oxfordshire and Gloucestershire.

That August a covey of poets had gathered on the border of Gloucestershire. I was down at the Chandlers one evening when Lascelles Abercrombie came over from Ryton, where he had a cottage, and turned the poets' duet into a trio; I think the projected Welsh holiday was discussed between them, as well as the Cadence, and the exotic Oriental dressing-gown of purple silk in which Ezra Pound had welcomed Robert Frost to London, and which Robert described in great detail. Nearer to Ledington than Ryton, Wilfrid Gibson had his home, to which the whole party of us were invited for a sumptuous picnic in the woods about it. I had not met either Gibson or Abercrombie before this holiday, and never saw either of them after it. My chief picture of the picnic is of the contrast between them, Abercrombie sprawling at ease and talking freely as he ate, and Gibson, shy and reserved, acting the host as circumspectly as if sitting at a damask tablecloth.

Literary fame was in the air, and the ebb and flow of poets suddenly went to Mrs. Farmer's head. One morning she presented herself with a request. Did I think, she asked with great dignity, that it would be in order for her to invite Mr. and Mrs. Thomas and Mr. and Mrs. Frost to supper one evening? I was sure they would be delighted. Then, would I undertake to ask them for next Sunday? I would, with pleasure. Did I think it would be the proper thing to ask Mr. Gibson and Mr. Abercrombie too? I undertook these invitations also. Still Mrs. Farmer lingered.

'Would you, Miss Farjeon, object to lending me your dining-room for the supper?'

Well, hardly, as I was to partake of the feast myself. I perceived that Mrs. Farmer was labouring under a sense of responsibility, and assented in suitable terms. She withdrew; and I ran down to the Thomases and up to the Frosts to deliver the invitations and warn them to come in their best, as this was to be an Occasion. Gibson and Abercrombie were duly advised. By the following day Mrs. Farmer had her acceptances, and got to work to prepare the entertainment for her literary lions.

On Sunday afternoon I was excluded from the dining-room, in which much shifting seemed to be taking place. I spent the day among the children as usual, and returned to my bedroom in time to put on my nicest cotton frock. Shortly before the guests were due I came downstairs, and found entrance to the dining-room barred by Mrs. Farmer, clad in her Best Black and an apron.

'The Guests will be sitting in the parlour before supper, Miss Farjeon, and as I shall be busy in the kitchen will you be so kind as to entertain them for me?'

So saying, she opened the door into the closed room; the double doors between it and the dining-room were still sealed. The back room was almost too good to be true; it was the stage-producer's dream of any middle-class Best Parlour in any Victorian play. It was crowded with more old-fashioned furniture than could be taken in by the late summer light which scarcely penetrated the shrubs against the windows, and the table-lamps which diffused yellow pools only on the objects that surrounded them on the plush covers. There was a scroll-back sofa and arm-chairs to match, and some uncompromising chairs; the mantelpiece ornaments and the pictures on the walls could not have been other than they were. The room smelt musty, but it was not dusty; Mrs. Farmer's massive arms had been at work. She indicated sundry books on tables and what-nots.

'The Guests may like to look at the photograph albums.'

It was complete.

I sat down on the edge of one of the smaller chairs, ready to spring to attention. In a few minutes I heard her greeting the Frosts and the Thomases in the hall, and they were ushered in. I rose, gravely greeted them also as she retired, and provided each of them with a Family Album. The Guests had arrived already somewhat under the influence of their best clothes, and Mrs. Farmer's parlour overcame them. We turned our pages of Cabinets and Cartes de Visites, conversing a little politely in hushed voices. Edward did not attempt to light his clay. Before long, Gibson and Abercombie joined us. Edward and Robert saw that they were provided with albums. I think we all felt bound by an unspoken conspiracy not to let our hosts down; there were moments when we dared not catch each other's eyes. Last, Mr. Farmer came—or was driven—in, uncomfortable in a thick suit and a collar. He sat down and sweated, and said the missus would soon have supper ready. We made conversation.

Then, for the first time since heaven knows when, the double doors were flung open by our Hostess. She had discarded her apron, and stood in full bombazine welcoming us to the supper-table, as if she had not already met her Guests at the front door.

And what a supper-table! Mrs. Poyser herself could not but have approved. The long table had been dragged into the middle of the room, and the dining-chairs were ranged along both sides; with Mr. Farmer's arm-chair at the top, and Mrs. Farmer's at the bottom. I found myself seated at my Host's right hand, some poet or other beside me. The table was loaded with huge shapes of food, a ham, a great joint of beef, a raised pie and birds, among dishes of butter and pickles and salads, and sauce-boats of dressing, and slabs of home-made bread. If ever a sideboard groaned that sideboard did, with fruit-tarts and trifles and cheesecakes, and at least two flagons of my favourite rough cider.

We fell to. To pick at the food would have been to insult Mrs. Farmer, presiding with complacent ceremony at the far end, pressing us to this and that, passing down platefuls that could not, in mere courtesy, be ignored, rising from time to time, an outsize Hebe, to replenish our tankards from yet another Jeroboam of cider. At first the clatter of knives and forks took the place of conversation; but tankard by tankard the talk flowed with the drink. It was a very hot night. As tongues wagged and self-consciousness waned, Mr. Farmer took off his collar.

'Father!' from his scandalized Better Half.

'Can't help it, Mother; I'm sweaty!' he beamed; and took off his coat.

For the rest of the meal he sat at ease in his shirt-sleeves, his tongue loosed with the best. Mrs. Farmer disapproved, but her party was being a success. All her poets were laughing and chattering about her. Meats were removed, trifles and tarts demolished in quarts of cream, tankards refilled again and yet again. At last she rose majestically, and from the sideboard produced an enormous Stilton in an advanced stage of ripeness. It was offered to the poets sitting beside her, and travelled down the board till it reached our end. I helped myself modestly, and presented it to Mr. Farmer, now chuckling fruitily and showing his black teeth. He winked at me as he dug in his knife.

'I likes it,' he said, 'when they looks out o' their little winders and wags their tails, but I don't like it when they squeals between my teeth.'

'*Father!*'

What did it matter? Everyone was wiping his eyes with laughter, and we finished the meal with the cheese. Mrs. Farmer rose. I rose, and Helen rose, and Elinor Frost. Mr. Farmer rose. The Poets attempted to rise, relapsed on to their seats, and regarded each other with comical consternation. They were perfectly sober, though exceedingly gay; but the gallons of strong cider, against which I had been inoculated, had gone to their legs, and not one of them could stand without support. I saw Edward and Robert stagger to their feet, clutch each other, and go down; they rose again with great caution, clinging together. On the other side of the table Gibson and Abercrombie were behaving similarly. Two brace of poets staggered out into the moonlight and went hilariously homeward like two sets of Siamese Twins. I have boasted ever since of the night when I drank all the poets in Gloucestershire under the table.

§7

Before I left Ledington, Edward was already bicycling northeast through the Midlands in search of local material for war-articles. From Coventry he sent me the words of 'Mr. John Blunt' and 'Au Jardin de mon Père', songs I had liked when he sang them at the evening sing-songs.

Postmark 4 September 1914
Coventry
Thursday

My dear Eleanor, Here are the 2 songs. I am too full up with the ales of Birmingham and Coventry consumed since I left that I can hardly do more. It hasn't been quite fruitless, but that is all I can say. Tomorrow night I go to Sheffield, probably till Sunday morning. Then I don't know how I shall move, perhaps to Liverpool and thro Bradfield to Newcastle.

You did go home on Wednesday I suppose? I think everyone was glad to have you and hope you were as glad to be there. I felt as if I were rather the grub in the apple.

Helen and the boys too got safe home I hear and almost simultaneously. I am finishing this scrap after a strained evening of chit-chat and recovery from my day's dissipation, but you know by this time that this is only a variant of my excuses for bad letter writing. Goodbye and give my love to Bertie. I hope he has got what he wanted. My own plans are more uncertain. It is obvious for one thing that I can't go away for an indefinite long time and have others to look after the family.
Yours ever
Edward Thomas

P.S. I should be very grateful for any war poems you come across, but don't ensue [?] them at all particularly.

Bertie was now in the Army. I think he had joined the Infantry. It hardly mattered to him what he had got in the War, because he had not got what he wanted in life. He aimed only at being sent to France.

Steep Petersfield

13 Sep '14

My dear Eleanor   I got back on Thursday. It was rather a sad
business as I couldn't get anything without deliberately seeking it in
ways I don't like. So I missed what I should naturally have seen and
liked except at Newcastle and perhaps Sheffield. I shall never forget
Newcastle's bridges, the river and the streets deep below at night.
The coast up from Hartlepool to Sunderland, a rocky one with a
lot of steep little valleys, and the sea very innocent looking and
shipless—I enjoyed a lot of such things in the train. Now I am
writing. The article is just a collection of trifles unexaggerated.
All depends on whether I get them into some reasonable or tolerable
order. When its done I shall find out what sort of soldier they still
want at Petersfield . . . I like the story of Bertie and the religions.
But did he really choose the Church of England rather than pick up
bits of paper. I am quite glad Joan is still in England. When shall
I see her and all of you next? Probably I shall make some excuse for
being up at the end of the month. Give Bertie my love.

Yours ever
Edward Thomas

I had told Edward how Bertie's Sergeant, when filling in a
form with his particulars, expected him to name a religion.
Bertie, who had none, said, 'Pagan'. The Sergeant advised,
'I wouldn't, if I was you. The Pagans do fatigue-duty, and
have to pick up fag-ends and scraps of paper in camp all Sunday
morning while the Christians are singing hymns. Better say
Church of England.' Bertie, rather surprisingly, accepted this.

Steep
18 ix 14

My dear Eleanor,   I wonder have you already gone to Greatham.
If you could come over we should all be glad except Bronwen who
will be in any case in town. Only there is just a possibility I too shall
be going to town. There is no particular reason why I should
or I wouldn't hesitate because I rather want to. But you say if any
particular day suits you to come over and I will answer at once.
Helen and I might cycle as far as Midhurst, if that suits you better.
I don't believe I was ever really in Coldarbour, though having been
in Newdigate and other places close to it I walked round about

and may have been. I think it is on Stane Street some way south of Leith Hill and north of Ockley. This gives a chance to your passionate quarrelsomeness. But a fig for it, for both its.

My article is finished. It had to appear on October 1. So I had to do what I could at once. Please send me War jingles whenever it is convenient, but not when you are not writing. It isn't worth it.

As I shall almost certainly be up next week or the week after I suppose I shan't see you in town. I must try to see Clifford and Bertie.

I was down at Guthrie's for a night and yesterday and had a swim.

> Yours ever
> Edward Thomas.

This letter was written under the impression that I had already carried out a plan to accompany Margaret Radford to Coldharbour in Surrey, and from there walk on to Greatham. But an unexpected turn of things at home kept me in London till the end of the month. Bertie had been drafted out of the Army with varicose veins, and was back in Fellows Road, a civilian. He might have been content to remain one, if Joan had not been leaving England. His determination to get out to France, if possible, held good, and he asked Godwin Baynes if an operation on his legs might make him fit for service again. It was doubtful, for their condition was exceptionally bad. The hospitals were crowded, but Godwin had influence at Bart's, and the operation was speedily arranged. Edward hoped to see Bertie at Clifford Bax's, before it took place.

Wednesday   Steep

My dear Eleanor, I can't be very definite. What I aim at is cycling up on Friday. If I can—it depends chiefly on weather—then I will come to Clifford's that evening. But if I can't get up till Saturday I doubt if I can manage anything as I have to keep the week end open. Supposing that Clifford will be at home all day Sunday in any event I might get over some time, if not on Friday. I would rather not see a lot of people. What I should like most would be to have you and Bertie and Clifford and Olga. So if you preferred to endure Friday evening with or without me let me know at 13 Rusham Rd., Balham where I shall call and leave my bicycle? I am very sorry to

hear of Bertie's being set back like that. Of course I have done
nothing yet—apart from the garden.

Then I expect I shall see you on Friday. Will you also let me know
if there is any time before the evening on Saturday that I could come
if Friday fails? I leave here possibly before Friday's first post for
the sake of the early morning.

Thank you for the poetry again.

Yours ever
Edward Thomas.

The changed handwriting is due to gardening not emotion	Helen is away for tonight at Guthrie's, cycling there and back

The meeting with Bertie wasn't manageable before the
operation. An incredible number of veins had to be taken out
of both his legs. We weren't used to operations and hospitals,
and Mother was upset and so anxious that Godwin, who was
attached to her, got the rules relaxed, and she and I were
allowed to see Bertie as he was coming out of the anaesthetic.
He was muttering and talking wildly, seeming to recognize us
in fleeting moments, then fading away again to some un-
approachable distance. The visit did nothing to help Mother,
who went home weeping; but next day we found Bertie fully
conscious, and in a state of indignation. The shortage of
nurses had let in a troop of V.A.D. helpers of all classes, and
the male patients had been told that when they required the
chamber-pot they must ask the nurse for 'a snowball'. The
reason given was that a number of young aristocrats were on
part-time duty in the wards, and the blushes of the débutantes
must be spared.

With Bertie recovering slowly in Bart's, I took up my dis-
rupted plans, and Edward's next letter found me with Margaret
in Coldharbour.

Steep
3 X 14

My dear Eleanor,   These few days at home have been too busy.
Some books turned up for review—Guthrie stayed here—I had
some apple-picking with Helen and baby for a neighbour—and on

Monday if it is fine I start cycling towards Wales. So I fear I shan't get to you. But Helen hopes you will come over from Greatham. I didn't see the doctor. The ear seemed to get quite well, only to relapse again. But I don't worry. My address in Wales mostly will be

> c/o John Williams
> 22 Eaton Crescent
> Swansea

I may see the Frosts on my way home in a week or 10 days. Mrs. Frost is still undecided and not well. I hope you will answer Margaret about Frost if she can stand the truth. Thank you for the poem.

> Yours ever
> Edward Thomas

His thanks for the poem, and, in the previous letter for 'the poetry', perhaps refer to 'War-jingles' that I may have sent him; or perhaps are the first mention of his own poems, which he was beginning to write, and which I typed and returned to him as they arrived. At first only Helen and I and Frost were allowed to see them.

Margaret Radford, the daughter of poets, was a delicate poet in her own right; she had vision and imagination, and she 'still had one foot in Paradise', as Jung told her some years later. But she was antipathetic to the things Frost wrote about. 'Mending Wall', for instance: by all means mend a wall if that was what you liked doing, but masonry was one thing and poetry was another. I reported this to Edward, who had joined the Frosts in Lascelles Abercrombie's cottage in Ryton, which had been lent to them for the winter.

> Ryton   Dymock
> 17 X 14

My dear Eleanor,   By the time I had done walking and riding and afflicting Helen with long journals I couldn't write in Wales. I left there on Tuesday by bicycle and came here in 2 days thro Brecon, a lovely ride over Brecknock Beacon and under the Black Mountains to Hay and Hereford where I got the first rain and first punctures. Now I am idling and making notes for another English Review article—on what country people say about the war and its effects—do you remember anything said by the Farmers? Mrs. Farmer told Lesley yesterday that the Kayser's hambition was to eat his Christmas dinner in London. Mr. Chandler has been home but only for a day. The children are well here but Mrs. Frost tired and Robert not very well. It is languid still weather which I enjoy completely in spite of a magnificent boil in a shaving place that makes a new man of me. We loaf and talk. I shall be glad to be home and wonder if you will be there. You didn't mention Bertie in your letter. Is he getting ready to leave Bart's? I heard from Godwin—that Clifford and Olga were going there. He wanted me to go but I couldn't. I must do some work up at the study and in the garden.

John Williams is an old retired schoolmaster. I am sorry your Geography let you think I could have passed you on my way west, but I went in fact by Savernake Forest, Salisbury Plain, Bath and Bristol, with a night at Avebury: so I was always farther and farther from Coldarbour and the theory that you should only mend walls and never write about it or (I suppose) about anything you really do, but only about what you might or would like to do, or perhaps what you couldn't and wouldn't ever do, except in verse.

Frost is writing to Viola Meynell by this post, I see. He is pleased she should quote the Pasture.

Ever yours
Edward Thomas.

Viola was as pleased as Frost at being allowed to use his lovely little poem on the title-page of her new novel. She had all the feeling for his work which Margaret lacked. When this letter arrived my stay in Greatham was coming to an abrupt end.

One beautiful autumn afternoon Viola suggested that we should walk through Parham Park and the little village of Cootham beyond it, to visit Phyllis Bottome. The house she was lodging in lay past Cootham Post Office, where any letters to be delivered next morning at Greatham would be waiting. While Viola strolled on I collected the mail. It included a letter for me from Bertie, which I tore open and read rapidly, as I ran. When we were abreast she saw that I was dazed. Was it bad news? I shook my head. Bertie and Joan were going to be married. He was leaving Bart's immediately, his nursing was to be finished at home, and the wedding was to take place as soon as he could stand. There was no question of his rejoining the Army. The letter was radiantly happy, and very tender. He found Bart's unbearable, and wanted to be where he could see Joan and us without restrictions until the day when he would leave Fellows Road for good.

I told Viola I must go home at once. Of that tea-time meeting with Phyllis Bottome I only recall two black eyebrows over two penetrating eyes, and the impression of an intense personality; but I was still so dazed with joy that perhaps I remember even these vague things amiss.

Steep

21 X 14

My dear Eleanor, This seems to me very good news. It didn't surprise me but it pleased me more than any other such news has done before. There is no one like Joan. You know this isn't ambiguous. I mean you know my mind about her. I would have written to Bertie but it would only have given him an impertinent letter to write a nice reply to. I must try to think of something to send to his flat when I know it is his and where it is. A breadplatter or a vase or something. Perhaps they are going to be quite comfortably off. But if there are any little things you know they want please tell me, so that I can avoid Tantalus iii and cruet x. Well, I am glad.

I can't get rid of Geography it seems. I am literal I suppose. Now I am reading the third bard who wants my opinion since September. The first 2 I spoke the truth to and they didn't thank me. This one will be the same I fear. Such a nice person with such nice 2ndhand admiration for youth and fire and life and all that, and doesn't show he possesses them or ever really saw them with his own eyes. 'Earth Triumphant' by Conrad Aiken, an American.

I got home on Monday night, riding to Cheltenham and from Andover home, with my usual luck in weather and punctures. Herewood Forest and Abbotstone Down (N. of Alresford) were the best things I saw.

I don't know how the Frosts will get through the winter. He isn't a bit well and she is too hardworked.

Thank you for the Norfolk notes. I believe they will fit in. I feel quite unwilling to go ferreting about, as I have several things that

I really want to write. But I suppose I must go and sit in a pub or two.

I don't know yet if I shall be up next week or later, but will tell you when I do, and will try to arrange a night at Clifford's if he is free.

Ever yours
Edward Thomas.

Far from being quite comfortably off, Bertie, when Sir Hamo Thornycroft asked what his prospects were, said that he had no job, no money, and was marrying on a borrowed fifty pounds from our mother. Sir Hamo was prepared to be generous. In the event this was not necessary. Bertie's brilliant gifts were becoming known, and he got a good newspaper job without difficulty. On October 24th Bertie and Joan were married in Hampstead Town Hall, with myself and Mother, and Lady Thornycroft and her youngest daughter Elfrida, as witnesses. Bertie, very shaky and leaning on Joan's arm, passed straight from the ceremony into a taxi, which took them to Paddington and their honeymoon in the west.

Postmark October 27 1914

My dear Eleanor,   Thank you for the watch. I wish I was going to take it to Bronwen; she will be pleased. And how much did it cost? I saw no bill. Your letter gave me qualms approaching selfsatisfaction. In any case I shall come to Bertie's and Joan's before or after the platter. Next week I shall be up I think for certain. I shall write to Clifford asking for Tuesday night if that suits you. Will you send me a word to say if it does or doesn't? Wednesday would do as well.

My Father is here and I have only divided minutes to myself,—if I haven't lost myself altogether in this strange company. Where we really agree is in talking about all the Jenkinses Bevans Howells —cousins in Wales where he had just been. He is retiring next month on his 60th birthday. But you won't be taken in by this excuse for a bad letter.

If Mrs. Meynell was so good that you won't part with the poem I ought to get it I suppose. I didn't see it. Thank you for the others which you could part with.

Yours ever
Edward Thomas.

He wanted to give Bronwen a silver watch, and had sent me some odd bits of old jewellery in part exchange, which I took to our local jeweller, a genial kindly German whom I had known from my childhood. I chose a pretty one, which he assured me was good. But Edward suspected daintiness, and would have preferred something more workmanlike.

Steep
Petersfield

29 x 14

My dear Eleanor, You excel in temperatures as I do in excuses. I wish you recovered from yours as quickly. But I will make it Wednesday in case; at least I am writing to Clifford to suggest it. I send the odd 7/6. The watch pleased everybody, except me, whom it was not meant to please. I am not used to these things, and it looked too toylike a watch. But Helen says it is excellent, and I am sure Bronwen will. No need to send me the bill. Oct. 10. Thank you. I will try to see Mrs. Meynell's. Begbie was in a hurry about Africa, wasn't he? Well, so was I. I only hope it isn't the beginning of much worse.

Excuse C IV. It is only 8 a.m. and I haven't had breakfast and am inclined to give you Esq as well as Miss on the envelope.

Yours ever
Edward Thomas.

October 10th must be the date of Alice Meynell's war poem which I wouldn't part with.

Although I could never knowingly destroy any note or letter Edward wrote me, I find only three more before the end of the year. But there must have been others, because now his poems were beginning to run.

9 xi 14   Steep

My dear Eleanor, It is all as clear as mud except that I don't remember whether I signed the cheque. Did I? I am now in the thick of Tipperary ii and an article on War Poetry, both to be sent in this week. Otherwise all's well. Moreover, Helen is going to town and elsewhere on Thursday and Friday and I may elect not to be left here alone and to come to Clifford's if he can have me. If so I shall see you. I am not more certain about the 20th because I have asked Davies to come soon. But should the visit to town

come off you wouldn't mind picking a later date, would you?
I had seen Hewletts absurd ballad. The man has gone clean off his
head out of compliment to the Kaiser. Of the 2 I prefer Wilhelm
because he sticks to prose and perhaps doesn't do that himself. I
shall be working part of the time at Clifford's, but free much of the
time. Shall I see Joan and Bertie? I do hope you will be well again
then.
Yours ever
Edward Thomas

When can I send the bread platter? Yours I take it is for their
country house.

Bertie and Joan had, of course, no country house. Joe and
Fan lent them a flat in West Hampstead while they looked for a
place of their own; they eventually found one in Antrim
Mansions, quite near us in Fellows Road. It was there that
Edward always saw them when he was in London, fitting in
glimpses of them on the days he came to see me and my mother.

A letter written shortly before Christmas contains the first
positive reference to his poems.

My dear Eleanor   Thank you for the poetry. I hope it won't seem
unkind to send you some poetry in return, but there are one or two
good things in the book. As for my own it isn't running just now.
I sent what I had to Monro asking for secrecy. He kept it 4
days and then said he hadn't had time to read it, so I took it back
rather crestfallen, tho its quite possible that he meant he hadn't
been able to get anyone to help him to an opinion. I want him to
publish some later on in a book.

I expect one time is as good as another for the Frosts unless the
Abercrombies were coming back. If only you get some bright days
there you will like that country as much as them. Mervyn and I
had such a day on Sunday cycling up to town. I had an engagement
for Monday and today. Tomorrow we hope to cycle back. I've
been doing up parcels a lot. But I am not ingenious. They are
practically all books.

We saw the Bone play on Saturday. Costumes and scenery
excellent and some nice groups, but tedious beyond words nearly
all the time. I've got to say something about it I suppose.

I hope you will have a good Farjeon Christmas.
Yours ever
E. T.

The Frosts had asked me to choose a time to stay with them at Ryton in the New Year. I had sent them, as well as the Thomases, a big 'Farjeon parcel' of all-sorts for Christmas. My presents to Edward included two bandanna handkerchiefs, patterned in reds and greens such as he liked; one twill (for weekdays), the other silk (for Sundays). I had also sent five drinking-glasses of various kinds, suited to each member of the family; Edward's and Helen's were choice.

Steep
26 xii 14

My dear Eleanor,   You did not say which was the Sunday one, so I shall vary them to avoid mistakes. But thank you very much all the same. They are my style—and Baba's—she plays with my handkerchiefs when I'm away. She also liked the swan, almost more than I did, especially when I wore it on the top button of my waistcoat, but I gave up doing that last night. The glass was excellent in itself and in its place in the series. Then unluckily I washed up the dinner things and tho I had not used the glass it was there. Well, I broke it. Lucky that nobody else did. I am sorry.

We had a pretty good day in the modified Thomas style, with fine weather and no bellyache. (Your box was opened in your style, by the way, which turned out very well.) I even wrote some verses which I will try to copy out by tomorrow. Baba and Helen and I got over to the Bones for a walk and Baba saw the prettiest half-moon at the top (or bottom) of the downiest white sky, coming home. But it turned to rain, and today most of us feel pampered. I am up in my study thinking about England. I've undertaken to write about what people (myself included) mean when they say England—for Harrison.

This is the first of my Christmas letters, but still it is one and can't possibly get over the page.

Yours ever
Edward Thomas.

1915

In the first months of 1915 Edward's letters are chiefly concerned with the stream of poetry which was now in flood, and his desire to follow Frost to America when the family left England in February. His indecision was only partly due to the fact that he couldn't afford it; a deeper reason was that he could not be satisfied while he was doing nothing for England. He had been trying this problem over for many months, and when, with seeming suddenness, he enlisted, it was the result of having considered and rejected any other course. At first he thought he might serve England with his pen; but articles and anthologies, of the most English kind, were not the answer. Then, having cleared his decks of the book in hand, he considered taking up some recognized form of Civil National Service. His decision to be a soldier followed sharply. Some doubts as to his fitness caused delays that chafed him. He must be either a soldier or not a soldier. His indeterminate position made him self-conscious, and he did not want his friends to be told anything until he was actually in uniform. Then he was put at rest with himself, as I don't think he ever would have been if he had decided to leave his country and go with his friend.

Until all this came to a head in July, his absorbing satisfaction was in the poems which he was now sending to me regularly as he wrote them. When minor points had been settled I typed them for him, but it was nearly another three months before he showed them freely to the men whose opinions he valued, and tried them with the good-class periodicals. The poems teemed in him every day as he walked up the hanger to his study. 'I can hardly wait to light my fire,' he wrote, in the excitement of new creation that was robbing the old unhappiness of its power.

§2

I had some country visits to make in the New Year; one with Arnold Bax to Wisbech, and another to the Frosts in Ryton. Edward hoped to join us there, but before the date was settled he sprained his ankle.

Steep
Petersfield
3   i   15

My dear Eleanor,
        I shan't be able to coincide with you at Ryton. The English Review article will only just be finished by that time and I am not sure how soon after I can contrive to get away, especially as I have just damaged my foot and am laid up quite immoveable. Now you will say I might write a letter. And yet I shan't. I won't even entertain you with my reasons. You had to cut Geoffrey Young after all. I kept my own copy.—I only told you about the glass to explain a lack of geniality in my thanks. I couldn't be lyrical even about the fragments. But I plead guilty to not having noticed the difference between the two handkerchiefs, tho my own are just linen.
    I shall envy you going to Ryton. Frost hasn't said anything about my verses since. I think I have got him in one of his raw places.

Yours ever
E. T.

Please remember me to Arnold and to Godwin and Rosalind.

In my answer I told him that Rosalind was ill, and the visit to Wisbech postponed.

Steep
6 i 15

My dear Eleanor,

Letters seem the luxuries they are now. I am in bed or in the same position in a deck chair for a week or so and then probably a fortnight indoors but downstairs. So the Doctor says, but the sprain is looking better and feeling quite easy now. When the article comes to be written I shall have got used to the position I expect.

I am so sorry Rosalind is ill and you robbed of your holiday for the time being. You couldn't go to Ryton earlier could you? Frost hasn't been well and is rather low. But the others must be in good form with your Christmas box and all. They are good at Christmas. We had all surprises and I had a beautiful letter from Lesley about the Leadon in flood and the shiny nights. Now Baba has to be consoled by drawing. She has been crying without pretending.

Now I have drawn the 3 blind mice running after the farmers Wife.

I did afflict you with Young in spite of sending you a cut copy. I believe you read him straight through and endured all his 'cumulance of repose' and his meaningless metricalities. But L'Isolée has something good in it and 'The Cragsman' (is it so called?). Probably he is faddy about capitals on classic precedents. Much of the good editions of Roman poets begin a line with capitals only after full stops.

If you don't go to Wisbech or Ryton this week could you come here for a little while. It could and would be contrived gladly. If you don't come do you feel able to put into words anything you thought (before being asked by me) about England, say in connection with any part of it or any event or saying or person? Please don't *trouble* about it as troubling would probably produce what I don't want—I had some delicious humbug from a friend who discovered he couldn't *love* his country because he depended on her for his living. I didn't want his intelligent discoveries.

Baba rhymes verse regardless of sense and makes verse without rhyme and equally without sense for a long time on end nowadays.

Yours ever
E. T.

P.S.   I have got out some of my verses, all you haven't seen. All except The Manor Farm are my only copies, so if you would like to keep any of the others would you make copies? I find typing at present too awkward.

Before copying the batch of poems, I had to tell him that I could not get to Steep.

Steep

10 i 15

My dear Eleanor,

Thank you for your letter. This is simply just to say there is no hurry for returning the MS. It was interesting to find you prefer my remarks unrhymed. You hit upon some passages I felt doubtful. But 'under storm's wing' was not just for the metre. 'As if they played' I was anxious to have in. It describes the patterns of the fish but it comes awkwardly perhaps after inlaid. I mean in 'Interval' that the night did postpone her coming a bit for the twilight. Night might have been expected to come down on the end of day and didn't. 'Held off' would have been stricter. As to 'sing and whistle first', I don't think 'to whistle and to sing' which is formally correct is as good. If I am consciously doing anything I am trying to get rid of the last rags of rhetoric and formality which left my prose so often with a dead rhythm only. If I can be honest and am still bad in rhythm it will be because I am bad in rhythm.

Now I am downstairs but worse off because I know how helpless I still am. I can only hop and am in a filthy temper and couldn't enjoy Stanley's song at all—I never heard it before.

I hope your mother is better this fine frosty morning.

Yours ever

E. T.

Stanley North was a mercurial artist in stained glass whom Edward had met at Clifford Bax's, and whose company he usually enjoyed. Stanley's ribald songs, appalling language, and atrocious manners could be extremely amusing or quite inexcusable, as you chose to take him. At this time he was very hard up, but in his successful later years his work brought him into High Society; and Princess Louise was enchanted to be told by him, 'Look here, old girl, come off it, you've no bloody taste at all'.

PLATE V

EDWARD AT HOME

Steep 16 i 15

My dear Eleanor

Thank you very much for these copies. I have now some later pieces you shall see when you come back, and I do appreciate having a safe in Hampstead in a road which the flashlight opposite thinks as safe as Berlin, I suppose. So you really are going to Ryton. How I wish I could. I am glad your mother is well enough and hope she took the soup. As to the party for Maitland it is most likely I shouldn't be free by then to any extent. I get on too slowly and am not sure I do get on. I had a setback owing to a slip. And if I am better by then I must try to get to the Frosts. I should like to see you and Viola Meynell and Maitland but a crowd is a crowd for me, I am afraid.

I am pleased you like 'After Rain' best. I wonder whether I can do anything with 'inlaid' and 'played'. The inlaid, too, is at any rate perfectly precise as I saw the black leaves 2 years ago up at the top of the hill, so that neither is a rhyme word only. No, I don't believe rhyme is at all a *bad* trouble. I use it now more often than not and always fancy I leave the rhymed pieces as easy as the rest, but tho I am so young a versifier I don't pretend to be sure.

The children are just beginning school again. We have had a lot of cards together after supper but not one walk. Baba has been very good. The other morning I told her I had dreamed about Frost. Do you mean the man Frost? she said. I used to draw for her when I was horizontal; now I do nothing for nobody.

Yours ever
Edward Thomas.

'The party for Maitland' was one being planned, I think, either at Dolly Radford's house in Well Walk or the Meynells' flat over Burns & Oates in Orchard Street; I can't remember what it was to celebrate, perhaps his having become at last a fully-fledged doctor. He was one of the most brilliant young men of our circle, yet he had had to sit three times for each of his medical exams. Long before he was a qualified doctor his gift for diagnosis was remarkable. His parents had been closely connected with William Morris, and Maitland preened himself on having been dandled in the idealist's arms. After this he grew up with his own ideals of socialism, which he was able to express when towards the end of his life he became chief Medical Officer of Health for St. Pancras.

It was when Maitland stayed in Steep with the Montague Fordhams, whose lovely garden was divided by a hedge from the Thomas cottage-plot, that I came to know him below the surface of the dancing wit which lit up our London parties. As we walked up and down between Gertrude Fordham's borders of Michaelmas daisies, we talked of ideas and facts and friends and Freud—

'Freud?' It was a new name to me.

'Haven't you heard of psycho-analysis yet?'

'No. What is it?'

'Tell me instantly what a geranium suggests to you.'

'A flower-pot.'

'Ah!' Maitland nodded his head sagaciously. 'So you are in love with the gardener's boy.'

He amplified a little this very short cut to the latest cult, which was soon to be a prolific gold-mine for the revue-writers, till it became an accepted discovery, when the playwrights took it over.

During our walks and talks I learned the deep integrity of Maitland's passion for truth. His swift tongue cut clean through sentimentality to the heart of whatever was under discussion, social or psychological. He diagnosed a character as acutely as he diagnosed a disease, and was illuminating, and sometimes disconcerting, about many of the people we knew in common. But I never heard his sense of fun used to *debunk* a friend in the way that was coming into fashion. He held the scales fairly, examined without personal bias, and once declared that you ought not to tear anyone to pieces unless you loved him. But he was firm in his rejection of humbug and compromise, and once said urgently, 'Whatever you do, Nellie, as you grow older—*don't go cosy*.' On the other hand, he warned me against destroying myself through sympathy. Why did he think I did? I asked. He answered, 'One day when I was going to visit Sylvia Lucas in the hospital I saw your face as you were leaving her room. You didn't see me.

I suppose one really has no right to look at anyone who is suffering, and doesn't know he is being looked at.'

I had begun to call myself a socialist, in a mush of feeling for the evils of poverty and the misery of the poor. Maitland would strip the feelings from the facts, and show me the hard core of the evil with a passion far more powerful than emotional identification. One night when he was seeing me home through the London streets he described some of the dire conditions he was working in; then stopped and turned his face towards the East End. 'Do you realize, Nellie, that you and I *are the exceptions*? There are *very few* people like us in the world.' He flung out his arm towards Whitechapel and Poplar. 'There are *millions* like them.'

§3

The Ryton week was fixed between February 16th and 24th. Edward asked me to salvage several of W. H. Hudson's books which he had lent to Frost in the autumn; he was afraid they might remain on Abercrombie's shelves when Robert left. My letters described walks I had taken with Robert, and much running about the village with the young Frosts, who made themselves at home everywhere; and particularly in the farm-house across the road, where Monday was not washing-day but baking-day, when the farm-wife kneaded a mountain of dough to last the appetites of the farmer and his men through the week. One of my Ryton memories is this woman's strong arms and hands at work in the dough on Monday morning, and of our fetching a load of warm loaves home in the afternoon. I never tasted bread so good, and it tasted better at the end of the week than at the beginning. The woman said baking made a harder day's work than washing, and Tuesday's tubful of linen made her arms ache less than Monday's tubful of dough.

When I said goodbye to the Frosts it was for the last time; they were leaving England in February.

Steep
24 i 15

My dear Eleanor
        I was lucky yesterday to have letters from you and Frost and
they gave me a certainty that you all had a good week. You had
the best of the weather too if you went down the Leadon and out to
Redmarley. After 10 months my 'Ross' map is one of my best used.
I am sorrier than I would tell them that they are going because
although I very much want to, I know how many things more
likely than not will prevent my going out to them. But I don't
think I ever pretended to be more certain than I was. I wish you
could have come here on your way back and to hear about them
and also because I don't know how soon I can see you in town. It is
like this. I am probably going up on Wednesday to town but with
no certainty of being able to walk more than 100 yds, and I go up,
instead of going straight to the Frosts, only to see the National
Service League in case they can suggest the right thing for me. They
may lead me a dance here and there. Also I might not be able to
keep it up. Otherwise I would say meet me at Miles [*Eustace Miles
Restaurant*] at 1 if you can. I go on to the Frosts, if the programme
stands the wear, on Friday.
        Just look at all these verses, mostly written since my ankle went
wrong 3 weeks ago. This will prejudice you against them. A man
can't do all that and be any good. Still here they are. I haven't
thrown away anything, even the worse version of 'Old Dick'.
        You knew that Mervyn was most likely going out with the
Frosts did you? It only depends on the man at the other end
answering Yes, in time, and we expect he will. I shall be glad for
him but sorry for myself because it means the end of any chance of
being anything to the boy. But I only hope I haven't been nothing
to him for too long now.
        Please give my love to Bertie and Joan and I hope you found your
mother well when you got back. My mother may come today the
first company I shall have seen except Bone twice. We five send our
loves to you.   Yours ever
                                                Edward Thomas.

Before the next letter I sent him Will Kemp's *Nine Days'
Wonder*. He had begun to compile an anthology that was to be
redolent of England, and I thought he might find something in
this Elizabethan curiosity which had pleased me for years.

Steep
3 ii 15

My dear Eleanor

Thank you for the books. I enjoyed reading Kemp. I think I had read him before but he is forgettable. His merit is not to say anything that stands between you and the facts which are entertaining. But he doesn't really create the facts and I don't feel sure I can quote him, unless it is about the stout girl who kept up with him for a mile. I shall read Chesterton but I don't expect I shall quote living people much if at all. There is not room and also I think I can get more unity and completeness by ending not later than Tennyson and Dickens. Is there anything of Dickens I *must* use? I have noticed a passage or two both on London and the country (Lincolnshire) in 'Bleak House' and 'Martin Chuzzlewit', but I am rather shy of taking them as I don't know Dickens well enough to be sure they are the right thing to show him by. I *should* like to see those songs of Henry VI's time, though I am using very little that is not excellent in itself as well as apposite, and that was a poor age and I have already got enough to fill a bigger book. But I haven't yet persuaded them to give me my terms, and it may fall through.

Please keep the Hudsons till you have read them. I am so glad you rescued them. The other books haven't come home and I almost expect they won't. I don't know what the Frosts are doing. Since his telegram on Friday I have heard nothing, and he hasn't appeared. Helen feels that perhaps they will disappoint Mervyn—and us. They are rather incalculable. I am impatient because my foot is really not well and I still can't go up to my study and time hangs and dies slowly. I am thinking still about cyclists corps, and get no less shy about the first steps, not to speak of expecting to dislike the life and wondering what would happen to my things and affairs. Well, you know about how serious this is.

I wonder why you were so firm against appearing in Aucassin? Is Bertie doing anything in it? But I haven't seen the play. I should think it would be good. It is within Clifford's range and he always does his conscious best. I must see it, but I hope I shall contrive to be spared the sort of show you went to to hear Gertrude and Stacy.

We have had Bronwen and Baba in bed with coughs and temperatures. They are now very convalescent in the kitchen. They send their love.

Yours ever
Edward Thomas.

'Why are you so firm against appearing in Aucassin?' refers to a stage version of 'Aucassin and Nicolette' written by Clifford Bax. Bertie adored this romance (which thirty years later, at the time of his death, we were working on for a musical setting by Clifton Parker); he intended to make a play of it in 1914, but had retired in favour of Clifford, whose version was charming. The play was to be presented at the Ambassadors, and some of our friends were taking part in it. The theme was enriched by Olga Antonietti's dark young beauty and dusky gold voice. It surprises me now that Clifford had proposed my taking part. I had a pretty singing-voice, and from my mother's side of the family had inherited a sense of theatre which served me in our impromptu charades; but my dread of public appearances was such that I would have shrunk from even walking on in a crowd. My steel-rimmed spectacles saved me; without them I was nearly blind, and with them would have spoiled the mediaeval picture.

Steep
9 ii 15

My dear Eleanor,   I hardly looked at the cartoon. The first glances were unmistakeable—'Kish' certainly awful. Of course I want to make money out of the proverbs but I didn't take to the idea of putting them in there even if with your help they could be got there. There is however a fairly sound reason too, against not doing it and that is that the 2 or 3 might give someone else the hint. So I don't think I shall. But the *real* reason is simply that I don't like the idea more than I do of serving at Selfridges. Not I believe out of loftiness, but maybe so.

I haven't made myself clear yet about the anthology. It isn't what Dickens 'says of England' that I want. Anything that makes us feel England particularly or which we could imagine making a stranger feel it is what I want—e.g. I am using Hotspur's ridicule of Glendower (and of all Celts) and also 'When icicles hang by the wall' from 'Love's Labour's Lost'—George Herbert's hymn called 'The British Church'—Keats's 'Autumn'. Does that make it clearer.

'Green Mansions' I felt certain you would like. And by the way I am glad you rescued those books. The others haven't come, Frost never mentioned them. There was 'Adventures among Birds' which Hudson gave me and Masefield's 'Mainsail Haul' and I think something else. It is a little inexplicable to me. I shall perhaps mention it in a note I am sending. They left this morning.

Your letter this morning Helen more or less answered. She was writing to you. The Frosts were going and I didn't think I was going to write just today. No I shall not be up this week but perhaps next. I will write to Clifford when I am surer, assuming that Mrs. Podmore is staying some time and will still be there. I have to do some days at the Museum and may as well do it now instead of sticking here lame and alone with Helen and Baba at the Ellis's and Bronwen at school.

No hurry about the poems. I am so glad you liked 'Tears'. I haven't yet made up my mind though to publish any of the verses except anonymously and don't know how to contrive that for periodicals.

I'll let you know about coming up. I must try to get to Bertie's, but I can't zigzag much.

Yours ever
Edward Thomas.

Steep
12 ii 15

My dear Eleanor

I have heard that tomorrow is your birthday. Have you already got this Song Book? If you haven't I must write your name in it; if you have I shall find you another book. I hope it will be the kind of day you like.

I expect to go to Clifford's on Wednesday but haven't heard yet. If he's very slow I can't go because I must arrange a few days beforehand. But if I go there I shall see you one evening. In the days I shall be at the Museum. I thought of staying till Friday or Saturday.

It wasn't a base place at all—'The Cartoon' I mean. If I were on the paper or in with them, or if I don't quite know what, I should send them. Also I suspect I don't like the idea of perhaps being *refused* by them.—Do you think 'The Purple Land' etc might have got among Abercrombie's books. Helen is going to suggest it to Frost and then if they are I can write. It is what Belloc calls 'extremely rum' to me. Well, I suppose you saw Helen and Mervyn today. I wish he was off and over.

My ankle isn't a bit better so I shan't get about at all and so shan't try to get to Bertie's this time.

Yours ever
E. T.

Postmark Feb 16

My dear Eleanor

Clifford can't put me up, so I may not get there at all. But could you meet me at the entrance to the Reading Room at 5 on Tuesday and we'll have tea? Or if by 5 the galleries are closed I will look for you at the gate. Don't answer if this is agreed.

It would have been nice to see you, and there would have been bacon and baked apples and a cake of my mother's. Bronwen rather enjoys our breakfasts and the evening hour before her bed. In a sort of way I am rather cheerful. But it is by a slight unconscious process of suppression. I can't write yet again.—I am sorry you didn't come and sorrier for the reasons. Still if it hadn't been your birthday it would have been worse perhaps.

Mervyn went off happily, but I guess Helen didn't come back so. And I haven't got the Frosts' address; I don't know if she has, nor if she inquired for the books. I think 'Adventures' about the best bird book there is, don't you?

A. E. Housman can't let me use him in my anthology because he has always said No to anthologists but he atoned by praising my Swinburne, which is the highest compliment I have had yet. You see I care more than 2 pins for myself.

Yours ever
Edward Thomas.

§4

Now he decided at last to try his luck with the periodicals. Conscious that his reputation as a critic might prove both for and against him, he decided to adopt a pseudonym. *Blackwood's Magazine* had begun to take some of my work, and as I had established friendly relations with old William Blackwood I offered to send him the first batch of Edward's poems, saying that it was the work of a friend.

Steep
Petersfield
20 ii 15

My dear Eleanor

Here are 4 poems by Edward Phillips for you to palm off on Blackwood if you can. I shall be enormously pleased if you can.

I have just got back again to my typing and to Bronwen. It is a beautiful evening but the solitude is multiplied, roughly speaking, by the number of people in Steep. Now I have got to describe Guthrie's character and deserts to the 'Professional Classes War Relief Council', and between truth and a practical object to be attained it is rather a nervous job. I am still hesitating about sending my verses to de la Mare and others—It is too much like begging for compliments. I shall wait.

Yours ever
Edward Thomas

P.S. Does anything in Adventures among Birds strike you as specially good for my Anthology?

He had chosen the pseudonym 'Phillips' because Philip was his second name; but I thought it would be wise to choose another, as Stephen Phillips was still in the firmament, though he had passed his zenith. Edward replied:

My dear Eleanor, Perhaps you are right about Phillips. What about Marendaz, which is a family name, and I think not that of any English writer—But would it be too un-English just now. If so, then it can be Eastaway, which is also a family name, and illiterate. You may choose.

I think the Hudson page good and remember it well. But I doubt if it would quite manifest itself all alone to the uninitiate, and I think I won't. And I have such a mass. I have just arranged it roughly. Until I have finished I am rather badly busy. Which is as well. It isn't much fun here even these 3 bright cold days— The snow is deep up there in the drifts.—Mr. Dodd is singing 'Glorious Beer'. (A new excuse for writing no more.)

Yours ever
Edward Thomas

MARENDAZ is the name.

But Marendaz was too un-English, not only 'just now' but at any time, for the poetry of Edward Thomas. Eastaway I liked, and he settled on it.

Steep
My dear Eleanor,   23 ii 15
        Thank you again and again. I can wait, I tell you. But
would there be any harm in having communications addressed c/o
you or of your mother? It would be awkward at Steep to be c/o
myself; or have I missed an obvious way?
        And I was thinking of a passage about Wells in Somerset. Two
whole pages would be too much. I believe I am laying up a lot of
rejections for the future. But if it would fill less than one sheet of
paper typed I should like to have it. Unless you have plenty of time
though, please don't, as I know at least 2 excellent things, have
already typed one, and can't use *more than* 2.
        I like that actress, but with Guthrie it isn't at all an accomplish-
ment. As for me, I am not a candidate yet and don't want to be.
        Helen is down at the Ransomes' now beyond Salisbury. We have
got snow here and there, and frozen roads, and the hills all snow
except the gorse and juniper bushes which look black. I suppose
Helen & Baba will be indoors mostly, drinking champagne &
smoking shag, a way they have at the Ransomes'. Bronwen looks
up from her mending and sends her love.   Yours ever
                                                         E. T.

So Fellows Road became the head-quarters for the 'communications' of Edward Eastaway, and the acceptances or
rejections of his poems.
        Edward's thirty-seventh birthday was approaching. I had
spent March the third with the family the previous year, and
he wrote on March the second:

My dear Eleanor,
        I have been badly pressed since Saturday with my Index to
do or I would have written. Is it too late to ask you to come here
tomorrow? I am not good for more than a short walk, but that
wouldn't matter. Would you stay the night too? Next day I go to
Seccombe's at Camberley and then have Friday in town but without
a free moment. I don't know about Saturday; it depends how early
I go to Coventry. Helen came back on Saturday. They had a
splendid time. Excuse all that I ought to have said; I haven't even
time to look at your last letter.   Yours ever
                                                 Edward Thomas
Tuesday 8 a.m.

I did not go.

I made ready at once to catch an early train, but when I told my mother that this was Edward's birthday and I would be spending the night at Steep with him and Helen, her distress became so great that I unpacked my knapsack. Her fondness for Edward had never diminished, but now for the first time her anxiety for me came to the surface, and she said some things she must have found difficult to say. I knew how little cause she had to fear, but I could not talk about it. I sent a telegram, and spent the day alone in great unhappiness.

§5

The next letter calls for some light on the important subject of Walking-sticks. They were bones of contention between us. Edward had numbers of them which were all, of course, the Real Thing. He declared that he would rather be seen dead than walking with a stick he hadn't cut himself. Going along a hedge, his eye never missed a straight limb of hazel or holly or thorn or ash standing up from a root that would plant itself in his palm as the perfect handle to the perfect staff. The green sticks he cut and seasoned had strength and character. Oak was the best of all. Now though I could not cut my own sticks, I also had an eye for the Real Thing, and no spindly weak-crooked stick picked out of a tobacconist's drain-pipe would do for me. But on my country walks I had spied three beauties in little country pubs, and I bought them for a shilling or two apiece; none of them new, and all well-used. One was a tall pale drover's ash, with a thick well-turned root to grasp it by; one a rough holly, brown and seamed like a gypsy's cheek with warts on it; the third a stumpy Irish blackthorn, french-polished from long use, with a stain of yellow on the oval knob. Edward had to approve of them all, and once said of the ash, 'I must confess I envy you that stick'. 'Try it,' I said. He looked from it to me with withering scorn. 'I wouldn't touch it with a barge-pole, thank you.' The stick of his I coveted was a warm-coloured hazel, with a down-tilted crutch that gave it personality, like a slightly-crooked nose on an honest face. But Edward never offered it to me, nor any other of his cutting; and we maintained the feud of the walking-sticks without compromise. After he died, when Helen gave me a choice, I chose the hazel which had fitted his palm so often and so well, and when I walked I felt his hand on it.

Now Maitland Radford too was a keen walker, and about this time he and I were once more to join forces with Viola at Greatham, for some tramping over the Downs to Singleton. He displayed to me with pride a stout peeled holly, the colour of Cornish cream, boasting, 'Edward has given me his best walking-stick'. In honour bound (on the nursery principle that Cambridge is better than Oxford) I spurned it in favour of my ash, which Maitland promptly belittled (*Oxford is better than Cambridge*). In describing the argument to Edward, I took my chance to pour scorn upon his whole tribe of walking-sticks if he really considered Maitland's holly his chef d'oeuvre.

                                                        Steep
                                                        Petersfield
                                                        (*undated*)
My dear Eleanor,

Here is the M.S. and not much else as I am badly pressed to get things done before we go. I hope you will get to Wisbech. It might be better than Singleton if you could get decent trains. But we hope you will come to Singleton. Do you know it? I often go there, and always on my way to Goodwood. If you come over to us, sometime we might get over to you.

How curious of Maitland to suppose me so curious as to give him my favourite stick. He must think me a great deal nicer than I am and much more ignorant of sticks. I assure you but not necessarily Maitland—still it is the truth tho it might be wise to be economical with it—that your stick is a thoroughly good stick in every respect, faultless of its kind, and that his may be so to him but is open to question as I do not think yours is—I mean as I *know* yours is not. No charge for this.

Goodbye. I am haunting Borrow now at a terrible rate too.

                                                        Yours ever
                                                        Edward Thomas

After this handsome admission walking-sticks ceased to be bones of contention, and became buried hatchets. Thenceforth we praised each other's generously, and continued to walk with our own.

§6

At Greatham I was introduced to the Lawrences. Viola had lent them 'Shed Hall', her cottage adapted from a long low range of cowsheds that stood at right angles to 'Humphreys' on one side of the courtyard. Lawrence was not well, and my first sight of him was propped up in bed against pillows. Viola had come to know him during the previous year and had volunteered to type his latest novel, in order to relieve him of an expense he could not afford. It was a long manuscript, the close work strained her eyes, and I offered to help her; and a portion of *The Rainbow* was typed on my Yost in Fellows Road. It included the stampede of horses which seemed to me epic, the work of a genius. I had read *Sons and Lovers* and *The White Peacock*, and had heard Edward envy in the latter observations on nature which he wished he had observed for himself. That first glimpse of Lawrence, pale and friendly, was a brief one.

Soon after I was in Wisbech with Arnold Bax, paying my postponed visit to Godwin and Rosalind. One day Arnold took me to Ely, a city he loved, and led me round the Cathedral, explaining its variety of architecture, about which I knew nothing. Under the lantern, as exquisite as a flower, my senses quickened and came alive to the beauties of 'frozen music'.

My letters from home included a long one from Lesley Frost, and the first rejection of Edward Eastaway's poems; Blackwood had returned them all. I sent the news off to Edward, enclosing Lesley's letter.

Steep
12 iii 15

My dear Eleanor

As we had virtually no letters we were glad to see Lesley's & didn't bother about Mr. Blackwood's. The fact is Mervyn was nearly sent back and Frost only wrote at the end of 4 days (in New York presumably) trying to get behind the law and at last (we hope) succeeding. As Mervyn said he was not seasick it sounds as if he must have been something else—bored probably. Frost was evidently too sick of the business to say more than that he believed it was over. Mervyn just sends a picture postcard each. Thank you for sending the letter. We still hope to hear.

I should like to read Artzibashef and Conrad but perhaps I shan't. I think I should prefer the Russian. But I am sick of reading at the Museum and then Maeterlinck's poems. I was glad to get back here and go up to the study again and write and have fine days for sowing the garden. I am not sure that I want to leave this part after all, especially as it would cost so much. The Ellises have a cheap old cottage just opposite them if we could resolve. If it were July, now, Godwin's pond would be just the thing. But I shall see him before July if he doesn't go away.

Am I right in thinking your mother won't mind my using her address for Edward Eastaway? I am sending the *Nation* one or two. Would you mention it to her in case she should not understand?

I suppose Blackwood just thought it looked very much like prose and was puzzled by the fact that it was got up like verse. I only hope the mistake was his and prefer to think it likely. But I am sorry he should go against your story, too, tho he doesn't sound like a man whose opinion one would wait for unless it had a money value.

Yours ever
Edward Thomas

A fund was being raised in Wisbech for the restoration of West Walton church. I was told that the church in decay was worth seeing. One morning I set out for it and on the road was overtaken by an ancient driving a dogcart with his wife beside him. They passed me, but drew up almost at once and waited till I came abreast.

'Will you ride?' said the woman.

She pushed up against her husband to make room as I climbed beside her. The old man was a spectacular cross between Santa Claus and Elijah, with jolly Christmas curves to his nostrils and ruddy cheeks, stern unsmiling eyes very deepset under shaggy brows, and an enormous flow of white beard over the great breadth of his old-fashioned best blacks. He did not offer a word or a look. His wife was talkative. She had been at Lynn during an air-raid, and described the buzz in the air that woke her up; so that now she never heard a motor-car pass in the night without wondering whether the Huns were overhead. At the word 'Huns' the old fellow rumbled Biblically in his beard; the rumbling gathered itself up in words, and speech rolled out of him as out of the prophets of old.

'A baad man, the Kayzer, a baad man! He shall sue for Peace and he shall not have it! Berlin shall not be saved. Roosher shall be one quarter of the Continent. There shall be land for France, there shall be land for England. We will take his money. We will take his ships. War he shall not wage for an hundred years. A baad man!'

He subsided into his beard again, and did not utter another syllable during the drive. I was put down at a point near the church.

It was indeed in bad decay, and well worth seeing; I hope it was never restored out of character, which was that of a fine old barn. On a slab in the floor I found an inscription which I copied for Edward, after jotting down the Ancient's prophecies.

THIS STONE
MARKS THE PLACE OF INTERMENT OF
WILLIAM ALFRED
THE INFANT SON OF
JOHN ROSE & BRIDGET WEATHERHEAD
HE DIED NOVEMBER the 19th 1826
AFTER SEVEN WEEKS

I wondered who was responsible for that plain statement. Did Bridget, by public confession of her fault, seek to expiate the tiny sin which heaven had recalled in seven brief weeks? Was it required of her by the relentless morality of her parents? Or exacted as a penance by the Church? At least the infant son of John Rose and Bridget Weatherhead slept in holy ground, and I hope did not wander in Limbo.

Steep
Petersfield
Tuesday
(*Postmark March 16th*)

My dear Eleanor,

Thank you for the letter Helen forwarded to me at Guthries. I was there just for last night. The weather was too fine not to get a bit of a ride. But it was very grey and one needed to be rather particularly well or not fatigued. It would have been better perhaps strolling at Ely Cathedral which I never saw with you and Arnold. There were some lovely moments though in crossing the downs. When I got back I found letters for Helen from Mrs. Frost and 'Mrs.' Scott. Mervyn had arrived—was out sweeping snow off the ice to make it fit for skating. I don't gather that Frost got there, but perhaps he did. Also I found the upper part of the paper rest of the Balaban, but it apparently doesn't belong; there are no slots in the lower part to put its legs into. You will solve it for me some day. Meantime the lower half is very useful. Perhaps I might never really need the upper in fact.

I am sorry about Bridget Weatherhead. I should think it rather likely the parson managed it. A person of importance enough to have her way would hardly be allowed (to make it public) by her family. But I should like to know. I would rather know that than meet your Elijah who thought the Kayzer a bad man.

If you should see Eastaway's name in the *Times* attached to 8 lines of rhyme, do tell me. They won't return them because I left out the stamped envelope.

I think you said you would be at home by the 15th. I may be up next week; if I am I will let you know, if I have more than a day.

Yours ever
Edward Thomas

The Balaban was a typist's two-piece support for manuscript; not, as one might infer from Edward's next, a dental appliance.

19 iii 15   Steep
                                                   Petersfield
My dear Eleanor,

I should have sent these verses before. If you still feel I might suffer from Zeppelins will you copy them some time, that is supposing they were up to the mark mostly. The Times didn't see my merits—it was a rejected thing you forwarded. But I am trying everyone in turn.

Please do not trouble about the Balaban. I wrote them an irritated note. For they began by sending another lower plate which I wouldn't trouble to return. I can get on quite well with the lower plate simply.

I am pleased to hear it was Watson they preferred to Eastaway; I shall have to cultivate a great voice I see, but I can't.

I suppose I was feeling haughty with my freedom from the need to use your Elijah. Never mind. I may yet have to. There is precious little else to do except in the garden, and the weather has been first rate for that, and we have both done a good deal tho I did steal 2 days to go over to Guthrie: and got back more dead than alive with fatigue. It has turned cold but cleared too. John Freeman is coming tomorrow. In little more than a week Bronwen breaks up and goes away with a school-friend. After all I shan't be coming up till then, about the 30th. In April if I can afford it I shall cycle to Glostershire and stay a few days.

I am just filling in some interstices in the Anthology.

Yours ever
Edward Thomas

P.S. If you do pass the Hampstead Library and discover that February review in the D.C. I shall be glad.

The poet John Freeman was another friend of whom Edward had spoken to me with affection, saying, 'He's a sort of angel, you know.' I understood this rare praise when I came to know John later on. He was gentle, with a fine sensitive mind, and qualities which made his plain features lovable. That day in March at Steep, John must have read for the first time some of the poems he was to see through the press when Edward went to France.

25.iii 15   Steep

My dear Eleanor   Petersfield

Thank you. I have some more, too. It has perhaps become a really bad habit as I walk up the hill and I can sometimes hardly wait to light my fire. I am glad you find some things you like. I like the Child on the Cliff. It is a memory between one of my young brothers and myself which he reminded me of lately. He

was most of the child and I have been truthful. I think I can
expect some allowances for the 'strangeness' of the day. I wish I
could cycle over at Easter but if I do go away I think it will be then
and I should go west. Still, I might, and I am not *fixing* anything
yet, and if I do the weather will intervene. I am still no walker
except on smooth roads. But I hope you will be quite well by then.
The weather has been tempting and tiring. We have done a lot of
gardening, and never had the ground in better order so early. We
expect Stanley this week end and shall look for news of you by
him. I have a number of things to do in town, but I think I can see
you on Wednesday or Thursday—next week that is: and I will
write again when I know.

My mother had such a good letter from Mervyn about his deten-
tion and his whist playing with fellow prisoners. Now he is bored
with Scott though.   Yours ever

                                                Edward Thomas

I hope Eastaway gets the only rejected MSS at Fellows Rd; he gets
them steadily.

He did indeed, and not a single acceptance.

The next letter is written after Easter, when I had sent the
usual family parcel in which Edward always had his own
chocolate egg. He had also a drinking glass, to replace the one
broken at Christmas.

Postmark 5 April 1915   Monday

My dear Eleanor

Baba and I thank you for the egg which we killed between us.
I must try sending you glass or may be I am immune as living in a
glass house and throwing stones. Now I have got to work. I
have practically accepted the filthy job—a book on the Duke of
Marlborough to be done in haste. I am coming up at once to the
Museum. One day I will have tea with you if you will have tea
with me, say on *Thursday* at 4.30. I could meet you anywhere
between the Reading Room door and the nearest Express Dairy.
This seems to knock all travel on the head this spring.

Did I tell you I removed the old Balaban and the Yost and I are
friends for ever!   Yours ever

                                                Edward Thomas

Tomorrow I shall be at

> 13 Rusham Rd
> Balham S.W.

Was that Bertie's poem in 'Punch', about the immunity of Hampstead people living in the midst of Heinrich, Hans and Hermann.

Bertie was already writing the satirical light verse which he developed so brilliantly in the post-war revues, but I don't think he was responsible for the poem in Punch, to which I myself was now contributing regularly my 'Nursery Rhymes of London Town.'

§7

After Easter the Lucases' cottage was lent to Dolly Radford; she invited me to go there for a few weeks with Margaret and a Miss Paget, who came to housekeep and cook for us.

The Meynell estate covered some eighty acres of meadowland and woodland stretched between the parishes of Greatham and Rackham. Under the comfortable broody wings of 'Humphreys' on the Greatham side, Wilfrid Meynell had built or reconstructed a clutch of little cottages for several of his children and their families. The Lucas cottage, on the Rackham border far afield, was a left-over from another time, simple, old and rambling, and I loved it best of all. Presently I stole it for my 'Martin Pippin' books. Coming out of the woods you discovered it like a secret, in a dip below a rough slope crowded with flowers, with grassland and a little stream beyond, and then the primrose woods again, and in the distance the saddle of Rackham Down. I can remember no other such enchantment of scent and colour as Dimpling and Percy Lucas had conjured in this dell between the woods.

The Meynell daughters went by family nicknames, freely used; Dimpling or Dimps was the Madeleine of Francis Thompson's 'Sister Songs', Viola was Prue or Prudie to us all, Olivia was Lobbie, to her father sometimes Robert. This seemed to treble their numbers to newcomers already dazed by the overflow of grandchildren from every household.

It was a memorably lovely spring, and to me most memorable because during it we saw a great deal of Frieda and Lawrence, who was on his feet again. There was a constant coming and going between Rackham and Greatham. When we supped at Shed Hall it was Lawrence, not Frieda, who dished up the meal in Viola's little kitchen, where he had painted all the common pots and jars with bright designs in stripes and spots. He made the simplicities of cottage life delightful, basting the mutton and stirring the onion sauce with the happy concentration of a child who is doing something it likes. Boiled onions did not contradict him, or baked lamb let fall remarks which excited his nerves to the pitch that sent Frieda weeping, but unsubdued, out of the room. His uncontrolled irritabilities astonished me at first, but I soon realized that one must know Lawrence all-of-a-piece or not at all. Nobody held back so little of himself, no matter in what company, or cared so little for the embarrassments he caused. I did not like this side of him, but I accepted it equally with the things in him which stimulated and fascinated me, and for which I felt both liking and sympathy. He could be vividly entertaining when describing persons and places; and although his nature and Edward's were quite dissimilar (one as self-expressing as the other was self-suppressing), they had in common a scorn of sham and hypocrisy, and what each gave you of himself was true. Lawrence gave fully, and expected your full self in return. I would have hesitated to confide to him my most intimate problems, but after any talk with him I found myself readjusting them, losing self-pity and learning better how to stand on my uncertain feet. I was still in the tadpole stage, and if I have learned how to become what a wise man called 'a Person', I owe most of my lessons at this time to Lawrence and to Maitland. Truth without illusion was *their* common passion; Maitland presented it with ardent objectivity, while in Lawrence it was hotly fused with his prejudices. '*Damn braces!*' might have been written of him. And although he had the fiercest personality I had yet encountered, I was not shy or self-conscious with him; he braced me even when he damned my enthusiasms. One day he damned me heartily for being, like my generation, drunk with Dostoievsky. I tried to defend myself. 'But Dostoievsky's a genius! Don't you think so too?'

'That isn't the point. You're all making a mistake. You all think he is concerned with God. *Can't you see* that his only concern, his only interest, *is in sin*?'

We were walking across from his cottage to ours, and I remember the very field-path on which he stopped and almost invoked the Devil by the deep drop in his voice, which had a startling variety and range; in fury and excitement it ran the gamut from a bass growl to a shrill snarl. When he was gay and friendly it could charm. On another occasion he inveighed against the facile use of adjectives, and condemned those writers who, he said, made them serve descriptively in the place of genuine perception. Verbs were active, nouns were forceful, but—'I would like to see all adjectives banned from the English language for twenty years, and writers compelled to describe things without their help. Unless,' he added reflectively, 'they had to describe a nigger with a red head of hair, in which case they could only describe him as "a red-headed nigger". That would be the exception.' He made me promise to send him some of my poems when I got back to London in May.

At the end of April I had to run up to London for a day or two, I forget for what reason. Very hot weather had set in, and Margaret said she would make me a cotton dress while I was gone.

Edward's next letter was to Fellows Road.

Postmark 28 April 1915   13 Rusham Rd.
                                                              Balham.

My dear Eleanor,

Thank you for 2 letters and the poems. I was rather ill for 4 days with a chill or I would have written—a chill and a boil together. And since I came to town on Monday I had meant to see nobody. But now I suggest we might meet on Thursday for lunch before I go home. Could you meet me at 1.30 at the Museum?

You were quite right. There is a line omitted in Lob:—

Jack-in-the-hedge or Robin-run-by-the-wall which connects the Jacks and the Bobs too.

Perhaps I shall be able to mend March the 3rd. I know it must either be mended or ended.

I wonder will your walk come off? I should like to see you all. But I promise you I am under a thick cloud of Marlborough mostly, tho I wrote a sort of a song in it;

> At poet's tears
> Sweeter than any smiles but hers
> She laughs: I sigh:
> And yet I could not live if she should die
> And when in June
> Once more the cuckoo spoils his tune,
> She laughs at sighs:
> And yet she says she loves me till she dies.

Does it make you larf?

Yours ever
Edward Thomas

We met in town, and I told him I would steal a couple of days from Sussex early in May, and walk across the Downs to Chichester, and through Singleton into Hampshire for a night at Steep.

Steep
Petersfield

29 iv 15

My dear Eleanor

Here is the revised Lob for Blackwood: but buttocks is surely fatal. I have mended March 3rd too, you see.

I am just back. All's well here and the cuckoo no longer conceals himself. It's a most beautiful evening and I hope you are going to have it like this in Sussex.

Yours ever
Edward Thomas

My cotton frock was ready for me in Rackham, a simple country-print which Margaret had found in the Storrington draper's-shop. The Lawrences came across to Rackham that evening, and I had to put it on for them. Margaret had run it up carelessly and prettily, and suitably to the place and season. I remember Lawrence looking me up and down with the friendly interest that narrowed his keen eyes, and pronouncing with emphasis, 'I *like* it'.

At the week-end a bevy of guests flocked to the cottages; Bertie and Joan, seven-months married, stayed in ours. Francis Meynell, the least-seen of the Meynell clan, came to his own cottage, bringing Bunny Garnett and Frankie Birrell with him. On Sunday there was a great gathering on the lawns behind Humphreys, cricket and croquet were organized, and I think it was Frankie who was responsible for a gambling-game, which consisted in throwing pennies at a jack placed at some distance, the thrower of the nearest penny taking the pool. Lawrence came out of Shed Hall to look on at us, and he and Bertie were introduced to each other. In the years following the *Rainbow* débâcle, when the Lawrences' serious poverty was the concern of their friends, Bertie lent them a room he had in King Street, Covent Garden, which Lawrence described in detail in *Aaron's Rod*.

That Sunday evening in May the whole party switched over to Rackham for charades and songs. Bertie and I contributed some numbers from the nonsense repertoire we had invented to amuse our friends; Lawrence sang the first Negro Spirituals we had heard, and set our brains jingling with an American ballad on the murder of President McKinley with words of brutal jocularity sung to an air of lilting sweetness.

Bertie and Joan returned to town next day, and I prepared to begin my walk on the following Wednesday. Meanwhile Edward had written to me from Steep.

Postmark May 5th

Steep
Tuesday

My dear Eleanor

I am afraid I may have to go up to town next week, on Tuesday or even Monday, to do another turn, I hope the last, at the Museum, and I thought I would let you know in case you might be able to come here before that or otherwise change your plans.

Did I tell you that I sent Monro a lot of verses in hopes he would make a book of them? Well, he won't. He doesn't like them at all. Nor does Ellis—he says their rhythm isn't obvious enough. I am busy consoling myself. I am not in the least influenced by such things: but one requires readjustment. I have stopped writing under stress of Marlborough, though. This 'April' is the last. I send 'Pewits' because I have revised it. Garnett thought it was nearly very good indeed in its way, and I think perhaps it is clearer now, and it had to be as clear as glass.

Helen apologises for delaying with this 2/6.

Are you enjoying the rain and sun and everything with your whole self as I do in spite of Monro etc with some fraction of me?

Perhaps I shall go to Clifford's for one or 2 nights if he will have me and we can meet there.

Yours ever
Edward Thomas

P.S. Just got your letter. So that is all right. Friday some time.
(*Written on flap of envelope.*)

That Tuesday night, when I was in Shed Hall, Lawrence asked, 'What time shall you start tomorrow morning?'

'About six o'clock.'

'I think I'll come with you,' he said.

The early hour was to allow for a long day; it was twenty miles to Chichester. I arranged to walk across from Rackham and join him at the gate on the Greatham road.

We met in one of those white Sussex mists which muffle the meadows before sunrise, lying breast-high on the earth, her last dream before waking. We set out, then, in a world still asleep, the known lanes and fields were strangers, as friends sleeping become strangers. The woolly haystacks and the sheep huddled against them were not yet actual haystacks and real sheep. They were still being dreamed by the land. If a lamb had bleated, one felt the dream must break, earth stir in her bed, and shake the sleep out of her eyes. We talked in lowered voices. At that time I walked with the long lope that matched Edward's negligent stride. He covered ground fast without any appearance of hurry. It was too fast for Lawrence, who soon said, 'I must teach you to walk like a tramp. When you are going to walk all day you must learn to amble and rest every mile or so.' We padded it gently to the foot of the Downs, walking rather as though we were tired at the end of the day than fresh at the start of it. The low-lying sun began to melt the mists as we climbed, unpacking the world from its lamb's-wool.

Lawrence was in his angelic, child-like mood. We found, followed, and lost the old track the Romans had made over the Downs to Chichester. We lost ourselves as well as the track, and wandered among curling valleys that led us astray. We only occasionally looked at the map. We sang scraps of songs, and every two miles lolled on the grass, where, till the dew had dried, I spread my green silk mackintosh. It was a new one, and Lawrence approved of it. We ate snacks from my knapsack, and talked when we felt like it. Our talk that day seldom touched on the things that irked him unendurably. In one of the deep bottoms, where the whitebeams looked like trees in silver blossom, he cried, 'We must be springlike!' and broke green branches and stuck them round our hats. I have sometimes tried to recall the things we said, but what I remember of that walk was its mood. Only a few spoken sentences remain. Of Bertie he said quite simply, 'I *like* your brother Bertie.' He paused. 'But he does not speak in his real voice. Scarcely anybody lets you hear his real voice.'

The day turned out extremely hot, more June than May. In the afternoon the food I had brought was exhausted. We became thirsty, and were lost still in the hills. At teatime when we took our rest we drowsed. Thirst grew intolerable, high among the Downs, far from the smell of a pub. When we rose to go on our way, '*Shandygaff!*' cried Lawrence, and as we walked began to complain to the world, 'I want my shandy-gaff!'

We made an immortal song of it, which ran:

> My shandy! my shandy!
> I want, I want my shandy!
> Shandy, shandy, shandy,
> I want my shandygaff!

The greater our thirst, the louder we vociferated our song, consulting the map-contours for a way out of the rolling hills and valleys. The next inn was all we cared about in the world. Suddenly I halted.

'My belt!'

'Eh?'

'I've left the belt of my mackintosh where we lay down.'

He eyed me. The resting-place was at least a mile behind us.
I said, 'It's a brand-new mackintosh.'

'I like it best without a belt,' said Lawrence.

> 'My shandy, my shandy,
>   I want my shandygaff!'

So my green mackintosh wore beltless to its end.

We climbed to a saddle of the Downs that showed us signs
of man again. Ploughed fields fell to a road where cottages
were, and, according to my map, an inn.

'That must be East Dean down there.'

We began to make our way down. A tractor was noisily at
work in the fields near the road, smoke rose from little
chimneys. Men were working outside, women inside. At these
first signs of civilization which we had seen for many hours,
Lawrence sank his voice to say, 'I know the people who live in
homes like that. I know them as I know my own skin. I
know what they think and do. I know their lives.' His voice
rose to a shrill pipe. 'I *hate* them!' It was the one discordant
note I heard from him that day. When we had dropped down
to the road and found our inn, he entered the bar like a bashful
yokel from another shire. We sat down on a bench against the
wall, among the few natives drinking their beer after work,
and Lawrence ordered our shandygaff in a rustic singsong.
We wished the Sussex men 'Good afternoon', they murmured
an answer, and while we drank with them Lawrence asked a
local question or two, and got their laconic answers. You
would not have thought that a quarter of an hour ago he had
cried 'I hate them!' of these men. He seemed, if not of their
county, at least of their kind, he knew the sort of talk they
would understand, and his speech had a tang of dialect,
whether deliberate or instinctive I don't know. We went on
our way again, and climbed the Downs round Goodwood, and
saw the loop of the race-course in the hills. It was growing
late, and in Goodwood Park we began to drag our limbs.

'*Please do not walk on the edges of the grass*' said small notices.
I was grateful to the peer who did not warn the footsore off his
grass altogether. On the last dull stretch of the flats into
Chichester I developed a bad blister on my heel, and entered
the town limping. We were dusty, weary, and talking little by
now. I had to find a lodging for the night, but food came first;
we stopped at a teashop and ordered tea and toast and eggs.
While we waited, Lawrence disappeared through some beaded
bamboo curtains, but soon returned to ask me for a penny.
I gave him one, and he disappeared again, then came back with
a sheepish smile. 'I can't make it work.' I went and managed
it for him, while he stood by like a very tired small boy.

Over tea he debated whether he too would sleep that night
in Chichester, but the place was crowded with soldiers, and
perhaps he did not like the look of the only lodging we could
find. A dour landlady perhaps did not like the look of us.
Lawrence asked me doubtfully, 'Will it do?' Neither of us
wanted to trudge further; I said it would, and Lawrence
decided to take the next train back to Pulborough. I went with
him to the station, where we had a long wait on the platform.
Then he talked, more than he had talked all day; differently, the
talk of the Lawrence who delved, gave you his truth, and demanded your truth from you. He knew me well enough by
now to know what an unformed life I had led, well into my
thirties. We were both very tired, and he put his last question
in a gentle voice.

'What do you want? A big personal experience? Or to take
part in some great social upheaval?'

'The personal experience.'

He nodded. 'Yes. First, I suppose, for you. But why not
both?'

The train came in and he leaned to wave through the
window, the spring-green branches wilting from his hat.

Next morning the blister had fulfilled its promise, and I
could not put my foot to the ground in my heavy walking-
shoe. Nor could I blame juvenile Chichester for being enter-
tained by the spectacle of a female with a knapsack on her back
hopping down the main street to a boot-shop. I shuffled out of

it in a pair of 'sneakers' two sizes too big, and tramping being out of the question, took the next train to Petersfield.

What with my heel and Edward's ankle there was no real walking that week-end. On one of the evenings Marston dropped in, and taught us sea-shanties sung by the Shackleton South Pole Expedition; in return for 'The Drunken Sailor' I taught them Lawrence's 'Mr. McKinley', which had to be repeated again and again.

When I returned for my last few days at Rackham, the Lawrences had gone to Brighton, and I went back to London without saying goodbye to them. Margaret remained behind with Miss Paget.

Postmark 12 May 1915
Wednesday   Museum

My dear Eleanor,
            I am afraid I may not be in town on Friday evening, unless I have to stay to bring Baba back. So—or in any case—would you meet me here tomorrow at 5 for tea? I have got Mr. McKinley on the brain now. I hope you have. Then we shall be quits. I am at Clifford's tonight but not on Thursday. What lucky weather you have had.
                                                    Yours ever
                                                    Edward Thomas

And this from Lawrence, two days later.

                                        Greatham
                                        Pulborough
                                        Sussex
                                        14 May 1915

Dear Eleanor,
            I'm sorry we weren't back on Tuesday, to see you before you went. But we came home by way of Brighton, staying there two days with Cynthia Asquith, who was down with her children.

We had a jolly walk to Chichester. Some time, let us take another walk, shall we? The country is now very beautiful, much apple-blossom and bluebells. I wish we were walking up that down again, or sitting in the inn at East Dean.

May I send you the MS of my 'philosophy' to type? Be sure and say no if there is anything against it.

Frieda is going to have two little rooms on Park Hill Rd, Haverstock Hill. So when we are in town we shall be neighbours, and we must be neighbourly.

Tante belle Cose

D. H. Lawrence

The philosophy was 'The Crown', which he published in the first three numbers of *The Signature*. I still have the printed slip announcing the appearance of this small venture, to consist of four numbers at a subscription of ten shillings, paid in advance. The contributors were Lawrence, Middleton Murry, and Katharine Mansfield, whose contribution was under the name of Matilda Berry. Only three numbers were printed; there were not enough subscriptions to cover the fourth.

I wrote that I would be glad to type his 'philosophy', and at the same time I sent him a small sheaf of poems, including a few of the sonnets which during those years I was writing without thought of publication. Only Bertie, Clifford, and Viola saw them all, and those I chose for Lawrence were the least intimate.

He answered almost at once.

Greatham—Pulborough—Sussex

18 May 1915

My dear Eleanor,

Thank you very much for the poems. I think there is *real* poetry in them. It is strange, in you, that you never seem to fight things out to their last issue; and things which seem to me so amazingly potentially good. You have a far finer and more beautiful poetry in you than Margaret has, even than such men as De la Mare and Davies. But they get theirs verily smelted out, and you never burn yours in the last fire. I wonder why. It is the same here as in Kol Nikon. But these are better than Kol Nikon. How beautiful Revolt nearly is, very beautiful, but for a faint tinge of sentimentality, a dross of smallness, almost cowardice, or disbelief, that should have been burnt out.

——but still in the cities of men

Thou shalt spin thy thread of existence in a pattern not thine own

That is very fine. But if you gave your real passion to it you would save your poems from their clichés of desolate waters and 'scale the steeps of the air'.

139

Underworld also has something very beautiful about it.

> I could believe the only voice that sings
> Is of the leafage sparkling into song

But never the last dregs of bitterness will you drink, never face the last embrace of the fire, in your poems.

I think I like the Sonnets best. But there is a tendency for anybody in writing the Shakespearean sonnet, to become facile. It is a form that lends itself to facility. But there is dignity and beauty and worth in these sonnets. I wish you had never read a line of Elizabethan poetry in your life, and then we might have had pure utterance from you. But I like them, I do; 'Certain among us walk in loneliness,' and 'When all is said.' 'When all is said' expresses you perfectly. It is very good. But it is not quite true. We *can* by the strength of our desires compel our destinies. Indeed our destiny lies in the strength of our desires. Why are you a little cynical, or perhaps even a little conceited. 'Destiny is the strength of our desires.' Let that be your line.

I have decided to try to type my MS myself. When I break down, I shall come to you for help.

It is sad, we have not got the Hampstead rooms; applied too late. But they were too small. We must try again.

Why don't you come down to Rackham Cottage for Whitsun, you and your brother or somebody you can choose. I wish you would.
Love from Frieda and me
D. H. Lawrence

I asked him to write out the words of 'Mr. McKinley'; the six verses were not so easy to remember as the tune, which, once heard, stuck like a leech. He did so, and included with them his last note from Greatham.

Sehr-geehrte Eleanor,
Thank you very much for the letter and greetings and stamps, all of which I lost. You had better have stayed at Rackham Cottage—Margaret isn't so happy and Miss Paget and I only quarrel. But it's my fault—I am rude and cross.

> On the first of May
> O fatal day—make a song of it.

Heart like greetings
D. H. Lawrence

Soon after this he and Frieda came to town, and settled for a little while in Byron Villas in the Vale of Health; where, being neighbours, we were neighbourly.

§8

Steep
Petersfield

My dear Eleanor
Thank you very much (except for spelling pewits 'peewits' which may be admirable but is not usual, I think). But I don't know if I shall be able to send any more out. I hadn't meant to, except to one or two people like Gordon Bottomley, who tells me I am still too much bound [by] my prose methods of statement. I suspect he is right, but of course I can't do anything but hope that experience and honesty will lead me to a better way if there is one (for me). Of course I have stopped now, though there are one or two things I did before last week which I still haven't shown you. I will try to remember to put them in with this. I am in the thick of writing—very slowly, but as I do 6 or 7 hours a day I have covered many pages already. It is mostly paraphrase so far with some bits of argument on points of character and conduct. In 30 or 40 such days, if I keep the pace up, I could put the blessed thing behind me, and yet I know I may find myself with nothing to do afterwards and nothing to hope for either. If it were right and reasonable to leave England in the present state of things I suppose I ought to go and really try to get something out of New York and Boston; also if I could seem to afford it.

I like your rainbow, but mine that I saw with Frost seems like the first that ever was except that I knew it was a rainbow. I can't imagine a painter interfering with either. Mine was too much of a pure rainbow, a new toy discovered by Apollo, for anyone to paint. It is more for a mythologist clad in skins.

Yes, Raymond Jeremy is the man. I should like to hear him again, but in a big room playing what I want.

The canoe party will be cheerful but I shall not want to leave Marlborough for it, I know well, after that Friday night. Well, I was sorry not to see you on Sunday.

I have sent your letter to Mervyn. We heard from him last week, but haven't yet this week.

Yours ever
Edward Thomas

The 'typescript' in Edward's next letter refers to the beginnings of his autobiography, which was left unfinished. It came to me in a copy-book, I think, which he appears to have shown to Chapman & Hall, and if so, I am not surprised that they 'complained'. Edward's writing could be difficult to decipher.

Marlborough still stood in the way of all decisions, but America was steadily gaining ground.

                                                    Steep
2 vi 15   Petersfield

My dear Eleanor
          Thank you very much for the typescript, including the letter. I wish we had some real haymaking here to offer you. But though the weeks have stolen a march on us in the rain we are not shorthanded except in typing. Can you really face these pages which Chapman and Hall complain of? They are more than I thought when I decided I would accept your offer, so I shall not be surprised if you send some of them back. In one case you will see there are 2 consecutive pages, with a bit to be transferred from the 2nd to the 1st. It will help if you can number the pages as they are in the M.S. I think they are about the length of a typed page.

If you do get to Haslemere or if you find you can get over from wherever you are on the 11th will you? I expect to be up on Tuesday and Wednesday. Shall I meet you on Wednesday if you are not gone to Wisbech? Say Shearn's at 1.30?

I got back yesterday with a long train journey and a short ride from Whitchurch, a little harassed by this Marlborough deficit, but the lanes were delicious. We were all together by 8.

America is still unsettled, but looks nearer as I go on.

I am sorry about the carpet and the continuousness of Bob and Bill, for I suppose they are really Alf and Erb as before.

                                        Goodbye.   Yours ever
                                            Edward Thomas

My mother had spilt a bottle of ink on my brand-new carpet, a piece of carelessness so unlike her, and so like me, that when I found her on her knees trying to efface the stains with half a lemon and her tears, I tried to comfort her with the assurance that I would have spilt it later if she hadn't spilt it first. Fellows Road was in the hands of war-time 'decorators'.

Steep
Petersfield

3 vi 15

My dear Eleanor,

Thank you for your letter. I could have wished it came a day later to let me know you have not been attacked by aircraft. We know nothing here. Perhaps you know no more. But you might send a line.

You should not have let my verses trouble you while your head ached and the paperhangers fought for their country—I never guessed they were such a devoted band. I am sending you some lines I contrived to write 10 days ago when I took a day's liberty. Are they the worse for Marlborough? You see how I had amended 50 Faggots before your objection to the last lines came. I imagine they leave it clear.

I do think Blackwood must be doting if he really thinks he sees Puckishness in me, but I hope he isn't and takes you instead. You mustn't lead these forlorn hopes any more.

If I could choose now I would have Peewit. So I always did write it. But I found it usual to write it Pewit and accepted—so long ago that I won't change, though if I knew the word as a sound not a name I should still write Peewit.

We had a cheerful letter again from Mervyn and one from Frost saying he is on the edge of taking a farm he likes with a mountain view. He is very brief and evidently engrossed but cheerful. It will become necessary soon to decide whether I can really go out there—with the idea of getting literary work mainly. If I thought I could try and might succeed probably I ought to go. And that is as near certainty as I can get.

Marlborough thickens, and I shall probably sit on here till it is done and then mount a bicycle if I still can. But should I come to town I will let you know.

Yours ever
Edward Thomas

I seem to have been sickening for something, but I can't remember what. The 'baby' who had also 'got it' was my brother Joe's Joan, the first of her generation to be born into our family.

Postmark 4 June 1915
   Sunday   Steep
My dear Eleanor
      I am very sorry you have got it. Perhaps it will not take a violent form in you or the baby, and I hope it won't. But before very long you will be able to go about without infecting anyone, won't you? Then you will come to Steep. I waited a quarter of an hour at Shearn's. But I think you would have been there at 1 if you were coming. I was sure you wouldn't come. But tell me, who did write those plain words? They look like mine and yet I can't remember them. Will you tell me?

We have got a cloudy windy day today. Baba had a temperature last night and we thought she was copying Mrs. Dodd who is in bed with German measles. Helen is nursing her.

The garden is in a sad way. Most of the seeds have failed and the slugs have eaten the green things and the weeds are doing as well as the Germans.

Please try any of my things on editors when you like. I don't know about a title for the blank verse. At the beginning 'the angle' should be 'an angle' and 'the yellow square' 'a yellow square'. What about 'The Last Team'? I can't be injurious to any purpose.

As to Me and Frost, I mixed up 2 forms of the 2nd verse. The 3rd sentence should be

        The to be
    And the late past we gave small heed.

Here is the last thing I did. The division into lines *looks* worse perhaps than it really is.

Now I have to do some typing, and some wood-chopping, and to go up to the study and light a fire before I leave again at 6.30. Margaret Radford is coming in to tea. Goodbye and I hope you will soon be well and free. Our love to you.

                    Yours ever
                    Edward Thomas

Mr. and Mrs. Dodds and their small son Tommy were the Thomases' neighbours, and occupied the other half of the semi-detached cottage.

The next letter is undated, but must have been written within a few days of the last, as he speaks of coming up to the Museum 'next week, about the 11th'.

Steep
My dear Eleanor,

What do you think? We have got a nightingale in our back hedge singing most of the day and night. It makes me wish the Frosts had stayed another spring. They never really heard it. He by the way writes another cheerful letter tho he hasn't found a farm yet. He likes Lob and seems to be showing it to the Editor of The Atlantic. Suppose it appeared simultaneous.

I suggest that Happersnapper Hanger should not lack as a Blackwood version of the disgusting line. So if you think it will pass will you correct? It is a Hanger over and above Harry Roberts' (HAPPERSNAPPER).

Don't trouble to type March 3rd, thank you.

Let me know in good time when you will come. I might pay my last respects to the Museum next week, about the 11th but would arrange it according to your time if you could be sure.

We shan't go to Essex I'm sure.

The Fordham children have been seeing Lawrence and liking him. I wish I could get over.

Please will you send me a good title for the *Proverbs*. 1st Prize 2/6.

Yours ever
Edward Thomas

The line in 'Lob' to be changed, to spare Blackwood's feelings, was:

> That Mother Dunch's Buttocks should not lack.

A nightingale in their hedge was a gift from heaven to Edward and Helen, but before the summer was over, when it sang all night, little sleepless Bronwen was heard to murmur, 'That *dratted* bird!'

Postmark 8 June 1915.
Monday
My dear Eleanor

Thank you again, but I didn't want you to trouble with Faggots. I am glad you liked the Sedgewarblers. Of course if I could really bring things pure and clear through verse into people's heads it would be a great thing. I rather fancy you doubt if it would necessarily be poetry. Well, I don't know either and I am not sure that I care. I am not trying to do anything in particular but only hoping that at last I have stepped into the nearest approach I ever made yet to self-expression. I expect that line ending in pair was to rhyme with 2 lines higher up—As to the 3-word line I thought it was right somehow, but there was nothing intentional about it. But I am up to the neck in Marlborough. 7 hours writing every day, and the rest reading in preparation and going over notes. I am afraid I ought to be on the top of Ararat or somewhere. I am getting a nuisance to mankind with my concentration on the silly thing. However I am rather thinking of finishing or all but finishing on Saturday week, and then cycling with a man whose holiday falls then up to Gloster and even Coventry—through Avebury maybe. Then it looks as if I must decide something as no other work awaits me except doing some tales of the English traveller-explorers which would be practically paraphrasing, which I do loathe. I have got no farther in thoughts of America. No, I don't think I would even so have asked you to let me have that money. I want to stave off dependence except in little odds and ends—very many they have long been—till I can do no more. It is wretched to be willing to work, to think I know what I can do, and yet not to be sure of £150 a year. I don't imagine I *deserve* anything but I am afraid I instinctively act as if I did and don't make the efforts other people seem to think I could make. I must read 'Self-help'. The point is I can do my own work without being told or directed, but I wait or can't do anything else unless I am not told. If anybody said You go and join the Royal Garrison Artillery and they will give you a commission, I believe I should go next month.

Frost's address is still Littleton. No letter from him this week.

The nightingales only make little remarks to themselves as they go about getting food I suppose for their young.

Now I must go.
                                                            Yours ever
                                                            Edward Thomas

Undated: I think Sunday, June 13   Steep
                                                            Sunday
My dear Eleanor

Thank you for the News and Leader. Let us know what train you will come by on Thursday and I hope it will be a train that is not cancelled, but on that line I should think the trains would be less affected. Bertie and Joan and Stanley and I had an amusing evening on Friday. I came back last night with Davies. And now for Marlborough.
                                                            Yours ever
                                                            Edward Thomas

The 'something objectionable' in his next refers to one of my frequent painful chest-colds which could only be 'settled' with violent applications of turpentine flannels. I suppose I had tried to assure him that this was not nearly as unpleasant as *Marlborough*, which I think he detested above all the books he had ever had to 'make'.

Postmark 18 June 1915   Steep
                                                                                      Thursday
My dear Eleanor,

I hope something less objectionable has 'practically settled' your cold or I should think you yourself will be practically settled, but I hope not. You don't mean to say you have to do this kind of thing every year. You—but I suppose your mother must be there and you have to be with her and the paperhanger and the firehanger. It seems, though, that somebody ought to be there with you. You mustn't imagine Marlborough was nearly as bad. I practically settled him on Monday. Then yesterday I had one day in town with the Acts of the Realm and now am having a day in Seccombe's library making last notes. Tomorrow and Saturday I shall wind up at home and then if the weather holds start cycling on Sunday towards Gloster though not much in a holiday mood. I have got myself to the point of thinking that America is a chance and that I see no other. Waiting for something to turn up is of course quite in my line, but I have done a good deal of it, and if nothing does turn up before the end of July I shall begin to decide how many days I ought to give to New York and how many to Boston. Frost can give me some introductions, he being well on his way, with his book in a 3rd edition out there. He has done some verses I hear but not sent them to me. He had all but taken a farm when I heard last Friday or Saturday and wanted to be addressed 'Franconia, New Hampshire' in future. Of course he wants me to go there, but I don't want to allow the pleasure of seeing them to influence me as I can't afford champagne. Also I should have to think of what it would be to leave them again, especially if I had done nothing to ensure going out again. But Frost tells me I ought not to go in on myself so much. I can't help it but I can help personally-conducted tours to the recesses. So I will not go on.

Bottomley sent me a letter about my verses the other day. He agrees with everyone about 'Lob' and is decided about it, but speaks in a way I can't be sure of about the rest. I imagine however that

I may have rushed along rather and taken very slight invitations sometimes when I could have resisted had I known. Well, I am not somebody else. That is what it comes to, and I need not try to see myself as if I were.

You are coming down in July, I hope.

> Yours ever
> Edward Thomas

The next undated letter is from Jack Haines's in Hucclecote.

> c/o J. W. Haines
> Hillview Road,
> Hucclecote, Glos.

My dear Eleanor

The word *draught* put me out. I thought only of a draught of air causing a cold.

I have just got here by Southampton and Salisbury and Avebury and Malmesbury and Tetbury. We are off to the Forest of Dean now, but this is my address till Sunday when I go to Bablake School Coventry for a day or two, returning towards the end of the week . . .

. . . Garnett tells me he doesn't think I have a chance of one (*N.B. a Pension*) but he will try if I wish. Of course I do wish. He advises me to go to America and change my nature and become warm and approachable, and give lectures, and like Americans. So the outlook is difficult. I am crowding an hour with letters and only send this now because in this little house I expect to be rather tied to my host.

I shan't go to America *before* the end of August I think.

The Frosts have their farm now.

Excuse this random scrap.

> Yours ever
> Edward Thomas

America had never looked so certain.

§9

29 vi 15   Coventry

My dear Eleanor

It was good of you to write after that scrap. Bicycling disqualifies me more than usual. I did a long ride here thro Stratford on Sunday and am still recovering. On the road I was making these verses, the first for a long time, but I think I should like them in any case. Luckily I got them done before I was informed that I had overestimated the length of my Marlborough by a lot. I hope it is their mistake, but am in dread of trouble.

I heard from Garnett towards the end of the week. Perhaps he went out at once. David was going then, but Edward was still in doubt.

I start away home on Thursday thro Oxford and expect to arrive on Friday and perhaps be in town the next week and see you, unless there is too much Marlborough.

I have just received Wilcox Phillips and Cammaerts but not Margaret Radford and I doubt if I shall get her. I wonder should I be blind to her.

Yours ever
James (Whitcomb Riley)

The three books which Edward reviewed under the heading: *Poems in Wartime*, were *Poems of Optimism* by Ella Wheeler Wilcox, *Armageddon* by Stephen Phillips, and *Belgian Poems* by Emile Cammaerts. He placed Miss Wilcox at the head of his column:

What does Ella Wheeler Wilcox say about the war? She is 'the most widely-read poet of the day,' yet the numbers who do not read her being still considerable, the question is of some interest. It is easily answered. She says what is being said, as she always does. She says, for example, that women are knitting. Her own particular contribution is rhyme:

> At the concert and the play
> Everywhere you see them sitting,
> Knitting, knitting,
> Women who the other day
> Thought of nothing but their frocks,
> Or their jewels or their locks.

It is simply an amplification of what a plain man would express thus; 'During this war all sorts of women knitted socks and mufflers for the soldiers.' She cannot ever stir an inch beyond what is being said. Thus in a poem called 'Justice' she says that though the hard-working man often remains poor

> Yet justice sways the universe of God.

149

She adds, as one who has been told by the voice of God, that eventually the illumined soul will wonder that it ever doubted the fact. Even so in 'My Flower Room' she informs us that in her 'flower room':

> I have met God: yea, many a radiant hour
> Have talked with Him, the All-Embracing Cause,
> About His laws.

I can only say it is improbable.

He found Stephen Phillips almost as platitudinous, but 'he has taste and literary knowledge. . . . Like Ella Wheeler Wilcox he echoes, but in his own graceful way, what is being said at a moment when people hardly know what to think, but must say something. . . . Mr. Phillips is the more refined and careful of the two. He will consequently have a smaller circulation.' Cammaerts he praised as a poet who really had his roots in his work, which is 'naturally patriotic, derived from the religion, the past, the soil of his country.'

Postmark 29 June 1915   Coventry
My dear Eleanor
    I have altered this, or rather (chiefly) put in 2 lines that got left out owing to the scraps I wrote on as I travelled. I hope you have had no more midnight telephone.
  We have got lovely rain that looks like preventing my ride.
  That beastly Marlborough is worse than any weather.

Yours ever
Edward Thomas

Then one undated, which must belong to the beginning of July, when he is coming to town, with America very much in the ascendant.

Steep

Sunday   Petersfield
My dear Eleanor
    You have been quick. I thought when I saw your envelope that you had had to return the MS. It is all very good. Loltum as you say is absurd. It was really Lottum.

I expect to come up on Tuesday. So 13 Rusham Rd. will be the best address for me. I hope I shall see you on Wednesday either at Shearn's at 1.30 or on your mottled carpet—I would bring clean shoes.

The Proverbs are now in 2 likely hands—with Duckworth and The Oxford Press, and I *hope* I can choose between the two.

I don't know how long I shall be up but I have a number of people to see and talk to about America. However, on Friday I shall be back here before evening.

We are having the Ransome baby for a time, but she needn't forbid you.

Yours ever
Edward Thomas

I suppose we did meet; I suppose he did see and talk about America to those numbers of people. But what was going on under his mind while it was making surface plans to leave England within the next two months? When did he *know* that he could not leave 'the past and the soil of his country', when did he consciously decide to do what he foreshadows in this letter of July 10th?

10 vii 15   Steep

My dear Eleanor   Petersfield

These verses are mostly instead of a letter. You will understand before the end of next week why I don't write. It is a plan that I don't want to speak of in case it comes to grief. If it comes off I shall have a longer interval from verse making than Marlborough gave me. The Proverbs, by the way, have had a home offered them. But Duckworth's £10 doesn't force me to decide for it at once, tho I have no reason to hope much from the Oxford press. I hope you are better. If you aren't or in any case don't hurry to type these, will you?

Yours ever
Edward Thomas

Postmark 15 July 1915

My dear Eleanor

The mystery was this. I have just seen the doctor and been passed by him and am coming up to town again on Monday to join

the Artists Rifles. I have lunch time free tomorrow. Will you meet
me at Shearn's at 1? You can't answer, so I will be there in any
case.   Yours ever
                                                   Edward Thomas

  13 Rusham Rd
     Balham, S.W.

Could you wire here early if you can't come?

I felt that I could not meet him at Shearn's, and wired to
him to see me, after his lunch, in Fellows Road. I rose as he
came into the room. He bent his head, and for the only time
in our four years of friendship we kissed spontaneously. He
sat down saying, 'Well, I've joined up.' 'I don't know why, but
I am glad,' I said. 'I am too,' he said, 'and I don't know why
either.'

Before very long I did know why. Self-torment had gone
out of him, and I was glad because of that.

Postmark 15 July 1915   Steep

My dear Eleanor
        This is the prayer and 2 other things you have not seen. I
won't say now they are the last. I am just home writing a lot of
letters. I hope I shall see you next week.   Yours ever
                                                   Edward Thomas

Postmark 21 July 1915   13 Rusham Rd
                                                  Balham S.W.

Tuesday

My dear Eleanor
        I got your letter and the typescript on Saturday night but
we had a visitor till Sunday afternoon and I was very full up.
Then yesterday I was attested and today I did six hours drill. There
is a great deal to tell you yet I can't promise to see you yet. My feet
have already given me the trouble I long ago foresaw. It may be
curable. I am to see the doctor about it tomorrow. But it puts me
in a rather miserable position if it can't be mended. However, don't
you worry. It's only silly to be in uniform and useless, but I shall
get over it one way or the other.

About 'Aspens' you missed just the turn that I thought essential.

I was the aspen. 'We' meant the trees and I with my dejected shy-ness. Does that clear it up, or do you think in rereading it that I have not emphasised it enough?

Don't think this only another of my excuses for not writing a letter, though it is an excuse for not writing now the one I could have written on Sunday if I had not been so occupied. I only send it because I have waited long already. Otherwise I should wait longer till I had seen the doctor. I only hope he won't give me leisure to think why I joined. Several people *have* asked me, but I could not answer yet.

You had a beautiful Sunday, I should think; we did, so warm, clear and fresh. But I am not writing weather rhymes again yet.

Yours ever
Edward Thomas

How all his letters show what the weather meant to him, how integral a part of each day it was. Other people talk about the weather, Edward lived it. The soldier and the poet now lived it in common, and the poet gave the soldier no rest. The long interval from verse-making, which Edward supposed he would have in uniform, was a delusion.

21 vii 15   13 Rusham Rd

My dear Eleanor,

I have just got to wait and see. The army doctor is giving me some treatment and some rest. But I can't manage anything this week because I have 2 books to do in my spare time. I was a bad prophet, because I have been perspiring these six hours over ten lines which perhaps are not right yet. But if you would type them for me I could see them better. They are

> What matters makes my spade for tears or mirth,
> Letting down two old pipes into the earth?
> The one I smoked, the other a soldier
> Of Blenheim, Ramillies, and Malplaquet
> Perhaps. The dead man's immortality
> Lies lightly represented with my own,
> A yard or two nearer the air of day
> Than bones of ancients who, amazed to see
> Almighty God erect the mastodon
> Once laughed or wept at what earth had to bear.

I suppose it should have been a sonnet, but I can't Rawnsleyise yet.

I believe you were right to be uncertain about Miss ———. I am so glad I wasn't there, though I should like to have seen you and Arnold and Daphne and Undine. Helen and I had a lovely walk. She will be glad to have you over from Singleton. I only hope I shall not be there. I do want to go on now. I don't want to see anybody till I know if I can. God bless you.   Yours ever
                                                                    Edward Thomas

Don't tell anybody I aren't a soldier yet tho I am in uniform.

Postmark 26 July 1915   13 Rusham Rd
                                                                    Balham S W

My dear Eleanor
          The exams rather exploded the verses, but I have a laugh of you for not detecting the rhyme of soldier and bear. However to please you I bring the rhyme nearer. I send you also 2 other rainy afternoon efforts. In case you are free tomorrow (Tuesday) at 1 I will come to lunch then at the Lyons nearest the top of Tottenham Court Rd. on the left going N. I will come through to the back. But I may have a very bare hour. Don't trouble to write even if you can't come. I will be there unless the sergeant says no.

                                                                    Yours ever
                                                                    Edward Thomas

So on Tuesday July 27th I lunched for the first time with Edward in uniform.

It might have been next year when we were walking in the country that I asked him the question his friends had asked him when he joined up, but I put it differently. 'Do you know what you are fighting for?' He stopped, and picked up a pinch of earth. 'Literally, for this.' He crumbled it between finger and thumb, and let it fall.

§10

9 viii 15   13 Rusham Rd.
My dear Eleanor   I had forgot the influenza in the glories of drilling with untroubled tendon and the horrors of inoculation (which I am getting over). I had 24 hours at home again at the week end and

expect another at the end of this week. I am now beginning to
wonder what regiment I shall get a commission in. But I shall
hardly get to camp in much less than a fortnight. So we ought to
meet in town. Part of me envies you getting about and envies me
of 12 months ago at Ledington, without a pang though. I have to
learn to keep my buttons bright. How can you walk in this weather?
I never knew it so close and these patent-leather-lined caps don't
improve it. Why shouldn't another soldier admire your stick too?
I have conspired with God (I suppose) not to think about walks
and walking sticks or 6 months or 6 years hence. I just think about
when I shall first go on guard etc. I simply can't do my one review.
Yours ever Edward Thomas.
I expect Guthrie would like to see you at Flansham.

This letter found me in Aldwick, during a trek across
Sussex into Kent. It was easy to deflect my route a little and
turn up from the coast to make friends with the Guthries—
lifelong friends, as it turned out. Edward bequeathed me three
great legacies of friendship in de la Mare, Frost, and James
Guthrie; and when Jimmie died in 1952 at the age of seventy-
eight, his legacy to me were his sons, Robin and John. 'You
are both Mummy and Daddy to us now,' John wrote from
Venice, where he lives. He fell in love with Italy and her
people in the Second World War, and they loved their enemy
as one of themselves.

Edward had spoken a great deal about James Guthrie and
given me a true picture of this whole-hearted artist-writer-
printer, whose Pear Tree Press had been producing beautiful
things since 1899: first at Ingrave in Essex, then at Shorne in
Kent, and last in Sussex, where its activities began in Harting
and found their final home in Flansham.

So much and so dear a part of my life are the Guthries, and
so much were they a part of Edward's, that what I want to say
about them covers forty years. Instead of dispersing it through
later books, I will pay my full tribute to Jimmie's memory here,
drawing on an article I wrote for the *Sussex County Magazine*
after his death. He was the first English poet to appreciate and print the poems of 'Edward Eastaway', and has earned
this place in their story.

After reading Edward's letter I decided to tackle the bug-
bear of the deep-rooted shyness which was a left-over from my
childhood, and to follow the Sussex coastline instead of the
hills I loved better. Flansham lay a little inland, a sort of forgotten corner amid cornfields; without post office, shops, or
church, or even a pub. Leaving Felpham I studied the lanes
in my map. In one of them I met a couple of young scouts,
not long past wolf-cubhood, with their bathing-towels. I
glanced at their kit, and they at mine: haversack, drover's ash-
stick, and green leather cap with some hedge-leaves pushed
into the band. We took each other in, and passed without
speaking. A few minutes later I was knocking at James
Guthrie's door, and he was opening it to me.

I began to explain myself. 'Edward Thomas told me to come
and see you, my name is Eleanor Farjeon——'

'Come in, come in, come in!' chirped Jimmie; rather like
a friendly Scotch robin, I thought, whose cheerful pipe put
shyness to the rout and made explanations unnecessary. Like a
Cox Pippin too (the robin's fellow in the apple-loft), the
smell of which invites you to sample its sweetness. When
Jimmie got talking, of things nonsensical or serious, he did in
fact seem to drip sweet chatter as ripe fruit drips its juice, and
in later life there was something fruitlike in the moulding of
his cheeks and deeply-dimpled chin. The *year* of our meeting
was 1915, but his welcome at the door was so instant, the
acceptance of myself so complete, that I hardly remember a
time when the White House at Flansham, with its inmates and
its interests and industries, was not in the texture of my adult
life.

He drew me in past the little parlour, with a couch and an
ornamental piano in it, but that wasn't where one sat in the
White House, and talked and joked and ate and worked and
lived. Downstairs the kitchen was the heart of the house,
where Marion Guthrie, tall, angular, fair, with a beautiful
dairymaidish skin, busied herself between table, stove, and
larder, and the scullery sink. I always felt that the scullery
should have been a dairy, with Marion churning butter after
milking the cows in the muddy byre on which the back of the

house looked down. She was a bustling housewife, hot cakes in the oven, sour milk in the larder for her scones. But the soul of the house was upstairs. While Marion was getting tea, Jimmie took me aloft to a long room stacked with presses and type and tools and easels and prints and books and paintings; the beginnings, middles, and near-endings of a dozen different schemes, showing me which he skipped from one to the next as rapidly as a bird hopping in a hedge. Before I had assimilated one, something else was thrust on me, but they were all of a piece with a purpose that was in being here. The place hummed with the activities of brain and spirit, and the intention to make a perfect thing of the job in hand, even if buying handmade paper to do it on meant going short of bread. For Jimmie's purpose involved a perpetual struggle with the wolf at the door. He could gird and grouse at the wolf, and grumble at a public which permitted it to haunt an artist's doorstep; but never once did I see him compromise with the creature. I went down to tea with a handful of exquisite samples from his press, a poem hand-drawn and coloured, sunk in its plate of fine paper, a little kneeling angel at prayer, some numbers of his magazine, *Root and Branch*, in which from time to time he and his friends expressed what they were after.

In the kitchen we were soon joined by the damp-haired scouts, fair Robin and dark John. Their greeting was: 'We knew you were coming here, you looked like Daddy's sort.' I liked this very much at the moment; in the years that followed, as I came to know and value Jimmie more and more, to be his sort was the best compliment his sons could have paid me. These sons adored their father. In that house of creation Jimmie Guthrie was the roots of the roof-tree, and his boys, Stuart and Robin and John, were its branches: his sap ran through all they did, or tried to do, in life. No artist can always be sure of a first-rate result; but no second-rate effort was ever made in the White House at Flansham. All the boys wrote, designed, printed, read copiously. Stuart, nicknamed Totch, was the one who, on the green piano which was Jimmie's wedding-gift to Marion, patiently figured out the nocturnes and studies of Chopin. Sometimes he wrote a

lovely simple poem, and he knew more about printing than
either of his brothers; but music was the love he hungered for.
He was less certain of his destiny than Robin, who had to be a
painter and nothing else; less vivid than young John, who, as
he developed, glanced and darted from theatre-design to
dancing, from music among the Dolmetsches to a close study
of literature. If Totch had lived, he would have travelled his
road more slowly than they theirs; but he would have drawn
his load with the lovable plodding patience of a shire-horse.
Probably no three boys in England were having so rich an
education as Jimmie Guthrie's three sons, and its richest part
came from Jimmie himself; from his sweet and wise co-operation in their varied work, and from the integrity which made an
inferior attitude to life impossible.

These were my immediate impressions of the boys. The
effect I made on them I should never have known but for a
diary kept by Totch in his teens, chanced on by Robin and
shown to me in 1957. Here is an entry made after I had taken
to dropping in at the White House as a matter of course when
I walked that way.

. . . And then the other day Miss Farjeon turned up and spent the
night and the gist of a day, so we have been quite flooded with
people. Miss Farjeon is great fun. She stumps along with her
knapsack on her back and her *chalala* [shillelagh?] in her hand,
looking for all the world like a pilgrim. And in she comes, straight-
way, and goes into the pantry and eats a pancake and a little pastry
off a tart and lights a cigarette—she lights a pipe sometimes—and
talks and shouts and laughs and turns the place into the very haunt
of merriment. She is one of the most marvellous personalities I
know. Her work is lovely and serious. She is fair and loyal to all
her friends. What fine people these are!

The boys, of course, had their own hand-press for their own
publications: a child of their father's Pear Tree, which they
called the Greenleaf. They invited me to write something for
them to print. Jack Yeats wrote plays for their toy theatre, the
passion of John's heart. Why shouldn't Miss Farjeon write
poetry for the Greenleaf? Miss Farjeon was barely at the

beginning of her professional career; but 'professionalism' didn't mean much to these kids. I was 'their sort', and it was natural that I should be asked, and should agree. I did agree; and presently, as I walked the Downs from Chichester to Alfriston, made a handful of songs on the way, which appeared under the imprint of the Greenleaf, with illustrations by Robin. I still have my copy of this little book, bound in gay wall-paper, interleaved with Robin's originals. Why he chose to depict me as a sort of H. G. Wellsian tramp in check knicker-bockers I could not understand; and neither, now, can he. *All the Way to Alfriston* was a limited edition, and may one day be a collector's piece; as James Guthrie's Pear Tree productions are now collector's pieces, watched for in, especially, the American catalogues, though achieved at a price so far beyond the public pocket that the wolf continued to sniff around the keyhole. But the wolf outside didn't matter, what you were doing on the other side of the door was what mattered—very much indeed.

One afternoon, when I was staying in the house, Robin demanded my hands for a big cartoon he was making studies for. He had not done with them by bedtime. Next morning I woke tormented with cystitis; I had to be got back home as soon as possible. Everybody was concerned—but Robin's concern outweighed all the rest put together. 'Won't she be able to stay till I've done her hands?'

I stayed, in agonies, propped in a corner of the sofa, the hands in position, till he, oblivious to my suffering, was satis-fied. I still hold it over the man; but I loved the boy for it, as I loved him for the way he disappeared for a whole day, no one knew where, in search of a lump of coal. Again for some cartoon he was absorbed in, he needed a rock of a shape not discoverable in the flat sunny cornfields that framed Flansham. I think he found what he wanted at last in some railway siding, spent all his pocket-money on it, lugged it home, and hacked his black 'rock' to the contours he saw in his mind. To me this incident symbolized his future; long before he became a light of the Slade, upon that rock Robin erected the church of his art.

The boys grew up, went their different ways, developed their different gifts, and always, from wherever they might be, came homing to the White House at Flansham. I went there seldomer after the twenties, held in London by my mother's long illness. But while any of the Guthrie boys were in town, my place was theirs, and I was theirs to call on. John ran his gamut of writing, lino-cutting, scene-painting, recorder-playing, ballet-dancing. The war took him to Sicily and Italy, and he gave those lands his heart. In England, Totch died, held in his father's arms. One of the brothers described that scene to me, and Jimmie's tender and unflagging strength, as he supported his eldest son in his last moments; the root still pouring its sap into its first limb. When the war ended, John settled in Venice, coming back yearly to see me and Robin in London, and his parents in Flansham. Then Marion died, in 1949.

What would Jimmie do now, at seventy-five? There was some anxiety about his living alone; but the young don't yet know how we old cherish our independence. Jimmie's roots, his work, his life were in the White House. He would continue to live there, and didn't mind living alone. He was happy, busy, his letters to me still looked forward, or, if backward, looked with a sense of the past out of which had grown the present, which was good to him. One of his letters, written a year before Marion's death, shows this so plainly that I must let it sum him up, better than I can.

I suppose I had been referring to some of the Essex names which Edward used in one of his poems, and this, thirty years after Edward's death, is how Jimmie replied:

It struck me that you might be interested to know more of the places in Essex, and might even go there someday. For me they have a special charm as they were my home—Ingrave, that is— when I first left home and took up housekeeping, so to speak, apart from the old family. Just then I was in despair of making a do at art: my people were against it, and the old home was somehow wrong in atmosphere. To be in an office was the limit of their ideas about what a young man should do: but I had always a firm impression inside that I was meant for an artist, foolish and all as I might be, and quite without training or capacity. In fact, I was in the wrong world, from which I could only very dimly believe in the other one where men painted pictures and wrote books. Besides, I did not know a soul who could guide, let alone cheer me. It was a truly miserable condition to be in: a condition I was determined to change. A certain amount of drawing for odd purposes I had done: had tried to get work to do for printers and in magazines. But on the whole it looked as tho I'd have to go into the City for good; a prospect which filled me with gloom and despair. Then I got an introduction to a man who did mural painting, stained glass, etc., who allowed me to go twice a week to be useful in his studio without pay or fee: which was very decent of him. He always said he liked me—why or how I can't guess, but it lasted a while, and suddenly he asked me to come and assist him with work in Ingrave Church.

It sounds ridiculous now, but to live in the country all the year round was an idea which attracted me immensely. It was equivalent to being in Heaven. Hallward proved to be a man of great charm. Not by any means a great artist, full of queer streaks in his nature, a true romantic of that time, he gave me the first kick off in a new life. We worked all day, and roamed about in the evening, stopping, I remember, to listen to the nightingale in the Park, admiring, loving nature. This all sunk in deeply into the willing soil of my mind, you may be sure. I still saw no way, but knew there was one, thanks to the warmth of this man's friendship and counsel. The angels are still on the wall, so far as I know, and are good angels even to this day. Hallward is still at work, at the great age of eighty-eight. I hear from him every now and again.

The upshot was that a cousin of mine and I determined to take a cottage and live there: he going to the City each day, while I did my work—in Pear Tree Cottage. For £12 a year we had that small cottage between us: and when he gave up, I stayed on. Instead of it being a tragic failure, prophesied by all, the folks used to come on holidays to stay with us. And I began to get a real grip of my work; a thing never before possible.

Marion's people farmed down on the lower parts, nearer the river, on the road to Tilbury. So I met her, and so the tale went on. At the back of the cottage stretched Lord Petre's park—Thorndon Park—with deer in it and all manner of fine material. Those days were among the very happiest days in my life. If I attach too much affection to Ingrave and its many charms, you will understand why: for it was probably the most important thing that could happen to me just then. A mere chance, maybe, but one can't believe that chance was the only element in anything so fruitful and so continuously inspiring.

There must be something in one's nature to take a certain course: to absorb certain ideas: follow certain lines: for none of my people have changed as I did . . . Nice they are too, of course, being my folks: but . . . 'to sell one's work is the real test,' I used to be told. And true enough as that is, it is not the whole of the truth. Success they could understand, not struggling to do things. Ours is a different world, somehow, modestly and kindly tho it may be. We understand them better than they understand us. The young man who did not agree was a sort of black sheep.

One is a bit of a fool too: for, after all, one had to learn by making all the mistakes first. There were miseries, but also a kind of glory in being free to find out what to do and how to do it. And in the long run others fail, even in business, and the poor artist is not any more in that inferior position. His sons . . .

But never mind what the poor artist said about his sons, what the root felt about the branches. They meant as much to him as he to them.

Jimmie concludes:

So when Edward discovered my patch of country, I had been before him by a good many years. And someday you should go there and look at it. Go from Brentwood on the Tilbury Road, two and a half miles out to Ingrave, Herongate, and the rest.

I chatter on.

Well, my dear, we shall be seeing you again soon, I hope. Marion joins me in sending love to you.

Ever your old
Jimmie.

The man who, after seventy, could review his life so truly from its unhopeful beginnings to the place where he now stood, need not be thought unfit to live alone. There is a sort of loneliness in which one's self lives fully. That this was 'my old Jimmie's sort' I am certain.

He lived surrounded by the evidences of the standard he had never lowered, or ever flown for a selfish end. Those lucky enough to own James Guthrie's *Wild Garden* know what fragrant childhood verses he could write, but these he did not print for himself. He used the printer's craft he had raised to an art to serve all fine writing wherever he could discover it, all poets, known and unknown, who were 'his sort'. When few had heard of me, he beautifully devised my *Sussex Alphabet*; he got on the scent of W. J. Ibbett, a poet as natural as Davies and as scholarly as Marlowe, who lived in great poverty in Dorsetshire—*Ibbett's Jessie* is one of the Pear Tree's sweetest fruits; he was first in the field with some of Edward's poems, when these had not yet been recognized; and his most tremendous achievements were among his latest: the superb *Frescoes*, a collaboration of Gordon Bottomley's poetry and Jimmie's pregnant visions, and the Blake *Songs of Innocence*, which was so costly to produce that he could only afford to bind the sheets as the orders trickled in. Fewer than twenty copies were completed. One of these was presented to the Kentucky University Library, for its collection of rare and beautiful books, in the month of his death. The report of this must have been his crowning joy; for Blake, his Felpham neighbour, was, of all visionaries, the neighbour of Guthrie's spirit in Flansham. Blake knew all about those angels Jimmie began his career with in Ingrave church, and those others invisibly limned on the walls of the White House as long as Jimmie lived.

No, Jimmie could not be lonely under that roof. And there were many human ties still pulling his heart-strings. He visited his relatives in other parts of Sussex; his grandchildren stayed with him; Robin and his wife went often to Flansham, and John wrote often from Italy. Our friend R. L. Watson walked over from Felpham to see him a few weeks before his death, and reported to me that he was still his happy, chattering, unpessimistic self. To another friend, in one of his last letters, he wrote: 'I keep very well . . . With things to do I must hang on for a bit. Still, I'm 78.'

Four days later he stopped hanging on; but not so suddenly that Robin and Debby could not reach him and talk to him in a Bognor hospital.

Just as they were leaving, swiftly and—as I at my age know
—beautifully, the roof-tree was felled.

The White House at Flansham will begin to grow another
life. It will be grown on the roots left by Jimmie Guthrie in
his homeground, his sap still running in them.

§11

The Guthries put me up for a night, and next day I went on
my way through my now almost native land of Sussex to the
foreign border of Kent; there to exchange the simplicities of
the White House at Flansham for the luxuries of The Leicester
Arms in Penshurst. Clifford and Olga had invited me to join
them there for a week. When I came in sight of its sumptuous
façade I felt I should have arrived by coach in a farthingale,
instead of 'stumping along with knapsack and "chalala" like
a pilgrim'; but I would have missed the excitement of walking
along a high ridge outside Cowfold that looked across to distant ridges on either hand, with a separate thunderstorm
raging magnificently over each. My father had taught me his
own fearlessness of storms—standing beside him at the door
when the air was dangerously charged I caught his exhilaration
(the same sensation served me in the Battle of Britain). It was
only commonsense that made me take shelter in a cart-shed on
the outskirts of a farm, where I ate my bread-and-cheese sitting
on the blue shafts of a wagon among cowering hens, while the
rain-darkened opening was torn by the flames and shaken by
the tumult of two tempests. I suffered from other forms of
fear in plenty as a child, but Sir Philip Sidney, my earliest and
best-loved hero, had allayed some of these by two lines in a
sonnet:

> Fear is more pain than is the pain it fears,
> Disarming human minds of native might.

It may have been because he knew how dear the Elizabethans
were to me that Edward once asked, 'What woman in history

would you choose to be?'—adding with a smile, ' "Sidney's sister, Pembroke's mother"?' So from Penshurst I sent him the lovely portrait of Mary Sidney with her lute.

19 viii 15

13 Rusham Rd
Balham SW

My dear Eleanor   I have been so busy at private soldiering that I couldn't write. I do route marches without discomfort now and am too conceited to trouble about other things except my 2nd inoculation which spoilt another weekend for me.   But I heard from Guthrie you had been there and was touched to see the photograph of Mary Sidney again that I sent Bronwen 10 years ago from Penshurst. We used to live at Elsie's Farm just outside the Weald village on the road from Penshurst station from Sevenoaks, a farm worth living in but probably not worth looking at. You may remember it in 'Set a thief to catch a thief'. I have been correcting the proofs of the Proverbs lately and indexing Marlborough filled up the small gaps of time. I hope you enjoyed the walk through Slindon and Amberley, I suppose by Bignor Hill and perhaps through Gumber wood. You will like the river and Penshurst Mile on days like today. Give my love to Clifford and Olga and ask them how much they pay for wiping their shoes on the mat at the Leicester Arms. I could meet you at Shearn's for tea on Monday or Tuesday *if* I am not on guard but I get short warning and perhaps could not let you know so tell me if you will run the risk of my not turning up and which day you prefer. I could probably be there (at the top) at 4.45 either day.

Yours ever
Edward Thomas

I hope to be at home Saturday night but again I *may* be on guard that day.

In a Penshurst pub, less heraldic than The Leicester Arms, I picked up one of my most treasured walking-sticks for sixpence, the stubby Irish blackthorn with the personality of a tramp sing-songing on an uphill road. The stick goes best up a hill, for it is really too short by inches, but I would never admit this to Edward.

5 ix 15   13 Rusham Rd
                                                        Balham

My dear Eleanor   Where are you these lovely days? I think you
said it was to be Wisbech, and you said nothing about being in
town in between. And I have been busier than ever—with night
operations and guard all extra. Helen is here for a few days. I
couldn't get to Flansham. I am not enterprising at weekends—or I
might go to Stanley at Missenden. It is still quite a holiday, tho I
don't like the men more. Perhaps the commission will not be so
long coming. The Artists have to provide 250 officers a month
now, so they are saying. At the same time somebody else says that
in France they are sure it will be all over in October. Camp is still
some way ahead, so I may see you in London before I go. Helen
sends her love, so do Bronwen and Baba.

                                               Yours ever   E. T.

Mine to Godwin and Rosalind.

Postcard postmark 13 September 1915

                                                     13 Rusham Rd

If you haven't gone to Steep yet I wonder could you come to
Clifford's on Wednesday evening? If not I could be at Shearn's on
Tuesday at 5 or about 5. Last week after Wednesday I was packed
full, and still no chance of camp. If I can I must try to get to Steep
to get our potatoes up. Helen goes there on Wednesday but she
isn't well.

                                                              E. T.

    At the end of the month he at last finds himself in Camp in
Loughton.

Thursday

My dear Eleanor,   It is not so bad, but now that the rain has come
it is worse. There is no comfort after work is over and it is dark.
The canteen is the only place, noisy and draughty and ugly. Everything is badly arranged, ugly and dirty. But one has an appetite
and can satisfy it, and the country is beautiful, and for a week the
weather was perfect. Helen will tell you everything. I was in town
just for Saturday night which I spent with my people. The end of
next week I hope I shall be at home and see them all. I only saw
Baba on Saturday. But I heard about Patience and how she re-
proached Bronwen and Margaret while they were dressing: 'You are
two proud sisters.'

I suppose your best chance with the rhymes is Christmas time and I fear you will be too late for it if Stanley hasn't all the drawings ready. It is a very good idea and ought to be a companion to my 4 and 20 Blackbirds.

No. Books are all off except a 6d one on Company Training, which I must learn by heart. They say we shan't be over 2 months here. Then I ought to be expecting a commission if I do moderately. I find I can learn some things yet, and I am just curious what I shall be able to do with a pen if and when I take to it again. Perhaps you will still be at Steep when I come.

Yours ever
Edward Thomas

Patience was the baby of Ivy and Arthur Ransome. They lived near Codford, where Helen and Baba sometimes stayed with Ivy; at other times Helen looked after Patience in Steep.

The rhymes mentioned in this letter were my 'Nursery Rhymes of London Town', which I thought I might offer to a publisher with illustrations by Stanley North. He enthusiastically produced a gay watercolour of 'Shepherd's Bush', in which the Shepherd under his hawthorn bush is bag-piping to a very lively lady on very green grass—and there the pictures ended. Publication by Christmas, even with a less erratic illustrator than Stanley, would have been impossible so late in the year. Meanwhile, *Punch* was accepting and printing the rhymes by the dozen, anonymously. Owen Seaman reserved the distinction of initials for the famous. The week in which 'Kingsway' appeared, Joseph Thorp, *Punch*'s second-string dramatic critic, bearded Sir Owen in his den with: 'Do you know you have a genius writing for you now?' 'No,' said O.S. Thorp thrust the current *Punch* under his nose, and pointing to 'Kingsway' demanded, 'Who wrote this?' Seaman refused to tell him. Thorp, a fantastic champion of whatever appealed to him, wouldn't let it rest, and presently discovered my name through the Meynells. He wrote to me out of the blue: 'These things must be published—will you leave it to me?' Before I knew where I was he had fixed up an interview with Gerald Duckworth whom he had already commanded to publish the book next year with illustrations by

Macdonald Gill. No one ever tried to resist 'Thorplet's' commands; he was a charmer, a sort of Puck whose touch turned sober commerce into fantasy. Hard-bitten company promoters lost their heads when Thorplet walked into their offices with some extravagant innovation he had just thought of to make business routine more enchanting. Alluring office writing-paper, expensively printed prospectuses, and attractive tube-posters owed much to him. He delighted in the crafts, and dressed in exquisite taste, a little outside the conventions. His wife, Netta Syrett's sister Nell, a woman of great artistic gifts and, fortunately for her, a strong sense of humour, accepted him as God made him, and adored him. When he turned life topsy-turvy, and friends threw up their hands—'But that's why I fell in love with him,' she said. 'Sometimes we haven't any money at all, and then all of a sudden we have a great deal. He goes away and brings it back. I don't know what he does. I often think he is a highwayman.' When they married they were lent a cottage somewhere out of the world for their honeymoon, and Thorplet insisted that they should carry their commissariat with them. They must not be bothered with going in search of shops. 'We drove away with an enormous hamper from Fortnum and Mason's. When I unpacked it I found it full of everything a schoolboy would have dreamed of for a midnight feast—candied fruits and jars of exotic preserves, brandy peaches, nuts and Turkish delight and potted pheasant, rich cakes and caviare, but not a potato or a scrap of bread. For the first week of marriage we lived on sweetmeats and pickles.'

This was the man who championed my nonsense, and launched me on the book-world without my having to lift a finger about it.

Here
Sunday

My dear Eleanor   We have just missed here. I didn't keep you waiting yesterday I hope. We were not dismissed till 5. And now I am leaving to go back to High Beech. Helen will tell you the change. I am only sorry because it means not being in town. It will be fully a fortnight before I get up again.

Are you quite well again? Typing for me somehow corresponds to your diseases, but I hope doesn't produce them. I expect you're right about the rhymes, most of them. The original version was in blank verse, but quite different. Hasn't Bronwen taught you tormentil, the tiny yellow flower in short hill grass, a flat buttercup or avens with rather separate petals? Tormentilla it is. The accent is on the 2nd syllable which doesn't (as I see it) affect the merit of the line whatever it may be; I mean doesn't tell against it. I suppose the influence of High Beech and the Artists ought to be clearer. I am going to slightly better conditions, but don't expect to write till I am disabled again. The knee is now well. My new address will be

> A Company
> Artists Rifles
> Suntrap
> High Beech

I go on Tuesday afternoon.

I believe I have floundered over refusing a wristwatch from Bertie and Joan. But I really didn't want one.

> Yours ever
> Edward Thomas

17 X 15   High Beech

My dear Eleanor Will you take some verses for a letter? I have been lame with an injured knee 2 days and this is what I have done with them and can't write a letter as good as yours that I got this morning. There's little to tell you anyhow. It has been a hard week with full evenings. If my knee is no better tomorrow I have some hope of getting leave to go off home for 2 or 3 days. But we may be starting musketry tomorrow and in that case I should have to try to do it, as it is the one thing they do well here. The rumours about a change of camp are not anything more yet. Most people hope to go to London and I should if we had done our musketry, as there would then be little to learn here that could not be as well learnt at headquarters.

How I envy you getting here and there in this fine weather as I used to do. If I am in town for a few hours I will try to arrange to see you.

Have you time to make some copies of these 21 lines?

Tchaikovsky it was, I expect.

Goodbye.

> Yours ever
> Edward Thomas

I have only a few of Edward's poems in manuscript, for I generally returned the originals with the typescript. The verse to Baba—'my daughter the younger'—is among them, with some slight scribbled changes here and there, in the faintest pencil now. Turning over a folder full of precious fragments I find, in Gordon Bottomley's hand, the list of seventeen of Edward's poems which he and Trevelyan had chosen for their Georgian anthology, the first public recognition of Edward as a poet. With it I find, too, a rejection slip from the *New Statesman*, one of the many which chance has not destroyed. I keep it as a comment on the change in valuations brought by time.

Postmark 18 November 1915

Hut 3 now

My dear Eleanor I am hoping to see you on Saturday. I have asked for the day. There is no leave, but I can get to Balham and then see you at tea time. From what you say I feel sure you can come to Shearn's at 5. You can come out, can't you? I am sorry you aren't well yet. Or you would have enjoyed the blizzard. I did so far as I could while it was taking my breath away. I much prefer them to Zeppelins which are so much commoner here.

I can't write in the Cafe tonight. I don't know why, except I suppose that I can't bring myself to regard answering letters as more than a necessity—I mean I never have any sense of communion except with people like Frost whom I cannot possibly see.

I thought you would like to see this list of the poems Bottomley and Trevelyan are to use. They run to more than 20 pages. Also I enclose the lines for Baba. All these place names are from this part of Essex—which I like more and more.

Goodbye—till 5 then on Saturday. If I don't get leave I will try to warn you in time.   Yours ever

Edward Thomas

Postmark November 23 1915

A Company still but not for long.

My dear Eleanor We are homeless here and most uncomfortable. But it's a lovely day and the post has reached me. I am glad London is mostly new. But this is merely to enclose 2 things I meant to give you yesterday. Can you type them some day? I don't know what they are like. Well, the future is uncertain. We are being shifted to a new company and may be robbed of some of our freedom.

I won't speak of the book to Baba. But when I asked her what I had given her and promised her 6d if she remembered she said, on reflection, 'A kiss', which in fact is all I did give her; so she earned 6d.

> Yours ever
> Edward Thomas

> Hut 23
> Harehall Camp
> Gidea Park
> Romford   Essex.

Wednesday

My dear Eleanor   I should have written before but I did not know where I should be. And I don't know now, but they say it will be here for some time, though our officer has gone back to London and expected we should soon follow him. We are having too easy a time, so that again I have reverted and written some verses. I am afraid they aren't finished. I never have any time really to myself and have continually to be putting my paper away. The days we spend in more or less formally examining the country with a view to taking classes out though we do not know that we shall have to do so. Beautiful cold sunny days, and the earth thick with clean snow. I will copy out the verses as they exist now and if you like them will you make a copy or two of them?

> There's nothing like the sun as the year dies,
> Kind as it can be, this world being so,
> To stones and men and beasts and trees and flies,
> To all things that it touches except snow,
> Whether on mountain side or street of town.
> The south wall warms me. November has begun
> Yet never shone the sun as fair as now
> While the sweet last-left damsons from the bough
> With spangles of the morning's storm drop down
> Because the starling shakes it, whistling what
> Once swallows sang. Yet I can forget not
> That there is nothing, too, like March's sun,
> Like April's, or July's or June's or May's,
> Or January's or February's great days;

August, September, October and December
Have equal days, all different from November.
No day of any month but I have said—
Or if I could live long enough should say—
There's nothing like the sun shining today—
There's nothing like the sun till a man's dead.

The camp is excellent but on the dullest flattest piece of a beautiful piece of country. I have a new set of people to get used to but have too transitory a feeling to succeed rapidly. Now a man has come along to talk and I must shut this up for tomorrow morning's post. The end of last week got full up and I went home again on Friday till Sunday morning.

Yours ever
Edward Thomas

Postmark 28 November 1915   Train to Petersfield
Friday

My dear Eleanor   Thank you again. Now I am going home and I will type the thing yet again because I have touched it again. I had great trouble to get leave this week end, but here I am in a train which ought ultimately to reach Petersfield. I tried to think how I could see you in town, but there is only Sunday and I have got to see my Mother and there is only Sunday afternoon possible and London then is not kind. The leave I half expected in the middle of the week didn't come off. I just got up to see the dentist, but without warning enough to let you know. With that interval this week has been much like the last, with some beautiful but cold weather that doesn't cure colds when you stand about drawing. Still we had always a solid hour for lunch in a farm or pub and got to know one another a bit. Next week may bring a change, a real job, and a move to a new company without a terrier for a sergeant major—but not to town it seems. With luck I may be home at Christmas but not to meet Mervyn. I only hope the mail won't cheat him of his fare.

By the time I am a sergeant I shall be really young I suppose. I wish I had gone on where the Proverbs left off. Probably I never shall, unless 'Lob' is the beginning.

Goodbye. I will finish this at Steep or at any rate add a copy of the lines.

Ever yours
Edward Thomas

'I wish I had gone on where the Proverbs left off.'

He feels a return to 'being young' in this folk-vein, and knows, rightly, that 'Lob' (a poem very close to his heart) is a return, in poetry, to the source he tapped in the prose of the Proverbs: richer because, being poetry, 'it is better than prose'.

I want to quote a bit from each of these, both redolent of English lore at its most English. First the prose; a passage from 'Birds of a Feather'. A Norfolk boy, Bob Dumpling, is being taken westward across England to Somerset, by a drover who must pick up a hundred head of sheep in Ilchester. They traverse the counties full of the evocative names of English towns.

'In the clear hard weather men were ploughing in the Thames valley below them as they passed by. The earth was turned up in rich, dark clods like the inside of a frosted cake, and on to the furrows descended hundreds of white gulls. When Bob shouted, the birds rose up and whirled in the air like snow. Wherever the fields had been striped black by the plough there was a dappling of white gulls on the black.

'The high downs on their left hand were white, but often dotted or blotched with black rooks. In the wayside thorn-bushes flitted scores of yellow-hammers as bright as flowers on the bare branches. "Birds of a feather flock together," said Bob. " 'Tis true, lad," said Davy, "though I never heard it before. 'Tis poetry, too. Some people are born to make poetry. Now, I have a little lass just gone two years old, and one day she sees a sparrow hopping close to the door and says to me; 'What is it?' and says I; 'A little cock sparrow,' and what do you think she says? Well, she says; 'Sat on a sallow.' A little cock sparrow sat on a sallow. That's poetry. But it isn't true. He wasn't on a sallow, and she doesn't know a sallow from an oak. But it's poetry, and so is yours;

'Birds of a feather
Flock together.'

I like that. Besides, 'tis true." ' "

(So her father enshrined Baba's couplet inside his prose.)

But here, in 'Lob' is Edward travelling Wiltshire in search of an old man whose face haunts his memory from years ago;

and the natives discuss what man it might have been, old Bill
Bottlesford, or Jack Button up at the White Horse, or Adam
Walker of Walker's Hill. The next man said:

> He sounds like one I saw when I was a child.
> I could almost swear to him. The man was wild
> And wandered. His home was where he was free.
> Everybody has met one such man as he.
> Does he keep clear old paths that no one uses
> But once a lifetime when he loves or muses?
> He is English as this gate, these flowers, this mire.
> And when at eight years old Lob-lie-by-the-fire
> Came in my books, this was the man I saw.
> He has been in England as long as dove and daw,
> Calling the wild cherry tree the merry tree,
> The rose campion Bridget-in-her-bravery:
> And in a tender mood he, as I guess,
> Christened one flower Love-in-idleness,
> And while he walked from Exeter to Leeds
> One April called all cuckoo-flowers Milkmaids.
> From him old herbal Gerard learnt, as a boy,
> To name wild clematis the Traveller's-joy.
> Our blackbirds sang no English till his ear
> Told him they called his Jan Toy 'Pretty dear.'
> (She was Jan Toy the Lucky, who, having lost
> A shilling, and found a penny loaf, rejoiced.)
> For reasons of his own to him the wren
> Is Jenny Potter. Before all other men
> 'Twas he first called the Hog's Back the Hog's Back.
> That Mother Dunch's Buttocks should not lack
> Their name was his care . . .

No wonder that the man who felt England so must fight
'literally' for a handful of her soil. 'By the time I am a sergeant
I shall be really young, I suppose.' Young with the youth of
the poetry of England, of Chaucer's England, Shakespeare's
England, the England no less of Greasy Joan and Mother
Dunch's Buttocks than of rose campion and ladysmocks all
silver white. Giving rein to that vein in him, Edward knew
that at eight years old, when Lob comes in one's books,
Traveller's-joy and Old-man's-beard are names of poetry as

true as wild clematis for the vine that rambles and smokes on the English hedgerows wherever a man may walk.

Hut 35

My dear Eleanor, Thank you very much. You will see I have made just 2 or 3 slight changes. 'This world being made so' is 5 heavy syllables unaccented. I hope you won't object but if you do I want to know. Thus far I had written when I began to be interrupted, and now it is near closing time. Tomorrow I am to see the doctor. I have been rather bad for 3 days and may get some days' leave and see you in the course of them; which must atone (if it can) for this short letter. We are now supposed to be fixed here though we still have to find our own work for the day. Some of the men are very interesting and altogether days pass easily—a little too easily. I prefer it to a lot of Gunn though. I know what you feel about Cliffords, in fact I think I feel as you do. Yours by the way, is the only reference I have seen yet to 4 and 20 Blackbirds. No reviews. No anything. But I am not complaining except of my cold &c which almost makes me write again—not quite, because it is too lowering. Who is the Scavenger Poet? Is he the last desperate effort of the people who discovered Davies had a wooden leg and wished he had 2? Helen sounds well again. But Frost is silent now.

Goodbye.
Edward Thomas.

Postmark 3rd December 1915   A Company now

My dear Eleanor   I wonder if you are right. In any case you have set me turning the thing over again and you will see the result in this copy. If you can bring yourself to, will you make a copy or two? The last line brings us two back again. But there is not much time now because we have really begun to work. We have a five days course, five days on end with a platoon of 50 men beginning (as far as possible) at the point where they left off at October in town. We don't have a Saturday class—all are out of doors—and I have now got into a new company with a sweeter sergeant-major so that I may get this week end and go to Coventry and see Hodson about Mervyn. Mervyn's last letter was largely about ships he might come by, and we shall soon look for news of the day of sailing. But I shan't be able to meet him. If I go to Coventry and have any time in London on my way I will try to arrange (if you are free) to see you. Goodbye.

Yours ever
Edward Thomas

Postmark 9th December 1915   A Company
                                                     Hare Hall Camp

My dear Eleanor   Thank you again but not for Daphne's title.
I am still not reading poetry except my own in your beautiful typescript. I hope Liberty won't be opaque to you always. But perhaps
it is opaque and someday I may see it. Now I am busy teaching
from 7.30 to 4.30 or later. We finished our first 5 days course today
and begin the 2nd tomorrow—a repetition of the first with improve-
ments if possible.

I got off on Friday night and we settled (as far as we could) about
Mervyn. He says he hopes to sail in the St. Louis on the 10th and
I hope he will. Helen says she will meet him. I can't ask for any
leave during the week, though I intend to try for this week and again
to go home to Steep. If Mervyn should be in town on Saturday
or Sunday week I might get up for the day only.

So Godwin is going out before me. I am no longer trying to
make up my mind what to do. I shall stay at this job a month or 2
for certain. If I get promotion which shows that I am some use I
may stay longer. But all B Company, and all my old squad, except
about 6, have been accepted by colonels and many have gone to
their regiments and I feel restless sometimes.

Suppose I go home on Friday and get back to town on Sunday
morning should I find you in at about 11? I shan't know till Friday
evening, so I couldn't warn you.

Oh, I don't thank you for George Sampson's opinion of my
cleverness. If he is right, it may explain my ingratitude. But never
mind; I don't feel 'arf buried yet really. We are really rather comfortable here. The two men I liked most at High Beech have joined
the map instructors and are sleeping here now. They are all crowding in. Goodnight. Give my love to Godwin.

                                                     Yours ever
                                                     Edward Thomas

Postmark 11 December 1915

                                                     Hare Hall Camp

My dear Eleanor   After all I can't see you on Sunday. They
wouldn't give me Friday night, but gave me till Sunday midnight,
so that I can come by the evening train from Petersfield. However
it is possible we shall get several days at Xmas. Then I can see you
going or returning.

The rain has upset work a good deal this week and everything
has been at a low level, except that Mrs. Hodson sent me a most

superb sweater and I had a letter at last from Frost. Elinor has been ailing a little all the time it seems and Robert hasn't been able to do much work on the land. He also seems to think I had better go on with my present work till I have to change—till I feel I must. Well, the camp is full of strangers now, except us seven.

My chest measurement is 39, or counting 2 sweaters and a cardigan and a jaeger waistcoat, 46. Is it for 'Who's Who'?

Goodbye. Yours ever,
Edward Thomas

I was trying to hit on a Christmas present that he would really like and had asked for his chest measurements with a view to some sort of good and desirable waistcoat. And if not, some good and desirable boots. But he was in a rejecting mood, and turned down every suggestion.

Postmark 20 December 1915
Sunday

My dear Eleanor,   We spent half the day trying to meet Mervyn, but he missed his train and I am going back without seeing him. Well I shall see him perhaps on Thursday—and you on Wednesday perhaps: if I can find time I will, otherwise, I will call about 5. If Wednesday is impossible it will be Thursday morning—perhaps. But about the boots, don't get them. Send back the waistcoat and bring something for somebody more grateful (and comforting). Really I don't need either, and it is a lot of money. Be as sensible as I am for a moment!

But I will take a cup of tea from you somewhere.

Yours ever
Edward Thomas

A cup of tea was not my idea of a Christmas present. Without asking for his yea-or-nay I ordered from Fortnum and Mason a superb pork pie, which was additional to the Thomas Christmas parcel, labelled with his name and my hearty curses.

Postmark 30 December 1915

Steep

My dear Eleanor   I got it in the neck all right yesterday. I was told I ought to open it at once. I did as I was told and we all took a turn at the pork pie all except Baba. It was better than boots, more convivial and I do hope less costly. But we can't thank you out of the depths of our hearts till tomorrow really as we have strictly abstained from everything but the pie. Baba, by the way, as soon as she saw the post, said, 'Oh, may I sit up and see you divide it?' They are all very well. Mervyn met me and I hardly knew him, he was so English, with hardly a trace of American accent. We are expecting a walk today if the rain is not too bad. Well, I do like your revenges and your curses. The only thing is they are not a great change from your blessings.

Have you already got the little Hudson I sent yesterday? If you have, tell me please.

Give my love to them all at 137.

Yours ever
Edward Thomas

P.S.   Shall I come over on Wednesday morning?

1916

§1

This is no case of petty right or wrong
That politicians or philosophers
Can judge. I hate not Germans, nor grow hot
With love of Englishmen, to please newspapers.
Beside my hate for one fat patriot
My hatred of the Kaiser is love true;—
A kind of god is he, banging a gong.
But I have not to choose between the two,
Or between justice and injustice. Dinned
With war and argument I read no more
Than in the storm smoking along the wind
Athwart the wood. Two witches' cauldrons roar.
From one the weather shall rise clear and gay:
Out of the other an England beautiful
And like her mother that died yesterday.
Little I know or care if, being dull,
I shall miss something that historians
Can rake out of the ashes when perchance
The phoenix broods serene above their ken.
But with the best and meanest Englishmen
I am one in crying, God save England, lest
We lose what never slaves and cattle blessed.
The ages made her that made us from the dust;
She is all we know and live by, and we trust
She is good and must endure, loving her so;
And as we love ourselves we hate her foe.

EDWARD's first poem in 1916 is the complete expression of his feelings about the war. For love of the dust of his country he cried 'God save England!' in 1915, as in 1415 he might have cried it at Agincourt. His hate-feelings were reserved for the Jingo Press and those who used its jargon in argument. His father was among them; these two, throughout their lives, never saw eye to eye. Edward had to write this war-poem, but having written it he did not include it in his book, when the time for choosing came later in the year.

Postmark Ilford, 7th January, 1916

D Company
Hut 51

Thursday.

My dear Eleanor   Thank you very much. I am not sure that 'love true' is a mistake, but perhaps 'love I will not' is, and I suggest

> . . . Philosophers
> Can see] I hate not Germans, nor grow hot
> with love of English, to please newspapers.

But perhaps it won't do. I am so busy now. The move to this new hut and company means a lot of new responsibility. Being senior corporal in the hut I am in charge of it, have to appoint men to clean it etc, call the roll and stop talking after lights out etc. Very possibly there will be more to do soon. Nor shall we have every week-end. Also every morning we waste over an hour in mere parade drill with our company. We can't get up just for the day on Saturday or Sunday as we could before. I am not enjoying it really. I have been out of sorts since last Saturday when I came up to town and saw my father and got into a very unpleasant argument. However I have some hope of getting home tomorrow night or Saturday.

I did write the couplets at Steep, but the others some weeks ago here. Helen won't like them a bit and I kept them by me undecided. I hope you are right.

Probably I shan't get to Coventry with Mervyn. When I shall get any time in town next, who knows?

Yours ever
Edward Thomas

D Company
Artists Rifles
Hut 51
9   1   16
Hare Hall Camp

My dear Eleanor,   I did get home on Friday night after some difficulty. In future it looks as if the difficulty will increase. However we got a beautiful day yesterday and did the usual things, lit a fire in the study, chopped some wood, dug some parsnips, and had a walk at sunset. The Bones were away and we saw only Mrs. Lupton. Mervyn and Bronwen were already in town so I can only see them today at Chiswick. I have written some more lines and amended those I sent you last. I am sending you both. Helen liked the lines about the war and wanted me to send them out but I am not going to entangle myself in that order of disappointments. The most I hope for is to have two things in 'Form' (which Guthrie has now left) and perhaps in a booklet or sheet which Guthrie wants to publish.

Yours ever
Edward Thomas

The artist, Austen Spare, whose drawings had a Yellow Book flavour, was one of the editors of *Form*. The two poems, 'Lob' and 'Words', which appeared in it were still by Edward Eastaway, and not by Edward Thomas.

At about this time Edward told me that his mother was in a nursing home in Beaumont Street, after an operation for cataract. 'Would you go and see her?' he asked, reminding me, as he gave me the address, how shy and reserved she was. I hoped that she would not feel ill at ease with a stranger whom she had never seen and could not see now. But Granny Thomas and I were at ease from the moment I sat by her bed and held her hand. Both her eyes were bandaged. One would always be sightless, the fate of the other was still in doubt. Beneath the bandages I could see where Edward's looks came from. Her voice was quiet and resigned. We had no difficulty in finding a subject to talk about. We talked of the son she loved best of her many sons. I promised to come again before she left the nursing home, where the days were sad and dull for her.

My dear Eleanor   I have let a long time go by. In the interval I have been home for 24 hours. That is all I could get, and I was really glad to get it, though not so glad by the time I was at Gidea Park again near midnight 5 hours after being home. We all had a long walk in the morning, did odd jobs in the afternoon, went to the Bones for an hour and then parted in a very black night—However my trouble is mostly over, and will be entirely if they allow me to have my 2nd Stripe this week as I should have done.

On the way home I got on with some verses I began last week or at last began thinking towards, and I have now nearly finished them. I shall try to copy them for you before I shut this up tonight.

There is not much that is new except these lines about roads.

Certainly I think your dashes would clear up 'Rain' a little. I will put them in.

I would have written yesterday in the train but thought there might be a letter from you waiting in camp and I mustn't write too many. I spend rather more than all my pay now. This is not a very intelligent remark. It simply means that feeling I ought to economise I hit upon the idea of two letters instead of three—And now I expect I shall have a letter as soon as I post this. I hope so.

So you saw Mother. You know I think she was more than pretty, don't you?

They asked for 500 volunteers for a draft to France today. 2 or 3 hours to decide. They might probably not have taken me. Anyway I didn't decide.

16 verses I see it makes. Helen is the lady in the Mabinogion, the Welsh lady who married Maxen the Emperor and gave her name to the great old mountain roads—Sarn Helen they are all marked on the maps. Do you remember the 'Dream of Maxen'? She is known to mythologists as one of the travelling goddesses of the dusk. But perhaps I don't convey much in my 16 verses.

> Goodbye. Yours ever
> Edward Thomas.

Towards the end of January I took Mother, rather war-weary, to Looe. It was my first taste of Cornwall. I had a new grey walking-skirt made against all the dictates of fashion, conveniently wide for getting over stiles and under barbed wire, and clearing the ground by at least six inches. In it I became the butt of Cornish youth, who today would jeer at ankle-length hobble-skirts. But I was growing more in-different to public opinion, more independent of my timidities, and I faced the young men out. The one fear I could not, and cannot, overcome was an abject terror of heights, inherited from my mother, whom the Swiss guides nearly put in a strait-jacket during the ascent of the Rigi on her honeymoon. My palms, like hers, sweat merely when *imagining* a height. One day I may drop down dead in the middle of Salisbury Plain, merely by thinking on the lofty Caucasus. And the Crowner will not know why.

One morning I made Polperro the object of my walk. I had heard of its charms from Dolly and Paul Corder (he was for several years the owner of Looe Island, bought for him by his father to play Robinson Crusoe with). In Talland Bay, on sea level, I was able to enjoy the rich Elizabethan associations of Grenville's little church, before I began to mount the coast-road to the fishing village. On my right was the cliff-face banked with gorse, on my left the sea, falling farther and farther below me. I managed to reach a considerable height, seeing nothing ahead but sky and the edge of the path, before I was attacked by the witless animal fright that forces me down on all-fours. (I once crawled out of a precipitous upper-circle seat in a West-End theatre, to the astonishment of the playgoers and the annoyance of the programme-girl.) That it was impossible to fall off the cliff-edge made no difference at all. The path was quite eight foot wide, and perhaps never got any narrower, but all I could see was steepness disappearing in space, and a sharp turn ahead, beyond which—— What? Safety? a gentle descent into Polperro?—or a steeper ascent, vaster space, and a sharper turn? I was never to know. Sick with fear I screwed myself round to crawl downhill again; and only then dis-covered that, pressed as far as possible away from the cliff-edge, I had been progressing by grasping the gorse bushes tightly, hauling myself upward hand over hand. My palms were full of thorns. Terror had deprived me of every sensation of pain.

Postmark Romford 30 January 1916

Sunday   Hut 15

My dear Eleanor   Thank you for your letter, the typescript and the photograph of the Island at Looe. I should have written before, but I have had a wretched week because I didn't get my stripe and the other man did. He was very nice about it and hated taking my place and assuming superiority in the hut and elsewhere. It seems my offence was taken much more seriously than I thought and intervention did no good. It has helped to make me feel dissatisfied with the work I do and more conscious of my failure to teach. Certainly we don't teach them as much as we should. Then came the dismal week-end in camp, with everyone away. Still it was very fine yesterday, and I got a walk, and now church parade is over and the hut has been inspected, and the captain didn't recognise me as the criminal and said it was a very nice hut—I being in charge while Vernon is away. But the news from home isn't good. Baba has been having stomach trouble again and Helen has been worried— she says it is better now.

The typescript is all right. 'They' in 15 refers to 'the dead'. Steep is right too in verse 6. I am glad you like it. I didn't think anything of it one way or the other. If I send it anywhere it will be to 'Form'. It will be a final proof of 'Lob' and 'Words' that will come to 137 Fellows Rd I expect. Spare doesn't seem to suspect me. I agree about his work. I only regard 'Form' as giving me a bit of public, though it will be very little help because I shan't fit in and shall rather suffer from the character of my company. But perhaps I will send them something else. They have got something already by E. T. I wonder what Clifford is doing.

I shall write to 137. I don't know the address at Marlow. It seems a long way off; so does Arnold. As for Althaea Gyles she seems as far off as 1895, and Olga with short hair almost as far.

Perhaps I shall go home next Saturday, but perhaps to Coventry to see Mervyn. I am not sure yet which.

I am being interrupted now all the time chiefly by a curious degenerate creature who lives in the hut and obeys nobody, almost besotted, very filthy in his ways, and very frank, by no means a fool, and more a gentleman than anyone else, and a little fond of me—he wants to take me out beyond bounds on his motor cycle to drink. By name Llewelyn. I'll tell you more about him later.

We are all waiting for dinner, most of us writing letters or reading papers, one man cleaning up. Llewelyn eating an orange after having cooked a haddock at 12. I must get another walk in the afternoon.

> Goodbye. Yours ever
> Edward Thomas.

'As for Althaea Gyles she seems as far off as 1895.' And so she remained to the end of her days in the forties.

This strange artist, a left-over from the Yellow Book set, had been found by Clifford Bax living in squalor in Paradise Walk in Chelsea. Althea had worked for, and been the mistress of, Leonard Smithers. Now she was no longer able to put her undoubted talents to practical use. She had a gift for writing, as well as for drawing and painting. In 1910, when Clifford Bax was producing his Theosophical quarterly *Orpheus*, he printed some of Althea's poems in it. I had never heard of her till the evening he said reflectively, over supper in his rooms in Jubilee Place, 'I think, Eleanor, you should know Althea Gyles.'

What he told me enlisted my sympathy and interest. I wrote to her, and on an appointed day went to the slum called Paradise, mounted a stair in a wretched house, knocked on a door, and was bidden to come in by a high shrill voice.

Althea Gyles was sitting up in a rumpled bed in surroundings of unspeakable filth and disorder. She waved me forward with the most exquisite hands I have ever seen, and the dirtiest. They resembled those of the Botticelli Venus in the National Gallery. There the resemblance ended. In appearance Althea was witch-like, with reddish hair, pin-pointed eyes, a large thin curved nose, and mottled cheeks. There was a touch of humorous inspiration in the stream of chatter she let loose in her piping voice; she fascinated while she stirred compassion. It was one's undoing. One ought to have fled at sight, for Althea Gyles was an Old Woman of the Sea. Sooner or later one had to shake her off one's shoulders.

I looked round for something to sit on not encumbered with rags, plates with last week's cutlets congealed on them, and other things one dared not investigate, while Althea babbled protestations of gratitude for my coming, commands I must fulfil for her, feuds I must settle and cudgels take up for her, mingled with tributes to Clifford, praise of a young misunderstood sculptor called Jacob Epstein, requests to see some of my writings, demands that I read hers. I continued to visit her regularly, supplying food, typing her charming fairy-tales, trying to clean her up, coping with her grievances, and enjoying her scintillating chatter about Aubrey and Bosie and Oscar (whom she adored). A silver-framed photograph of him, his picturesque head rising out of a fur-collared coat, stood among the combings on her dressing-table. It was, she said, an agreed thing between her and her friends that in a crisis she might send them unstamped letters, and that they would pay the supercharge—and come. Even Bertie, less at her beck but as fascinated as I was, came with me sometimes to spend an evening in Paradise Walk. We brought fruit and cake, and Althea brewed us perfect coffee in a cracked jug with her Botticellean hands, and told tales of Oscar in Paris. Leonard Smithers wanted to publish a new edition of *Salome*; Althea was to decorate it, and Smithers sent her to France to make Oscar's acquaintance. They met for the first time in the Gare du Nord. She was hungry, and he led her from bistro to bistro, feeding her by colour-scheme, calling for a green drink with a rose-pink sandwich here, a purple drink with a yellow sandwich there. They seemed to pass several days and nights of enthralling talk doing this. He died before Althea had accomplished more than a sketch or two for the new *Salome*.

Bertie and I each bought one of her paintings for five pounds: he an enchanting milk-white unicorn against a clear blue sky, I a dusky faun adoring the stars among chimney-pots. The Unicorn was devised for an alphabet which she intended to complete one day; she had begun with the letter U, and never gone backward or forward.

Althea's needs and claims went on for more than a year. Before I was quite drained my mother and Harry protested. I continued to try to help her from a distance. Presently, to my relief, she removed to St. Giles Cottage, Half-Moon Street,

Shepherdswell, Kent; from which pretty address she sent me pretty stories which I submitted to Mrs. King for *The Vineyard* in vain. When a publication such as *Form* swam above the horizon, it seemed the very field for Althea Gyles of the Nineties, until it sank out of sight. But Clifford reminds me that even for *Form* 'Poor old Althea' was too long out of date.

Postmark Battersea 8 February 1916   13 Rusham Rd
Tuesday   Balham

My dear Eleanor, I have been kept here with a chill. These verses, however bad, won't tell you the wretchedness of it. Except the Ash Grove I wrote because I couldn't read or talk or sleep or rest during the day. I am better now, but fit for nothing. My hope is to be able to go out on Friday and to get leave to go home instead of to camp. If so I will let you know and we could meet in town. I did hope to get back soon or I would have written to you at once. But the doctor says I can't go out yet and I don't begin to want to, though the days are so fine.   Goodbye. Yours ever
Edward Thomas.

Postmark 13 February 1916   Steep
Sunday

My dear Eleanor You have rounded me up properly with a third letter. I meant to write to prevent you copying those verses because I had begun changing them—but I was tired. I did write when I got here Friday night but the letter was obviously tired and I thought I would wait. Well, I got some sun yesterday and a long sleep and I am better though groggy on my feet and still with a nail in my chest apparently.

I have made several copies of these so don't you trouble to make any will you? I think perhaps the Ash Grove is really better and I know the sonnet is (you didn't realise it was a sonnet I suspect).

We get till Wednesday here, that is if I don't have to stay later to be well enough. Could you take us on your way either tomorrow or Tuesday? We will expect you when you arrive. Otherwise if you are to be in town on Wednesday I could meet you in the afternoon from 3 to 5, say at Shearns.

It is another bright day today and I must get out while it is still morning.   Yours ever
Edward Thomas.

§2

At the end of February I was making my first visit of the
year to Greatham. Viola had never met Helen, and we wrote
inviting her to Shed Hall for a week-end. She had a map for
the walk from Pulborough Station, and I told her to take the
long way round through Coldwaltham instead of trying the
short cuts by Hardham along the river, so lovely in spring,
but now impassable with the snows and endless rain. It was a
dreadful day for walking, underfoot and overhead. We expected her in the afternoon, and kept a big fire in the sitting-
room, and a kettle simmering for immediate tea, but hour after
hour went by till we grew anxious. Long after dark she
stumbled at the door; she was drenched and spent, and almost
in tears from wandering lost in strange fields in the relentless
weather. I turned on a hot bath and put her to bed. Of her
only meeting with Viola I remember nothing but her woebe-
gone arrival.

Postmark Romford 27 February 1916
Sunday   Hut 16

My dear Eleanor   How nice to go to Coldwaltham (nicer to up
Waltham). We are kept much indoors by weather unsuitable for
mapping. This is Sunday a wet thawing Sunday and not really a
holiday but just a day when few know what to do unless they are on
leave. Somebody said something about homesickness the other
day. It is a disease one can suppress but not do without under these
conditions.

We are all in a turmoil of speculations. We are to have a new
(and worse) sergeant major. The instructors are to be shuffled
about and some (I expect) to go. Men over 30, they say, are to be
transferred to fighting units as unfit for officers.

I can't write a bit. I am restless till I can. Can you and do you,
in the snow? I am hoping everyone will clear out of the hut soon
and leave me alone. The snow is all dirty again and I can't walk
alone here and nobody wants to walk. You will have Helen down
when this comes perhaps.

You will both be at Steep this day week, I hope. But I already begin to see it will be an absurdly short day. Measles, too, may intervene. There are many new cases today and only this hut has entirely escaped in our company. I am quite well again and unable not to take a cold bath.

It's snowing again now. 'Is the canteen open?' is the cry. I must make some tea.

Goodbye. I must end this and allow myself to get so bored that I must write something or go out.

Tell Helen I shall write to her tomorrow. She should have had a letter before she left home and I hope she did.

Yours ever
Edward Thomas.

Postmark 1 March, 1916
Wednesday   Hut 14

My dear Eleanor, If you are back on Friday this will find you at Hampstead. It is chiefly to say I very much hope to go home again on Saturday and to see you on the way. As you probably can't answer in time I will come to Shearn's as soon after 1 as I can on Saturday. Nothing is certain here but I am promised leave. There are more chances of leave this week than there are men expecting it, so I step into an extra chance, or hope to.

Dillybrook is like Cockridden no less because it isn't in a rhyme. But it would have been nice to have another Spring with you. Nice even to think of here where we are losing more and more of our liberty. We had a walk this afternoon—Wednesday always is a $\frac{1}{2}$ holiday. Thursday used to be a holiday for us while the rest did engineering. Now we may be landed.

I have leisure to feel what I am missing. Still I don't miss everything—and what did I ever do more than not miss everything. Goodbye till Saturday.

Yours ever
Edward Thomas.

I sent Edward various parcels of ginger and all-sorts for his birthday, and because Hudson often mentioned it in his books, a tin of maté with the outfit to brew it in—a sort of decorated gourd with a metal tube. And I also promised him a monocle to wear with his newly-won Corporal's stripe.

Postmark 10 March, 1916

Thursday

My dear Eleanor, I didn't know where you were till to-day. I thought you might be at Steep or at Greatham or at Hampstead. Then your parcel came yesterday and I simply couldn't delay. Your ginger has completed to-day's lunch at 'The Bear' for six of us— we are six instead of 5. As to the chocolate I couldn't confine it to instructors. It was rather funny seeing the men all take one of the large ones, except Benson. The day has been as it were one grand sweet song—with dates to begin with at breakfast. I must be 39 or 40 by now, with this fresh birthday or birthdays. I have felt like it once or twice, but not on account of your parcel or your letter. The changes haven't really begun to take place. The possibilities would take an age to mention or explain. In short we are all fed up.

And now I can't get more than a 24 hour weekend. They have so far only given me till Sunday evening (usual early hour), and that from Saturday I may contrive more. And now Helen tells me you won't be at Steep. You didn't say when you could get to Steep again. In any case this weekend was available so I took it or hope to take it.

I was looking forward to quarrelling over my M.S.S. But I hear you have made a selection and I shall have to argue it out through Helen unless it is just my own.

New people will do signalling, with me between. We are learning signalling in case the changes compel us to teach it, as it may be we shall.

We had Dr. Saleeby on personal conduct last night. I wanted to ask him if he could find a white rabbit in my cap. He looks a perfect conjuror.

The monocle will be splendid. When is it coming? The only thing is I doubt if a lance-corporal can wear one except in the privacy of the hut. It will be a great success there. I am glad I shan't have to share the Maté with the other 25 men.

Goodbye, if you do come I shall be glad.

Yours ever,
Edward Thomas.

Steep

Undated, probably March 11th   Saturday

My dear Eleanor You won't be coming I suppose. It is past 4 now and Helen says she doesn't think you could manage this week-end. So without giving up all hope I will send these verses along for you to see. I wonder if you like the smallest.

I did get away after all, and yesterday too. It was our last day with Pearce. He is transferred to town. I suggested he should get me there too. Of course, if our fellowship were not going to be broken up I should in many ways like to stay—largely for the out of door work. But if we are split up I should prefer town. I don't think there's much chance. However, if I do get put in charge of the mapwork in one company (as I may) I shall perhaps be a sergeant all the sooner and wear a bayonet and get photographed.

It is fine and wintry here, very dirty though underfoot. The hills look impassable and make me think they must have looked like that 2000 years ago. I should like to *see* your floods.

Well, Monday or Tuesday or Wednesday I suppose our tangle will be untangled. I will let you know what happens. It would be fun if I came to town.

All our loves to you.

Yours ever
Edward Thomas

P.S. I haven't tasted the Maté yet. I forgot it yesterday.

In his next he thanks me for the 'monocle', which, as I remember it, was a large chocolate disc wrapped in tinsel.

Postmark
15 March, 1916   Wednesday

My dear Eleanor, Now I have a letter and a monocle to thank you for. The letter came just after I had written to you sending some verses, so I waited a few days in case I had news. But there is nothing really. Only we are lecturing all day for some weeks. It is good practice but tiring and indoors of course.

The monocle is excellent, rather large, but really better than the glass thing which is more usual, though one can't see thru it. It is fully as decorative, too. In fact I am not sure if I ought to wear it without another stripe, and that is a long way off. I was ticked off yesterday for having hair too long, which grieved me because I am not seeking any compromise between long and short. These little things just make the difference.

I told you I sent off 40 poems to Bottomley, didn't I? Some will soon be out in a booklet by Guthrie—6 by E. E. I shall remain E. E. till I find if people like him at all. Out of your 30 I should think I retained 20. I brought in some you rejected. I wish you had been there to argue it out. It could so easily have been done, if only I hadn't delayed writing to you and eaten away at your box. It was a nice weekend. The Sunday was warm and fine, though we had plenty of snow left for snowballing. I left out the Ash Grove. We tried the maté, but it was too strong or something, and we only learnt that it resembled tea.

Bottomley hasn't told me yet which out of the 40 he has taken. I want to have the last word over them. Apparently the book is settled. So E. E. will have some show. I hope he will be distinguishable.

Yours ever (and I hope this reaches you before you go away again)

Edward Thomas.

Postmark
20 March, 1916

Sunday   Hut 15

My dear Eleanor,   I hope you are better. You should not have worried with all those lines. I wish I could have seen you. But we are more tied up than ever. No one had leave this week end. Quite likely I shan't get away next week end. However things are being cleared up. I am in charge of the mapping in D Coy with one man to help, but I have no immediate hope of promotion. The Captain still remembers my offence. Still I have work up to the eyes. I am to take charge of the hut again and as Vernon (the full corporal) is going to another company, I have to lecture all day which I am getting used to.

Helen is going to town she says—just as the weather changes. It has been lovely for most of 3 days and today perfect. We were out all day. But from now we have ordinary N.C.O.'s duties to perform at weekends. It will be a further tie. Still, some men are worse off. Some were detailed for France on Friday without warning. Some are to go to fighting regiments willy nilly. If I can lecture satisfactorily 6 times a week for 2½ hours I shall not complain. Goodbye and I hope you are better.

Yours ever
Edward Thomas.

Postmark
2 April 1916
Sunday   Hut 15

My dear Eleanor,   I have left your letter so long unanswered that
I can't answer it but just ask you for your news and send you mine.
Are you better now and where are you? I have really been very busy
and am likely to be more so and be left in charge here as I expected
before. They have given me my second stripe, so the fine weather
makes me content and I have written some verses, one set for
Mervyn and one for Bronwen. If they are not too bad, will you
type them?

Helen is home today I expect, after seeing her brother-in-law
buried. Bronwen goes away for part of her holidays to Deal on
Tuesday, so I shall miss her if I do get any leave this month.

Let me know if you will be in town on Saturday in case I could
see you on my way through—if I go.   Yours ever
                                                  Edward Thomas.

I typed the verses, filled with the Essex place-names which
his pleasure in them turned into poetry. Here is the little one
to Bronwen; I love it for the sweet names, and for the happy vein
his 'daughter the elder' always induced in him; the vein in
which he vied with her in finding the first things of the year in
the Hampshire hedgerows.

> If I should ever by chance grow rich
> I'll buy Codham, Cockridden, and Childerditch,
> Roses, Pyrgo, and Lapwater,
> And let them all to my elder daughter.
> The rent I shall ask of her will be only
> Each year's first violets, white and lonely,
> The first primroses and orchises—
> She must find them before I do, that is.
> But if she finds a blossom on furze
> Without rent they shall all for ever be hers,
> Codham, Cockridden, and Childerditch,
> Roses, Pyrgo and Lapwater—
> I shall give them all to my elder daughter.

These were soon followed by the poem to 'my daughter the
younger' and the trilogy for his children was completed.

16 iv 16   Hut 3

My dear Eleanor,   Thank you for the typed copies of Baba's verses.
I am on my way back to camp now after an unexpected week end.
Unexpected but struggled for. There is still no regular leave, and
I fear no hope of Easter leave. Still, it might come off. Then I
shall see you at Steep. I very much wish it could be. All the
children should be there: also my elder sister-in-law, who is staying
till near the end of the month.

There is no news. We have had a poor week, with only one day's
real work, which is quite another thing from having a holiday,
though we did spend most of the time out of doors, doing no more
work than we liked. It makes us feel unnecessary, and also helps
the bad impression they have of us map-readers as truants, which we
don't want to maintain.

I am asking Bottomley to consider putting 'Aspens' or 'After
Rain' in place of 'Wind and Mist', and sending him the verses to the
children.

Things are moving in connection with the Civil List. But the
opinion is that I am too young for a pension. A grant seems more
possible. They are collecting letters from the great on my behalf.
                              How are you now?

                                                      Yours ever
                                                      Edward Thomas.

§3

I don't know who it was—very likely Gordon Bottomley—
who started the idea of getting a Civil List Pension for Edward.
Edward had many friends whose names carried weight, but he
did not know Alice Meynell, and I asked him if he would like
me to approach her when I was next in Greatham.

Postmark 8 May 1916

Thursday   Hut 3

My dear Eleanor,   There is no hurry about the verses. I hope you
will like some of them better when you see them again. Somehow I
thought 2 or 3 of them were all right, particularly 'Go now' perhaps. They are the last I have written. This fine warm weather has
given me enough to do enjoying it. Last week we wasted too much

time to enjoy it as much as I wanted to, though we had 3 good long walks. This week has been busier and the intervals have been far pleasanter. There are nightingales all round the camp. The may has been out more than a week. There have been glorious warm still evenings.

No news, except that Benson and Mason have gone to other companies, and Vernon and I are left to work with D. The worst of it is he is going out into a billet with his wife and I am to remain (probably) in charge of this vile hut.

No hurry about Mrs. Meynell. You do as you think best. De la Mare isn't a bit hopeful, so I need all the help I can get. He doesn't seem to think I shall have anything at all.

I doubt if anything will come of the Welsh Army job. It looks too much as if the Welsh press wanted someone to send them 'Eyewitness' stuff, which I suppose I could do, but with difficulty and not to suit Welsh taste. I only wish it would come off, because it is unlikely the work here will be better organised in the future, and unless it is I shall be always sick with either uncertainty or idleness.

I am expecting to go home tomorrow, perhaps just till Sunday morning, tho if the weather settles fine I may walk to Haslemere and catch the 4.20, I think it is. Is there a chance of your coming over? If I knew I was coming by the 4.20 we could meet in town *if* you are to be in town. I should have a couple of hours to spare.

Yours ever
Edward Thomas

This letter crossed one from me saying that Mrs. Meynell was writing in support of the pension. I mentioned that E. L. Grant Watson, who had once been a master at Bedales, was staying with me and Viola in Shed Hall. He and Edward had a good deal in common as field-naturalists.

Postmark 8 May 1916

Hut 3
or rather 13 Rusham Rd

Sunday

My dear Eleanor   We hoped you would appear yesterday but perhaps you were already in town. It was too late to arrange to see you today. Have you thought better of the verses, or any of them? Here are still more for you, the short one being half Baba's.

I forgot to give you a message for Peter Watson which I am very sorry for. I like him tho I am not sure how I should get on with

him. It would have been very pleasant to see him again. Is he a
fixture at Greatham? Because if so, he might be willing to walk
over or half way over some week end. It seems that ordinary leave
starts again now. You will come down with me some Saturday,
won't you? Or are you perhaps to be with Mrs. Simon?

Please give my love to Bertie and Joan and your mother.

> Yours ever
> Edward Thomas.

I had already met Grant Watson, whom we all called Peter
(it was the universal nickname at that period), at Godwin's in
Bethnal Green; a tall, strong, good-looking man, not yet
known as a writer, whose varied life had included adventures
in Australasia—I don't remember where. He was very frank
in describing to me and Viola his experiences on some island
where life was 'brutally primitive'.

Peter Watson was a magnificent swimmer. A swimming-
pool was now under construction at Greatham, and well-
muscled week-end guests were roped in to help. Peter no
doubt contributed his quota, but the pool was unfinished;
and though it has been for forty years one of the best of
private pools, it would always have been too confined for
Peter's prowess. One rather imagined him thrashing round his
island before breakfast, scattering sharks and swordfish in all
directions. That is how I am sure the Meynell children saw
him. They admired him with good reason. Every day he led a
tribe of them to the river, plunged in, and made them plunge
after him. The vigorous fearlessness which those children now
pass on, year after year, to their children and grandchildren in
the Greatham pool (under the eye of a grand St John the Baptist
on a stone plaque), owes much to Peter Watson. But our
greatest cause for gratitude was what he did for darling Sylvia
Lucas. She was precluded from the active sports of her
cousins by the accident to her leg two years ago. Peter took
her to the river with the others, carried her in, and invented a
stroke that overcame her disability. He made her practise it
every day, and she became one of the best of the swimmers.
I have always thought with warmth of Grant Watson for this

determined kindness to a child. We have met seldom, not, I think, since 1917, when he came to see me in a cottage I had found for myself between Amberley and Arundel. As we wandered among the trees on a high chalk cliff above the Arun, he did his best to teach me the bird-notes all about us. Edward had sometimes tried to, but I was a poor pupil. I can no longer distinguish the 'acid' note of the wren. I am reasonably certain of chaffinches, blackbirds, and thrushes, and I have only once mistaken a super-thrush for a nightingale. Poultry excepted, cuckoos and owls are my certainties.

Down below us came a harsh croak from the river-bank. A moorhen, perhaps? 'What waterfowl is that?' I asked Peter.

'A goat,' said he.

On a similar occasion, Edward and I were standing at the top of a road running downhill through Epping Forest. Suddenly he pointed to the crossroad at the foot, perhaps a quarter of a mile away.

'Look! there's a deer running across the road.'

'Where? Oh—I've missed it!'—but I knew that at most I should only have discerned some flicker of movement. And then the flicker cut across my sight. 'There goes another! I can see it now!'

'That one,' said Edward, 'was a motor-car.'

Postmark 28 May 1916
Sunday   Hut 14

My dear Eleanor, We are only free in the evenings nowadays. They won't let us alone. We have to do all the usual duties. Every N.C.O. is to be made universally competent. No doubt it is very good for us as well as for the country and I really am determined not to mind much.

The new hours give us a longer evening, so that we can still walk a little. I have even written several things which I send you.

Trevelyan threatens that the Annual with my verses in it may not appear. Constables are offering miserable tyrannical terms. I wish I could make something out of my work. It is more and more necessary with my money dwindling and—I fear—the pension so improbable. Thank you for securing Mrs Meynell. She might just do the trick. As to the Welsh job, I expect I shall hear nothing more.

I may have leave next Saturday and I may have to wait another week, that is till Whitsun. The rumour is we are to have a little more time off at Whitsun. Could you come at either time? I may get both.

If you see Clifford, tell him I believe recruiting is just reopening at the Artists (Duke's Rd., Euston Rd.).

Can you enjoy the fine weather?

Yours ever
Edward Thomas.

Mrs. Meynell's letter did not do the trick, but it helped to secure a grant from the R.L.F. Edward was grateful and disappointed. What he wanted was some security for his family. Did this failure affect his decision not to go to France without a commission?

In June I had a slight attack of whooping-cough. I only whooped once, but had to be kept in quarantine.

June 9, 16.

My dear Eleanor,   Thank you for your letter and the typescript. I am glad you liked the sonnet, I suppose it was one. My fear was that it ended with a click. 'One' is, I suppose, a weakness.

Fancy that phrase coming in the autobiography, and fancy my not putting in the whooping cough—Helen says I did have it, but I only put down what I remembered. So I can come to see you when I have a chance next. I am so glad you aren't whooping.

They are to give me £300 instead of a pension. So I can set Mervyn up for a time. He may go to the London United Tramway Works at Walthamstow if I can arrange lodgings there. I don't like his being just anywhere and on his own with so little of his own apparently. One of my brothers thinks he can get him there as an apprentice with every chance of learning.

I do hope David will escape. I have been trying for an artillery commission but without military influence it looks as if I might have a long wait. Luckily we have been quite busy here and I have had less to complain of.

I expect to go to Steep again next week. If I have any time I will rush up to Hampstead on my way. Or could you come out and stay out? Is that allowed? Goodbye.

Yours ever
Edward Thomas

Tuesday

My dear Eleanor, I suggest we should meet on Saturday outside Shearn's at 1 and then walk into Regents Park and eat some lunch sitting down or walking about. There would be no time for me to get to Hampstead.

It is raining here now most of the time. We 'carry on' indoors somehow or other and get rather bored and sleepy and illtempered, but not very. We are restless again. Four or five of us may all take commissions. I have just had my name put down for one in the R.G.A. or Anti-Aircraft. If I am accepted I shall be at the Artillery School at St. John's Wood before very long. Then I could see something of you. But the influence is new and remote and may not take effect.

Mervyn is getting on better now at Coventry. So he says. It is almost fixed he is to go to Walthamstow on Sept. 1 as an apprentice in the motor works of the London United Co. Hodson has not said anything about Mervyn yet except that he is livelier with the boys than with him. If only he can find good lodgings and not be bored and thrown on the street too much he may enjoy his new life at Walthamstow.

Did I send you the short lines on a pond? I am sending you a sober set of verses to the tune of Rio Grande, but I doubt if they can be sung. Are they worth copying? Also I am sending you Davies' new book.

If it is wet on Saturday I shall not expect you. Goodbye.

Yours ever
Edward Thomas

Postmark 19 June 1916

Hut 14

Monday

My dear Eleanor This was the thing. Well, I got home and tried not to be hurried in my 24 hours. I wanted to sit in the study for example and could only light a fire and go on to a picnic. The lady's slipper was lovely where we sat but I had to be back to write letters and look some things up and shave etc. Also I had to take Bronwen back so that she should miss Tommy during an infectious stage. She is with Mary. There is no more news here, except that practically all our N.C.O.'s are put down for the next School to take commissions. So if I do stay here I shall have plenty of work to do. I imagine I shall be always on guard.

I wonder would you get me 'Form' unless you have a copy to forward to me? Please. I do hope you weren't any the worse for bustling about in the sun on Saturday. And will you send Mrs. Meynell my thanks when you are writing? It would be most difficult for me to thank her directly.

Yours ever
Edward Thomas

§4

Postmark 24 June 1916
Saturday   Hut 14

My dear Eleanor   Look what I have done. I have been 3 days sick and confined to the camp, practically to the hut and this is the result. I have altered Rio because I feel you are right. I have cut out the 3rd and 4th verses and the only refrain is

> 'I'm bound away for ever
> Away somewhere, away for ever'

Does that do it any good?

I am better now and just going out for the first time and hope I can get a walk tomorrow and be fit on Monday.

There are more changes ahead and in case I should be robbed of it I am trying to arrange my leave to begin next Saturday. I have got to move my books from the study. Mrs. Lupton has turned me out. After that Helen and I are going to the Guthries, the Ellis's, and finishing up in London. If you were at Greatham we could call there. I suppose there is a place to put up at. Otherwise we should see you in town.

It is most satisfactory that Duckworth has altered his terms in the right direction.

I remember when all the animals in the Zoo seemed to be in the moon. They were all roaring and howling together under a rising full moon while we were doing night operations in Regents Park last summer. I thought it was some horrible mob. I wonder what your baby did see there.

Goodbye. Yours ever
Edward Thomas

Edward's 'Four-and-Twenty Blackbirds' and my 'Nursery Rhymes of London Town' were both being published by Duckworth in the autumn. His book was dedicated to me and Clifford Bax, and mine to Joan, the baby he speaks of at the end of his letter. She was now three years old—rather young to be taken to the Zoo during the war; yet at some time when she was very small she did have a ride on the elephant whose round tour passed under an arch. It was the big thrill of the ride for me and my brothers, when *we* were very small. So it may have been in 1916 that one day, having dinner at Fellows Road with Mother and Harry and me, Joan startled us by staring fixedly at a pastel portrait of my father on the wall, asking, with an odd emphasis, '*Who's* that?'

'It's your grand-daddy, Joan,' said Mother.

'Yes, *I* know,' she nodded, 'my *old* daddy. He comes when I'm alone and plays elephants with me.'

I heard Mother catch her breath.

When Harry was about Joan's age Father played elephants with him. He stood a-straddle in the middle of the room, and said, 'Come and be an elephant, Harry', and Harry crawled under the archway of his legs.

Joan was now eating her dinner quietly. We did not question her. When we told Joe about it he was as surprised as we were. He had never spoken to her of our father, and had quite forgotten the elephant game, which had been specially Harry's.

Postmark
29 June 1916
Wednesday   Hut 14

My dear Eleanor, I wish you were well. It is a long time since you were. Is the war preying on you or do you write like that because you are out of tune? I wish you could shut your eyes to many big things as I do without trying. If they do prey on me I don't know it. But then I wasn't in a bad mood when I wrote those lines you thought sick—I think you meant the longest of those 3. I thought it was more than a shade heroic. Bob's Lane I liked, but I am glad you liked the sonnet.

About seeing you, can Helen and I see you at lunch on Thursday next week? We hope to reach town on Wednesday night. But it might be Wednesday morning—would Wednesday lunch suit you better? Will you write to Helen and tell her which day and whether 1 at the Strand *Cottage* would do? I only get from Saturday till Thursday 9.45. We shall have to modify to suit the weather as we can't carry anything. How I wish we could fish on the way!

This is the latest. A wet warm free afternoon. The forest is a fragment left 6 miles from here, the best of all this county. I go there every time I can. There is a cottage not far off where you might like to stay some day. The people have been there 53 years. You can't imagine a wilder quieter place. Goodbye.

> Yours ever
> Edward Thomas

Postcard, postmark 2 July 1916

> c/o H. Hooton Esq.,
> Newquay
> Red Down Rd
> Coulsdon

(on Tuesday night)   Surrey

Your card has come. Hoo-ray. Will you dine with us on Wednesday at Brice's on the left hand side of Old Compton St. as you go from Tottenham Court Rd at 6.30. Or if you prefer another place send word here or to 13 Rusham Rd where we shall go on Wednesday morning. All well but flustered.

> E. T.

Postmark 10 July 1916

Hut 14

Saturday

My dear Eleanor,   At Ellises I could not help writing these 4 verses on the theme of some stories I used to tell Baba there. The other 3 I believe are no good, the forest is perhaps a too obvious metaphor.

Now there are fresh excitements as soon as I get back. I am being tried with several others at the School and if I succeed I shall at once be a Sergeant Instructor. They want one for mapping, but the test is simply drill. They want a man who can move small parties about in a smart satisfactory way. So it is at least 4 to 1 the man chosen won't be me. If I don't go to the School I may still stay on here for a short time to see what turns up. I was demi-semi-officially told something might turn up.

I did enjoy Boris Goudonov. If only I hadn't to see it or to hear anything but the instruments.

If I have time in town on Saturday shall I see you at Shearn's? I may be going to Coventry unless I go home to arrange my books.

When is your book coming? I have not seen anything like all of the poems yet. If you have got them all together I would like a copy.

The weather is good again, but everybody is away, and I haven't been able to make up my mind for a walk today. Tomorrow I shall. Goodbye. Will you remember me to Stanley and to Clifford some day, and of course to Bertie and Joan?

Yours ever
Edward Thomas

I answered this letter from Whiteman's Green, a part of Sussex new to me, where Joan and Bertie were renting a primitive farmhouse that summer—'Mizbrook's', near Cuck-field.

Postmark 17 July 1916

 Hut 3   Sunday

My dear Eleanor, I have only just realised I can't reach you in Sussex now. I am very sorry I did not write before but it was impossible to write more than a postcard. Things have worked up to such a state of anxiety here for everyone, probably due to the great demand for officers which is likely to increase and must somehow be answered. I can't make up my mind whether to go at once. But if they do make me an instructor I shall feel thoroughly justified in staying. Even if they don't, I am more necessary than ever because 4 men have left us—practically all (all but one) of the men I liked most. Nothing has even begun to be decided yet. This week perhaps will see it over. To add to my unrest I have been put in charge of another hut, mostly very new inexperienced men and the place has to be organised. By the way, among the new men just come down are Scott James and Blanco White. Blanco White is in my Company but I have not met him yet.

I got home yesterday, have been arranged [*sic*] all my study books and doing odds and ends in the garden. Helen is not well. She is nervous and anxious, so I have agreed with her to move if possible to the neighbourhood of Walthamstow and to have Mervyn at home when he begins work. We shall begin to inquire at once for a neighbourhood that would be convenient and yet be out of the crowd. You don't know that part, do you? I don't want to go, but Helen does. She wants to be with Mervyn and she thinks he ought to be at home if it can be managed. I think it is probably right and we can afford the move, because the Commission is going to allow me £1 a week so long as I am disabled from earning a living—the Civil Liability Commission. This would cease if I became an officer.

Helen is thoroughly sick of Steep people. But I think she is in a state which would make her sick of most people who are not friends.

We shall have to find another school for Bronwen, tho Bedales suits her very well.

Once I walked by Whiteman's Green and along to Balcombe and Worth and Horley. But I have forgotten it. I don't even know if it is in the South Country. How I wish it were possible to fish and be at ease thoroughly. Our old pleasant days in Essex seem to be past quite. Work is the best thing. It is fairly frequent tho irregular. Many days have been wasted in reorganization and in interviewing the Company, man by man, to see what material there is, I suppose, in case of necessity. Perhaps fine weather would make a difference.

What is Stanley doing? I shall not be astonished to see him here soon.

Goodbye. Yours ever
Edward Thomas

Saturday (*probably July 21*)   Hut 15 now!

My dear Eleanor,   I have got 2 hours to myself in the hut, having set free the man who was supposed to look after it till all came in. Half are away on week end leave and all that I care for. All day I have had nothing to do and no freedom to go more than 2 miles out. I did 2 panoramas for practice, but it was a beautiful day thrown away. These 2 hours I didn't really know what to do with. This conceit is the result;—

> The clouds that are so light,
> Beautiful, swift and bright,
> Cast shadows on field and park
> Of the earth that is so dark,
> And even so now, light one!

> Beautiful, swift and right one!
> You let fall on a heart that was dark,
> Unillumined, a deeper mark.
>
> But clouds would have, without earth
> To shadow, far less worth;
> Away from your shadow on me
> Your beauty less would be,
> And if it still be treasured
> An age hence, it shall be measured
> By this small dark spot
> Without which it were not.

Is it worth typing? I sent you 2 others last Sunday on my way home. It was the *Thrush* that Helen didn't like.

I got into trouble soon after my return. Mason was away till the same Sunday night and was not in at roll-call, but feeling sure he would be in by the next train, I reported him present. He didn't return till 7 a.m. on Monday, by which time I had reported him absent in a fluster. So we both had 2 serious talks with the Sergeant Major and an Officer, and my position isn't improved. I shan't be a full corporal just yet.

So you have a white blackbird. Good luck to you and it. It is certain to be a white blackbird. It will have a better chance in Hampstead than ours had at Steep. We saw it for 3 years though.

Things aren't at their best. The new responsibilities and the trouble upset me. Then Christmas perhaps. And the new rule against going more than 2 miles out of camp makes Saturday and Sunday days of imprisonment. I only hope I shall get off next week.

> Goodbye. Yours ever
> Edward Thomas.

Postmark 25 July 1916

My dear Eleanor, I should like to have that copy of 'Form' to show Pearce. Could you bring it with you on Saturday?

I don't mind people knowing really. I don't mind anything much except that I can't learn mathematics (or not in hurry). The interview is to be on Friday and I shall know whether they want me or not.

And I forgot to tell you how much I liked the dedication of your poems. It was very much. But I am in a hateful mood now. Most

things are disagreeable here and the ridiculous worry of the hut
puts the lid on it. Also mathematics all day without result. Blanco
White is no great teacher.

That line should be just 'the thrush *repeat* his song'.

Forgive this.

I am ever yours
Edward Thomas.

For more than a year before the first book of London
Nursery Rhymes came out I had been singing them to Joan,
making up tunes on the spur of the moment as I walked about
with her in my arms before bedtime. I had sent Edward some
of the verses in manuscript, including the dedication to 'my
baby'.

> *Joan was born in West End Lane,*
> *And when she was born she was young;*
> *Joan was born in West End Lane*
> *While the nine-o'clock bell was rung;*
> *And if little Joan had never been born*
> *These songs would have never been sung.*

Thursday, July 26   Hut 15

My dear Eleanor,   I suppose it is the fact of measles getting into
the camp, coupled with a strong cool wind, that makes me more
cheerful. Two out of the 4 Companies are already isolated, or
several of their huts are. We are still clear but are working with a
platoon that is half infected already. If I get away this Saturday
I shall be lucky, and it may be my last for some time. Well, we are
working anyhow and this morning I actually lectured for nearly
an hour on scales. Think of it. I shall have to do it again and again
till I am not afraid, and then try something more interesting. But
Lord how I did dislike it, looking from face to face to see if anyone
was inclined to grin, and fixing a stern gaze on the face most inclined. However it is over now, and somehow or another I have
been clearer with my section this week. Gradually we do learn a
little of how to teach. You were quite right, I did see things from a
bit of an attitude when I saw them so black. Now I see them really
grey. There is a beautiful strong wind and we shall have no
Zeppelins. On Monday night we heard them and had an hour or
two of darkness in the hut.

By the way, it was largely because the stripes were pure decoration that I felt the miss of them so. If I had been sure I was doing well the mere lack of outward signs of approval (especially as they aren't really that) would have mattered less I am sure.

It is fresh tonight as I said before, but I went and re-sprained my ankle on Monday and had a couple of days lameness and have now got to be as careful as ever for some time. So there is no walking except down to the café at 7 to stay till 8.15 or so when we return to clean buttons and boots and shave. I may get as far as Steep on Saturday if there is any leave. It was to be Coventry but probably Hodson wouldn't want me from an infected camp. But I feel sure of not taking it home. If I have an hour or 2 to spare in town I must see my Mother. So I can't promise to see you on Saturday. You will be back, I gather. If I should stay on in town and not go to Steep I would come in on Saturday afternoon on the chance. Goodnight. I have some exam. papers to look over now. This is a recent addition to our work. We really earn our 1/5 a day now.

Goodnight and I hope your Mother is well again.

Yours ever
Edward Thomas.

§5

In August Edward wrote from hospital, on Y.M.C.A. paper with the heading: 'For King and Country'. The letter brings the first mention of the cottage in High Beech which was to be his and Helen's last home.

Postmark 11 August 1916

Hospital—Thursday

My dear Eleanor, I entered this place on Tuesday morning and ever since have been too bored to do anything but wish myself out. I can't read. This afternoon I had to write something. I wrote these 2 verses, which I am afraid may simply make you think them perfectly true. There is a faint hope I may escape on Saturday with some leave. Then I shall go home. I am much better, but my arm isn't. It might take quite a long time.—The latest is that Irene has found as the most likely cottage one a few yards from my old billet at High Beech, a beautiful situation but rather lonely for

Helen and with a mile of forest for Bronwen to go through to school. One of our neighbours would be Arthur Morrison who wrote some East end stories—were they?—years ago. He and his wife were very hospitable people. You won't come over from Selsey will you? I ought to be at home on Sunday and Monday.

Yours ever
Edward Thomas.

I was, as usual, rambling all over Sussex; first at Selsey with Margaret Radford, then taking in the Guthries en route for Greatham, and ending up at Mizbrook's Farm again, this time with Rosalind Baynes and her second baby Chloe. He wrote to Selsey while he was convalescing in Balham.

15 viii 16   13 Rusham Rd

Balham

My dear Eleanor,   Mother wants me to thank you for her letter. The Public Man read it to her. She was really delighted with it and perhaps you can't imagine how glad altogether she is that you came to see her and came again. She is really much better. Now the rain has laid the dust she has been out and that has done her good. She doesn't like many things indoors. She doesn't like wearing smoked glasses by the way. She doesn't like not being able to write this letter.

What did you do about the rain yesterday? I thought of trying to catch you with a letter at Guthries but the rain perhaps hurried you on.

My mother and I are alone here, the P M having gone off to Wales. It is a lovely calm evening after rain and not a little sun. I came up and sold some books and had tea with John Freeman and de la Mare and a brother in law of his who may publish some Eastaway in a volume.

Selsey sounds just what I imagined it on seeing it from Flansham except that I did not imagine the houses nor yet Pound. But you know all about my imagination.

I wish suddenly I was an Officer going out now. I am most impatient. Yet the book on Artillery instruments I am reading is not a thing I could master in the boat train, neither. In the meantime I am busy hoping I shall be in London for a time and not at John o' Groats.

Frost hasn't written for an age.

Mother says she hopes to be able to read your next letter herself which does not mean she hopes it will be a long time coming. She deciphered some of Helen's writing this morning.

Yours ever
Edward Thomas.

Please remember me to Peter Watson and say Alix Florence was asking me about him at the Fordham's 2 weeks ago.

How casually he mentions the teatime with de la Mare's brother-in-law, Roger Ingpen of Selwyn & Blount. The possibility of 'some Eastaway in a volume' soon changed into the certainty of a book of poems by Edward Thomas.

His next letter is posted to Greatham from Steep, where the house is in an upheaval for the move into Essex, though the cottage at High Beech is not yet finally settled on.

Monday (*August 20, 1916*)   Steep

My dear Eleanor, I have been here since Friday night and go tomorrow. Most of the time I have been preparing for the move, burning books and papers and packing boxes of books I decided I would sell. I could almost sell the lot. At intervals we have been out and I have read some of your poems. They are like china shepherdesses &c. They all surprise, yet not too much, just enough to make one wish one had invented them oneself—the slut Kensal, for example. And yet I can hardly read except what I have to, such as Gunnery Formulae simplified. I do look forward to the new work. It is likely to begin about the end of the month; whether at St John's Wood or not is quite uncertain. You go roaming about. I hope it is as pleasant as it sounds. Did you chance on Bronwen in a caravan near Littlehampton. Hardly, perhaps. She is thereabouts for a week. Helen doesn't know where she is going.

Don't you worry about typing those 2 verses, in which I have changed 'August blue' to 'harvest blue'. I was glad to have them to write anyway—shall be lucky to do more till the swifts are back again. If I go to St John's Wood or Handel St. do you think I could work at Fellows Rd of an evening? We all get sleeping out passes and can come in at midnight or for the morning parade. I go on Wednesday to look for cottages near Chigwell &c.

Goodbye and good fishing to you.

Yours ever
Edward Thomas.

The next two letters came to Mizbrook's Farm. The second enclosed a letter from Granny Thomas.

Hut 3
Postmark 21 August 1916   Sunday

My dear Eleanor, There is a man here talking to me about religion. He went on till it grew dark. He is one of those hateful people whom I never can say a word to to reveal my hate. Well, all I can say now is that at last I am leaving here. I report at St John's Wood on Friday. 13 Rusham Rd should henceforth be my address. For I expect I shall go from here on Tuesday and stay there till Thursday and then probably return here in order to go formally next day to St John's Wood with all the others. Mrs. Blanco White was here today. I had to stay in camp all day on duty. It is so dull and I have a poisoned hand which makes me useless and wretched.

I shall see you next week then. Thank you. I shall probably be able to arrange to go to Fellows Rd of an evening *unless* I am really not to be at St John's Wood but at Handel St. Is it possible I can think of anything but gunnery there? This place I shall be glad to see the last of, tho not of Wheatley and Benson. In fact I hope I shan't soon see the last of them. I may get this week end because reporting on Friday can't mean beginning work before Monday. Helen will be at Flansham, but there would be no room for me.

I have sent off some Eastaway but had none of his latest by me.

Goodbye.

Yours ever
Edward Thomas.

13 Rusham Rd.
Balham S W
Aug. 25. 1916

Dear Eleanor. How good you are to me, and how well you write! I read your last letter all myself, and without any discomfort, so you see I really am getting better, though I am not supposed to do much, and the field of visible things is still very dark to me.

Well dear, I hope you are really having a good time, and storing up pleasant recollections, apart from the sleeping problem. I don't like to think of you doing those tramps all alone and finding such inhospitable folks when you look for rest. I should like to know how you fared at Henfield and on to Mrs. Baynes?

Perhaps you know that Edward left the Romford Camp on Tuesday, and has to report at St. John's Wood this afternoon. Poor boy, he is not at all well and has a bad abscess on his right hand, and ought to have a few more days for rest, and I should love to have him, but in these days the powers that be show no mercy, tho' I am not without hope he may return tomorrow. Now he asks if he may add a postscript and of course I agree knowing well it will make my letter less dull.

This is all I can say dear and so Goodbye and happy days be yours.

With love from
Granny.

This was Edward's postscript.

My dear Eleanor, Thank you for your letter. You will find one waiting at Mizbrook's Farm, I hope, from me. I am just off to St John's Wood. If I am kept there I shall look you up soon. My address had better be 13 Rusham Rd. Am I impudent in asking whether, if I am to be billeted out, I might possibly be billeted at 137 without inconvenience? I don't know what the billet money would be but it might be enough to cover the cost of my living (minus the champagne). You will tell me as directly as I ask, won't you?

If I am any good I will call and see your Mother tomorrow. But my poisoned hand has simply left me a wreck, good for nothing at all, in spite of 3 days rest here.

This is only a P.S. to my mother's letter.

Yours ever
Edward Thomas.

I don't know why I was going to sign myself Edward Garnett.

Mother would gladly have put Edward up in our spare room, but the constant changes of plan during army training removed him almost at once from St. John's Wood to Handel Street. He was now Cadet P. E. Thomas.

From Cadet P. E. Thomas
Royal Artillery School
Handel St
27 viii 16   W.C.

My dear Eleanor,   If I possibly can and I think I can, I will come round immediately after I am dismissed at 6 tomorrow. Then we can have dinner out or in as you like. You see I am not at St John's Wood. All the R.G.A. men are here. It is too far off for me to sleep out, but I hope I can work at your house sometimes. There will be a great deal to do. Thank goodness my hand is mending fast, and so am I. I have been resting yesterday and today at Rusham Rd. We get practically every week end. The result is I got tired of logarithms and wrote 8 verses which you see before you. When I come I should like to borrow about the last 12 things I have written. I want to send them to the prospective publisher I told you about, with these if they are good enough.

Goodbye. I hope you have a waterproof today.

Yours ever
Edward Thomas.

September was a restless month for Helen and Edward, she coping with the complications of the move, he uncertain of his chances of going to Trowbridge for artillery practice. The move was delayed from one date to another, and Helen was still in Steep at the end of the month, and Edward in Trowbridge, as he wished to be.

Postmark 13 September 1916

13 Rusham Rd
Wednesday   Balham   S W

My dear Eleanor,   It seems we are to get off tomorrow for the weekend and Helen and I may go to Steep on Friday. If possible I will come straight to you tomorrow, tho it can only be for a short time. It seems we may *all* go to Trowbridge next week. I shall be glad for my health's sake. If I don't see you tomorrow I will let you and Bertie know about Tuesday. Goodbye.

Yours ever
Edward Thomas.

Wednesday

R. A. School
Handel St   W C

My dear Eleanor,   Thank you for sending me the estimate and for getting it. I wrote at once proposing Sept 21 tho Goodness knows if Helen can manage it then. She says they have had some good weather. Mervyn remains silent.

I meant to come over tonight, but an arrangement for tomorrow night had to be altered, so I hope I shall find you in tomorrow night instead.

By the way, you misread that poem you didn't so much like— about the swifts—missing the point that year after year I see them, *realising it is the last time*, i.e. just before they go away for the winter (early in August). Perhaps it is too much natural history.

Yours ever
Edward Thomas.

Postmark 21 September 1916

Wednesday

My dear Eleanor,   I don't know yet whether I am going. The exam was easy but I expect others found it so too. Of course if I don't go to Trowbridge I shall see you before long. In case I don't could you send me a copy of those last verses—the Blenheim Oranges—of mine? I can't find one or the original. You will see I have written some more too—if you *can* see the faint type. Perhaps one of them is better than the others.

Before I send this I will make sure whether I am going to Trowbridge. My address there I believe is just

Royal Artillery Barracks
Trowbridge
Wilts.

If you call me

P. E. Thomas
R.G.A.

perhaps it will be all the clearer.

I wish I had seen Bertie, but hope he is not going to trouble to write about it.

Helen can't move till the 8th. Did I tell you? I expect Bronwen will go down and Mervyn will the last half of next week, when he has a holiday.

Yours ever
Edward Thomas.

P.S.   I have got to go to Trowbridge. I hadn't allowed for the
fact that some people aren't as plain as others. Well, I am sorry for
several reasons. But it can't be helped. Will you mention to Bertie
that I can't be free yet awhile? Goodbye.

Postmark 25 September 1916
Monday   Royal Artillery Barracks
                                                        Trowbridge.

My dear Eleanor,   It isn't bad and the weather is lovely. Moreover
the Saturday and Sunday were almost free, so I walked both to
Dillybrook and to Bradford by the fields. We are in tents and so we
see the night sky. The trumpet blows for everything and I like
that too, tho the trumpeter is not excellent. We have had our cos-
tume criticised a good deal and have had to buy gloves and so on.
But it is not so bad as it was painted. I have met Hooper once or
twice, in fact he was one of the Bradford party. I like him. I like
men with that easy free manner better than clever men.

I may get home on Saturday tho it is an inconvenient roundabout
journey by Salisbury and Portsmouth.

I hope you liked some of the verses.

Bertie did write, but of course it will be some time before I can
go there now.

Are you quite well now? If so, you will be going away blackberrying or something, won't you?

                                                   Yours ever
                                                   Edward Thomas.

§6

Edward's letters have been an index to my whereabouts for
all four years, and those for October are lost. So I don't know
if I did go blackberrying anywhere, and I can't fix the exact
date when he dropped in on Mother and me on one of his
flying visits, with not much time to spare; and asked after tea,
'Could we go to see Bertie and Joan for an hour?' But it must
have been before he was an officer, still wearing his rough
khaki.

We walked round to Antrim Mansions. Bertie opened the

door to us. He was surprised and delighted to see Edward, and said, after shaking hands, 'Mr. Earle is here'.

I have already mentioned George Earle, the English master at King Alfred's School in Hampstead. Among his pupils were not only the three Cox children with whom Edward had stayed in Selsfield House at the end of 1913, but their cousins, Joan and Rosalind Thornycroft. I had heard Mr. Earle spoken of glowingly before Joan and Bertie were married, and afterwards met him once or twice at their flat. He was forty-five years old, and had been teaching at K.A.S. for fifteen years.

When Mrs. Cox said, 'Mr. Earle is the finest teacher I've ever known, and perhaps the only teacher,' she was speaking of a man so individual that it was impossible to liken him to anyone else. He was the son of the philologist John Earle, Rector of Swainswick near Bath, who held the Anglo-Saxon Chair in Oxford until he died in 1903. George Earle had inherited his father's genius for finding a kingdom in a word, from its roots in the soil to its flowering in the air. He was alight with the love of the English tongue and its literature, and in the classroom he talked to the children out of the store within him. A lesson may have begun with some set theme, but its end was never in view. Words streamed off his tongue like flying birds, uttered with a swift felicity that could never be remembered or recorded. One bungled trying to repeat what he had said. What remained was the spark he had fired in the mind of his listener: a child, a charwoman, a poet, a garage-hand, a Don, or a gaol-bird. Some of his last classes were held in Wandsworth Gaol among old lags. At the end of the term their spokesman stood up and said, 'We want to thank you, sir, for sharing with us the treasures of your mind'.

This inspired, unworldly schoolmaster was also a master cabinet-maker. In the school workshops he showed small boys and girls how to sharpen their tools while he sharpened their wits on the nature of a metaphor. He left in them a love of words and of wood.

When Edward and I came in he was in full spate, sunk in an armchair, a finger crooked round the stem of his briar. He broke off to smile at me, and be introduced to Edward. 'Mr. Earle—Mr. Thomas,' murmured Joan. We sat on the sofa facing the arm-chair. Edward took out his clay and began to stuff it; Mr. Earle puffed his briar and caught his interrupted thought out of mid-air. I forget what he talked of, William Barnes perhaps, or Chaucer or Whitman or Isaiah; the doctrine of the Trinity or the Cerberus myth; or he may have been pulling some line out of his thousand pigeon-holes—'There is a budding morrow in midnight', 'If there be nothing new' (a sonnet he made peculiarly his own), one of his prime loves leading into another. Presently he was talking of Traherne, and in his ardent, beautifully toned voice, began to quote the immortal passage about the orient wheat.

Edward stopped puffing his clay to say quietly, 'Have you got it quite right?'

Mr. Earle stopped as though struck by a stone from a catapult.

'Isn't it,' said Edward, 'so-and-so and so-and-so?'

Mr. Earle thumped his knee. 'By God! you're right!' He stared at the soldier in the ranks who could correct him on Traherne.

Bertie murmured in his ear, 'It's Edward Thomas'.

Mr. Earle's blue eyes lit up. He leaned forward to roll the golden apple of talk to this writer of fine English. Edward rolled it back. There followed one of the most wonderful hours of give-and-take that can ever have created itself between two men to whom poetry was the breath of life. The rare thing was that they listened as intently as they talked. In the interchange with the man sitting opposite it was as important to hear as to be heard. Briar and clay glowed, went out, were relit; the talk went up on smoke-rings. I can't remember a single word of it.

Edward looked at his watch and knocked out his pipe. 'I must go.'

He had a train to catch. He said good night to us all, and Bertie saw him out. Sunk in his chair George Earle said, 'By God, what a man! He calls to mind that description of Carlyle's, "wearied yet unweariable".'

The next time I saw Edward I told him this, and he laughed a little. But I knew from the sound of the laugh that he found the description apt. I remembered it twenty years after, when we were trying to choose something from his own writing for his memorial stone. It was R. L. Watson who found, in 'The End of a Day', Edward's self-description:

'I rose up, and knew that I was tired, and continued my journey.'

§7

Postmark 2 November 1916

R. A. Barracks
Trowbridge

My dear Eleanor,   This is only a word to say it seems an age since I saw you or heard from you—also to send you some verses I managed to write before the end of my leave. I did something else too coming down in the train on a long dark journey when people were talking and I wasn't, but I have got it still to finish.

I had a word from Frost but only to enclose 2 photographs and say he hoped I would send him duplicates of my verses when Ingpen has made his choice, which he is slow in doing.

Now I have another exam on Saturday the last that is at all serious and might drop me back a little. I think I know the work but I may easily make slips. At least I always do in my exercises. I expect to be home just for the week end. I wonder could you come over on Sunday? Next week should be my last here. Then I go to Wanstrow for a week and after that (so they say) we have leave to get our kit &c.

De la Mare goes to America on Saturday. I hope he will see Frost. Maitland wrote that he had none of his kit left that was any use. Goodbye.

Yours ever
Edward Thomas.

The next letter contained the first draft of 'Lights Out', to me his best-loved poem. It 'goes into the unknown' of himself further than any other. How can he wonder 'is it nearly as good as it might be'? He must have known that it was.

Royal Artillery Barracks
Trowbridge
6. xi. 1916

My dear Eleanor,   We did expect you. Baba and Mervyn and I
went down some way to meet you, but we were quite prepared to
be disappointed. Also we escaped drowning. They were all well,
but I arrived late after being inspected by Sir William Robertson
and it was more of a rush than usual.

Thank you for typing the verses. I see that 'At the age of six'
is a rather rough way of explaining who speaks. But he did tell me
he was six too and seemed to realise he had a long way to go. Now
I have actually done still another piece which I call 'Lights Out'.
It sums up what I have often thought at that call. I wish it were as
brief—2 pairs of long notes. I wonder is it nearly as good as it
might be.

I am thro the exam comfortably, and now I have only 4 days more
here: then a week at Wanstrow, where I suppose my address will
be; 'R.G.A. Wanstrow, Somerset'. After that I shall possibly have
10 days leave. Sunday I shall spend at my Mother's. On Monday I
may go to see Gordon Bottomley after some shopping; on Wednesday to High Beech. Will you come there one day? We are very
full at present, having a friend of Bronwen's filling one room, or I
would suggest a night or two. But I daresay I shall be in town again
as there are many things to buy.

Hooper is at Wanstrow and I miss him. I saw him often last
week.

I hope your Mother is better before this comes to you.
Goodbye.

Yours ever
Edward Thomas.

Then came 'The Trumpet'. This poem is pencilled on cheap
paper dotted with calculations, that I suppose have to do with
his lessons on 'pulleys and weights'. The flimsy sheet stands
witness to how hard self-consciousness died in Edward. He
did not mind poets knowing he was a soldier, but he did mind
soldiers knowing he was a poet. But would his messmates
really have taken notice if Edward lifted his hand from the
paper to scribble his poem on separate lines, and would they
have drawn any deductions from it? I doubted it, as I found

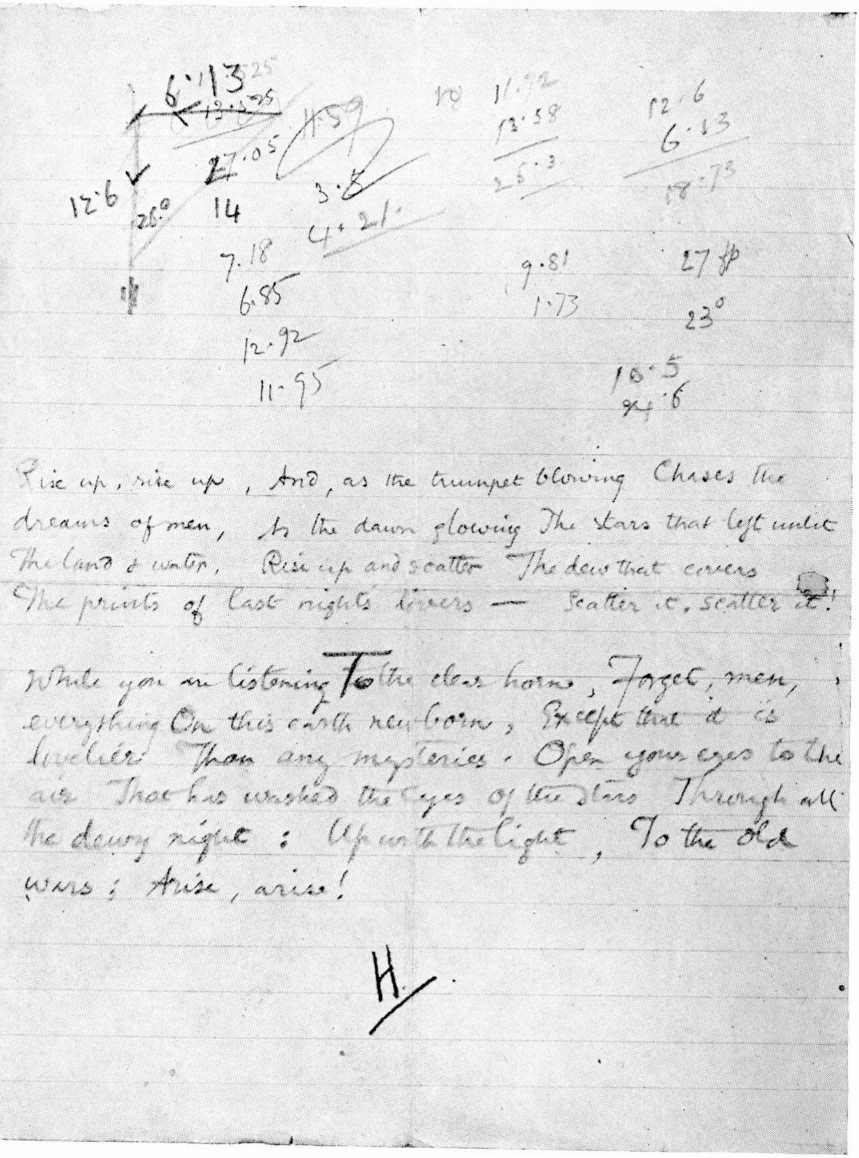

PLATE VI

6·13

12·6   27·05   1·59

14   3·8

7·18   4·21·
6·85

12·92
11·95

10   11·92
13·58
25·3

12·6
6·13
18·75

9·81   27
1·73   23°

10·5
24·6

Rise up, rise up, And, as the trumpet blowing Chases the
dreams of men, to the dawn glowing The stars that left unlit
The land & water, Rise up and scatter The dew that covers
The prints of last nights lovers — Scatter it, scatter it!

While you are listening To the clear horns, Forget, men,
everything On this earth new-born, Except that it is
lovelier Than any mysteries. Open your eyes to the
air That has washed the eyes of the stars Through all
the dewy night; Up with the light, To the old
wars; Arise, arise!

H.

THE FIRST DRAFT OF 'THE TRUMPET'

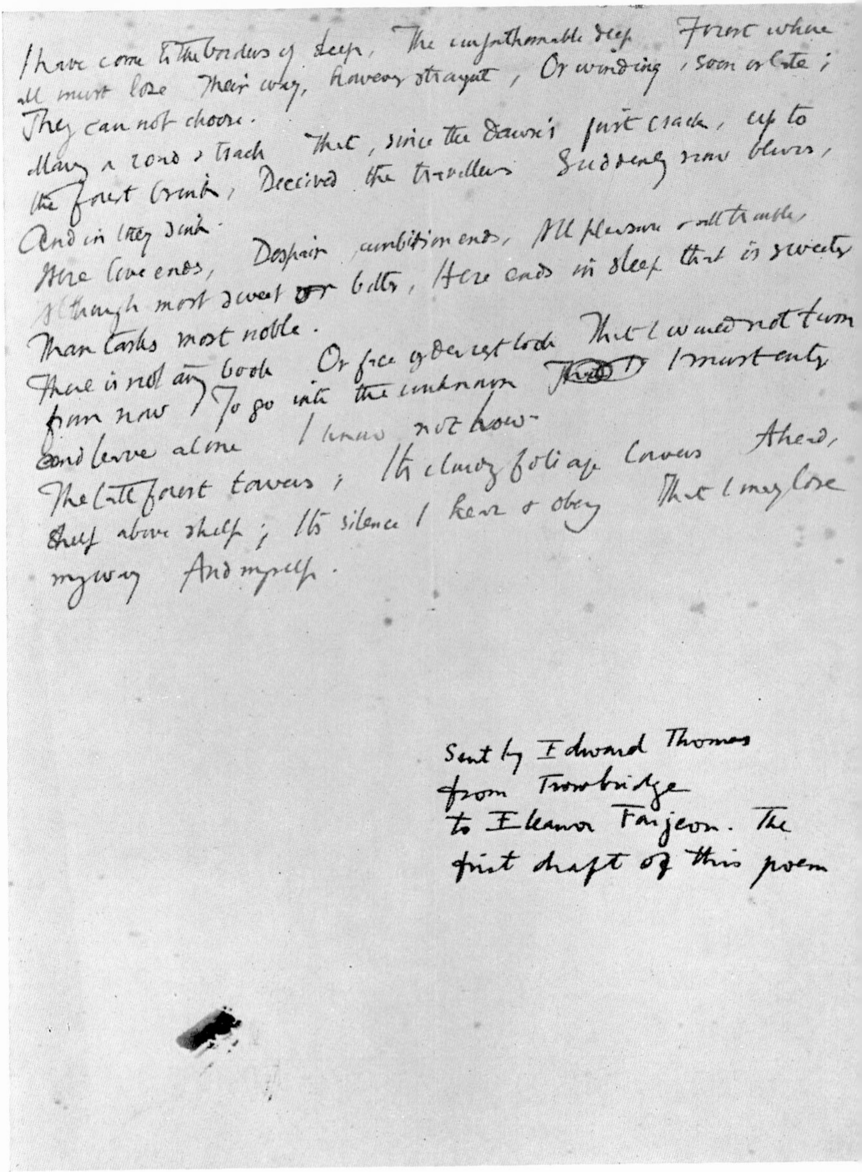

PLATE VII

THE FIRST DRAFT OF 'I HAVE COME TO THE BORDERS OF SLEEP'

the initials in the running paragraph, and typed the verses as they were to stand, the first poem in the book now under way. He was making his final choice from poems as he wrote them, discarding others he did not like so well.

Wednesday

My dear Eleanor, Thank you very much for everything. But I am so sleepy I don't know how much more I can say. Lectures nearly all day make me sleepy. It is rather difficult, too, to learn about pulleys and weights and the teaching is mostly almost useless. It is only 12.30 but I hardly know what I write, now or in making notes. So it is difficult to see how I shall manage it. Partly, too, the very violent physical drill explains it, and a night partly spent in trying to keep rain out of the tent. I think I told you we had some walks on Saturday and Sunday, but all the week we are practically confined to the barracks as we work till 7.30 and can't go out unless we are in our finery, which is hardly worth while changing into. However you can see I have some ease, because I have written some verses suggested by the trumpet calls which go all day. They are not well done and the trumpet is cracked, but the Reveillé pleases me (more than it does most sleepers). Here is the result. You see I have written it with only capitals to mark the lines, because people are all round me and I don't want them to know.

I like Hooper, but he is in another squad and I don't see much of him.

Yours ever
Edward Thomas.

I am still Cadet P. E. Thomas.

Postmark 12 November 1916

Sunday

My dear Eleanor, Thank you for your letter and all the type-writing. On the whole I do like the trumpet verses. If they have to be named 'The Trumpet' will do. By the way the actual trumpeting grows worse not better. I am not sure what you mean about not being successful with 'The Forest', which I suspect is a bad Maeter-linckian thing.

I am writing now because I am on a long slow journey back to Trowbridge and shall most likely have no other opportunity. I had to leave Petersfield at 11 (or rather 11.30 the train being late) and just caught the only train to Trowbridge, and that going to take 4 or 5 hours I see and I can't read about pulleys and levers and sleighs all the time. I am very very slowly overcoming the impossible difficulties, so that after all I may pass the next test in a fortnight's time. I may get to High Beech that Saturday and so I suppose may you—it will be the only chance of meeting. To add to my work they have made me a bombardier, that is to say I wear one stripe. I have to take charge of a guard and do other duties, tho it gets me out of menial jobs. I wish I were not so slow. I think other people can concentrate more on these things than I can with only a quarter of my mind willing to work at them.

Mother was so pleased that you came to see her. I am afraid she has many things on her mind.

Oh, Granville Barker is in my room now, but is just being shunted off to a School for Coast Defence. I suppose his friends have urged his country not to risk his life. I hope I shall always be as eager to risk mine as I have been these last few months.

Now we are at Eastleigh, which is a station.

If it keeps fine up to Warminster I shall get out there and walk the 10 or 12 miles via Dillybrook. So you see I have some luxuries thrust on me. It seems odd to go down those roads with spur chains jingling on *my* feet.

They were all well at home, and the house in a pickle. Mervyn was there, too. I think he is getting thinner. If they can get to High Beech safe and everything safe I shall be pleased. It is to take 3 or 4 days—I suppose for lack of petrol.

I see a little of Hooper. I think I could get on very well with him, but he is in a different squad and not in my room—I am out of the tent now and in barracks.

Goodbye now. I must eat my lunch and read again.

Yours ever
Edward Thomas

About the time when Helen was making the long-delayed move to High Beech, my Nursery Rhymes were published. Edward had been temporarily moved to Wanstrow and I wrote there to say the book was on its way.

Tuesday
Wanstrow

My dear Eleanor,   Thank you. It was nice to get a letter out here, where we are billetted in a big empty house with 2 basins for 42 men. If it rains, I don't know what will happen. But it is beautiful country that I know a little. We work from 9 to 4 and then as much as we like. Personally I like to walk 2 hours in the evening. Then we rehearse for the concert, 4 of us are singing 'Mr. McKinley'. Don't come down.

I am worried about the impression the willow made on you. As a matter of fact I started with that last line as what I was working to. I am only fearing it has a sort of Japanesy suddenness of ending. But it is true, whether or not it is a legitimate switch to make. I will think of it as much like somebody else as possible.

It now seems likely we shall not leave Trowbridge on Saturday in time to come over to you. But later on there will be time, apparently.

Thank you for 'Lights Out', and thank you for your book. I look forward to having it. When I shall read again is quite a serious question, whether I write again or not, and apparently I may. But not here.

Goodbye.

Yours ever
Edward Thomas.

R.G.A.
Wanstrow
Somerset

My dear Eleanor,   Are you better now? I shall be so glad to see you again. That will be in about 10 days time or perhaps early on Saturday evening. On Saturday begins our leave, which may last anything from a week to a month. After Sunday with my Mother I am going up to see Gordon Bottomley. I shall be at home probably from the Thursday (23rd) onwards. You must choose some fine days. Also of course I shall have to be up in town shopping. There are many things I must get besides those I could get.

Your suspicions about the back of this page are right. I am an unconscionable time becoming silent, I feel. But this last week was not a pleasant one and I had to do something to avenge myself. Yet another exam at the end of this week.

Hooper's gone and I am very sorry. But I must get him to come with me to Bertie's some day.

Well, if I can, I will come and see you on Saturday any time after tea—unless my luggage is too much for me. I hope I shall see your Mother quite well again.   Yours ever
                                                Edward Thomas.

This letter was written on the back of a sheet on which he had typed the first draft of 'The Long Small Room'. The first line ran:

The long small room that showed the distant west.

In his next letter, posted at Carnforth Station, on his way to Gordon Bottomley, he changed the line to:

The long small room that showed willows in the west.

Postmark 20 November 1916

Carnforth Station

My dear Eleanor, Blanco White had some other callers, so I couldn't do what I went there for till about 6.30. It was most tiring. And I never thanked you for the book. But I can now much better because I read every one in the train coming here. I can only say I liked more than half very much and thought practically all the others very good too. It may be that I should have liked all equally if I had not read them straight through—a very absurd test to put them to. I agree that your illustrator is appropriate and never takes the upper hand. If you have any luck you might do well at Christmas.

Well, I did most of my shopping this morning without much enjoying it, as I kept on getting the 2nd best of everything. I shall be back home on Thursday evening and we will suggest some days for you.

By the way if the first line were 'The long small room that showed willows in the west' would it make a difference.
                                                Yours ever
                                                Edward Thomas.

Three days later he is spending the rest of his long leave at High Beech with the family, where they are now settling in. I was to go for two nights to see the new home before he left for Lydd.

23 xi 16

High Beech
Loughton

My dear Eleanor,   Thank you very much. I am glad you think the change made the difference. I showed it to Bottomley in the new form and he seemed to like it. He enjoyed reading your book. I remember he particularly liked 'Kings Cross' and 'London Wall' and 'Cheapside'. And he took to the pictures. Your name reminded him that Lady Alix Egerton was an admirer of your stories, by the way.

Helen suggested Sunday. I would prefer Monday as I might have to go out to meet Wheatley on Sunday or he might come here, whereas I am quite free on Monday and Tuesday. Will you stay at any rate till Wednesday? Or would you stay on a little longer and let Helen and me go over for a day and a night to Chelmsford?

I did get a sleeping bag, not quite the best. But I did not get a leather waistcoat. I thought you might like to triumph over me by getting that. It is the only thing I can think of at the moment, unless it is a flashlight or a collapsible stove of some sort. No, not a breast plate. I won't be the first or 2nd.

I enjoyed every hour at Silverdale and then went and wrote something about the house there, which I will try to copy tomorrow morning before we go over to see my mother and the John Freemans (till Saturday morning).

Yours ever
Edward Thomas.

§8

Long before I met Gordon Bottomley, I knew him, through both Edward and James Guthrie, as a man who gave himself generously in friendship. His physical condition partly immobilized him and obliged him to live with great care, but he never allowed it to confine his interests, or to spoil the pleasures of companionship. When Edward died we wrote to one another, and he sent rich replies to letters I had occasion to write afterwards. In 1921 Guthrie was again in distressing straits, and I asked Bottomley's advice. Not long ago I turned up his reply by chance; its opening so bears on Edward's last visit to The Sheiling, that it seems to have been lying in wait for this place in the story.

The Sheiling
Silverdale
near
Carnforth   19th April 1921

Dear Miss Farjeon,

A letter from you this morning gives me great pleasure. I remember very well the last time you wrote to me, but every time I think of that sad hour I think also of Edward and the many things he wrote and said to me of you and your genius and your friendship. And when I read your delightfully best book, All the Way to Alfreston, I remembered Edward's last days here and his eagerness for me to like your book of London verses—then just out and conveyed hither in one of those pockets of his new officer's tunic which his sergeant-instructor had insisted must not be used lest they should bulge and spoil the ideal officer-contour.

So that nothing could feel more appropriate than that you should write to me about Guthrie: for I was the cause of his and Edward's meeting, in the days when he still lived at Harting and Edward had newly settled in Hampshire at Berryfield Cottage. It is a thing of very real concern to me that Guthrie should be hampered either in the use and development of his unique and splendid and profound inspiration or in assisting his plainly marvellous boys to mature and exhibit their promise and gifts: and if it had not been that the pressure of this grievous time and my paralysingly expensive health lays as heavy a burden on my resources as they will bear, I should before now have done everything I could personally to ease his straits.

Two more pages are filled, in his clear ornamental script, with kindness and counsel; ending—

If at any time it occurs to you that I can do something in some definite quarter, you have only to tell me and I will do all I can.

Long ago Edward made us sure that you have two friends upon this lonely hill-top: and my wife and I join in sending our kindest regards to you.

Yours very sincerely,
Gordon Bottomley.

Later on he and Marjorie Gullan often used my 'Singing-games for Children' in the Morecambe Festivals, but it was another eighteen years before we met. Bertie and I had just produced our *Elephant in Arcady* at the Kingsway Theatre, with a wonderful cast divinely led by Irene Eisinger. In the first week of the run I had this unexpected letter.

Hotel York
Berners Street
London, W.1.
12th October 1938

Dear Eleanor Farjeon,

What a delicious dramatist you are; you are as good, as enchanting as Die Eisinger herself (and *doesn't* she take with both hands the chances you give her.)

My wife and I wallowed in Arcady last night: praises would be just an inclusive catalogue, so I will only say Thank You for everything. I do hope it will keep on until the next time we are in London.

I looked about in each entr'acte—so far as one could in dress-circle and foyer—for someone who looked like you: but I couldn't make up my mind if you might be one of them. (You certainly couldn't have been just any of them!)

We are here on our way home from Dalmatia (where we spent the Crisis), and must go off in a day or two (day uncertain yet); but, if we have to go off quickly and without a chance of seeing you, you will be first on our list when we see London again.

Many regards and thanks from us both.

Your years-old friend
Gordon Bottomley.

Before he left London I had tea with him and his wife. It seemed natural to find this calm-faced black-bearded poet reclining, rather than sitting up, in a deep armchair in the hotel lounge. Edward had portrayed him for me expending as little effort as possible on a chaise-longue outside The Sheiling. While we talked—of the play, of music, of children and speech-training, of poetry, and of Edward—he emptied the hotel sugar-basin, lump by lump.

'To conserve energy?' I asked.

He smiled blandly and crunched another lump.

I am glad I didn't miss this chance of seeing him. There

never was another. Our letters became still livelier after it. 'O, Nellinor Farjeon, Nellinor Farjeon', he begins in November 1939, when John Moore's life of Edward had just come out. He praises it, though he feels that the 'large pieces' from Helen's books embedded in the text present too different a focus from the biographer's. He would have preferred Moore 'presenting all from his own vision . . . but he has truly set the real Edward, as he lived and loved, before those who have not had the blessing and illumination of knowing him'.

§9

I spent the last week-end in November at High Beech. The journey from Liverpool Street was marked by a small adventure. I caught a non-corridor train which stopped once near London, and then ran without another stop to Loughton. There was the usual bustle of soldiers, but the station was not very crowded. I found an empty carriage, put my knapsack on the rack over the far corner seat away from the platform, and settled myself. A pretty young mother and her little girl got in; the child took a window-seat near the platform, and the mother sat beside her. At the last moment a small party of soldiers hustled by, glanced in, and hurried on; but just as the train began to move, one of them rushed back, flung open the door, and fell into the corner opposite the little girl. He grinned affably at his *vis-à-vis*, then at the pretty mother, and the train pulled out.

It was soon obvious that he wanted conversation. He was a big Australian, who should have been husky, but looked, in fact, gaunt and ill. The mother was pleasant but reserved, and changing his tactics, he began to talk to the child—or rather, through the child to the embarrassed mother. He was oncoming but not in the least offensive. The child answered him bashfully; the mother smiled but said as little as possible; and when the train made its single stop she said, 'Good day—we get out here'. He helped her with her suitcase, lifted the child down, and the pair disappeared from sight; into, I felt sure, another compartment. The soldier blocked the window until the train drew out. As soon as it was well away, he walked over to my end of the carriage, and said, 'Gurl! there's sumpin' I been wantin' to do ever since I got in. D'you mind?'

I said I didn't and hoped I wouldn't. To my relief he tugged a flask out of his hip pocket and gulped down a big swig of whisky. Then he offered the flask to me. 'Have one?'

'No, thank you,' I said amiably, 'I don't drink it.'

He put the flask back, sat down opposite me, leaned forward, and said very earnestly, 'Gurl!' (He slapped my knee with the back of his hand.) 'Gurl—I don't want you to think us Aussies is all larrikins. You won't, now, will you, gurl?'

I promised him, as earnestly, that I would not, and asked him what part of Australia he came from. Sydney, he said. What had he done there before the war? He had worked in the sewers. I played my strong card with larrikins from Down-under, and told him that though I had never been to his country my father had emigrated there in the 1850s, following the gold-rush from camp to camp, and having adventures without number. I did not have to invent the adventures, either; my father's stories were extremely exciting, and enlisted the soldier's interest. By the time I'd exhausted them a third of the journey was done, and we were practically larrikins together. Every now and then he took another swig. I kept it all very pally. Where was he going? To the station beyond Loughton, to say goodbye to the nuns in a hospital there. He had been sent back to Blighty with his inside torn out. He described his dreadful wound fully, and spoke with tears in his eyes of his nurses. He was returning to Sydney next week, and he couldn't go without saying goodbye to those good women. He was taking them presents.

His ghastly pallor was explained. I felt great sympathy for him, and rather liked him, but I wished he wouldn't swig his flask quite so often.

I asked about his family—had he any? Yes, a wife and two or three kids. 'I'll show you, gurl.' He pulled out a bursting pocket-book, and littered the seat beside him with snapshots and letters till he found what he wanted. I admired the children and asked their names. He had something else important I must see. He strewed the heterogeneous contents of his kitbag over the carriage: things he was taking home for trophies and souvenirs, loot, documents official and private, pitiful mementoes of an experience that would sear him when they were faded—ah! here at last was the bit of shell they'd dug out of his guts, other bits that he had picked up in the trenches, for his friends—'would you like a bit, gurl?' I spun out my questions. He wanted to shift the key, took another swig, was a little baffled, and began to fumble with his bag, looking morosely at his scattered junk. After one or two attempts to stow it back, he gave up.

'Aw!' He flung the bag into my lap, waving a large hand over the muddle on the seats. 'Purr 'em away, *purr* 'em away.' He emptied his flask.

I made the job last as long as I could. He watched me. There was still one station to go. At last everything was somehow stowed back in the bag. I gave him the pocket-book filled with his poor home life, and knew that the final swig had effected the change, that my larrikin's confused vision mistook me at last for a woman, no longer for the mate who had dug gold and ranged the Bush with him, and worked in the sewers of Sydney.

'Gurl! I tell you what.' He leaned forward from his corner and pinned my knees with his. 'You goin' to Loughton, I go on to the next—tomorrow you walk halfway an' I walk halfway, an' we'll meet.'

'I'm sorry, I can't. I'm staying outside Loughton, with a friend who's soon going to France. I'm sure you'll see that I can't take time off on a short visit.'

He wanted to get angry, but didn't know how to yet. 'Well then, gurl, give me a kiss before we part.'

'No,' I smiled. 'I'm sorry.'

'What, not one kiss from them ruby lips?'

'Not one.'

Now he did begin to get ugly. 'Grrr!' he growled, 'I could get better kisses than yours from the gurls in France.'

'I'm sure you could,' I agreed. 'Do you want to go back?'

He growled again. The time for words was over. He had my hands firmly, and the rest of me hemmed in the corner. I knew I mustn't make any movement of escape, but I wasn't frightened, and that baffled him too.

The train slowed up. Porters' voices called Loughton.

'My station!' I glanced out of the window. 'There's my friend. Would you help me down with my knapsack?'

Drunk as he was, old custom was too strong for him. A train on the run was one thing, but no larrikin could keep a gurl pinned in her seat with the train at rest. He stood up and heaved down my knapsack sulkily. I shook his hand, and said 'Good luck!' Then I jumped down from the carriage and ran to meet Edward, who really was coming along the platform in his officer's tunic. I suppose I was panting a little, for he glanced inquiringly as he took my knapsack from me. 'Nothing much, it's all right.' My larrikin had disappeared from the window. Poor man with his guts torn out because of this war. Who could blame anyone for anything? I didn't want to talk about him, and Edward asked no questions. We talked of other things on the long walk to the new home, a very dull walk through Loughton to begin with, but the last half was good, uphill through the spreading trees, now almost bare.

Yes, the Forest was good, but the house itself was bad; it was dismal and poorly-planned, and felt—what indeed it was— too temporary to settle in. It would have taken months of happy living to give it the heart and soul of a home; the few snatched days which Helen and Edward shared in it were not enough to grow roots for her when he was gone. Edward was restless, his centre had shifted, his military quarters had more meaning for him than this unfamiliar rather ramshackle dwelling. The move had left all sorts of jobs to be attended to; he was busy with them as he would have been at Steep, with his thoughts on the little study up the hill. But now, while he chopped a woodstack for his family against the winter, we all knew that he would not burn it with them, and while he busied himself his mind was on France. His mood was a little perverse. A trifle of talk at a meal lingers in my memory. Somehow or other *Tristram Shandy* came into it. Edward praised it as one of the greatest books in the language, but Helen was prejudiced against it, and exclaimed vehemently, 'I can't *bear* it!'

Edward said shortly, 'No woman is able to understand Tristram Shandy.'

I protested, 'But I read it again and again.'

'No woman *ought* to be able to understand Tristram Shandy,' he said, still more shortly.

It was one of the moments when to laugh might have been the wrong thing; I hope he smiled, at least, in recollection at his own perverseness.

When I got back to London I ordered a large kit-bag he had asked me to get for him, and suggested a lined waistcoat to follow, as a gift from myself. He acknowledged it on a postcard followed at once by a letter.

Postcard postmark 2 December 1916

Friday

I go to Lydd on Sunday. My address will be

2nd Lieut. ——
R.G.A.
Lydd   Kent.

I got the bag and everything, thank you. So it is still the interlude. Did you all arrive safe? I hope so.   E. T.

Postmark 3 December 1916

Saturday   High Beech

My dear Eleanor,   Thank you for the shadow of the waistcoat. And the typescript of 'The Trumpet' which I have copied. 'The Child in the Orchard' I had. I sent a card last night saying the telegram came yesterday while I was out. It was just a little too early—Sunday. I shall just have time to fill that bag. It is like a big stocking. I doubt if I shall ever want more room. For Lydd I really don't want nearly all.—I am out of sorts with everything except my job now. I am sorry if it made this week worse than middling. Are you really better at all? Bronwen is more cheerful today knitting while Baba plays about in her room. They send their loves with mine.

Yours ever
Edward Thomas

Then came the letter which told the news we dreaded, and he desired.

Officers' Mess
Tin Town
Lydd   Kent

7.xii.16.

My dear Eleanor,   Thank you for your letter—the one for East-away. This is only to tell you just a few facts. One is that they asked for volunteers to go straight out to Batteries in France and I made sure of it by volunteering. Don't let Helen know. Of course I may not be wanted. I may not pass the doctor. If I do I shall have some leave first. If I go to a Battery in England I may go straight there from Lydd. Thank you, the bag was all right as far as you or I could tell by looking at it. But it turns out too clumsy and will get very rough usage by being pulled about along the ground &c., so I must find a substitute.

Hooper is here and in the same hut. But as he comes in at night as I am going to bed, and I am going out in the morning as he gets up, I don't see much of him. Also he is in a different mess where he spends most of his time. He says he is going to fail.

I shan't come home this week end. I shall just walk over and see Conrad, who is only 12 miles away.

We have beautiful clear weather and for a few days (at any rate) I can enjoy this flat shingle and the long rows of low huts &c enormously. Lydd itself a few 100 yds away is beautiful—an old group round a very tall church tower and a line of elm trees, the only tall things in all the marsh at all near to us. I find though that nobody else likes it as much.

Goodbye. I shall see you if I get home after Saturday week when the exam is over, and I shall try to see Bertie too.

Yours ever
Edward Thomas.

The news of his going went round among our friends. 'He won't come back you know,' said Arnold Bax. It was what many of us felt.

Those who never knew him, in whose thoughts Edward may live as a man who died, unfulfilled, too soon, I would ask to read again attentively the last paragraph of the letter which came to us as the forerunner of his death. It is not a startling paragraph, and has none of the special beauties which he turned into poems when he stopped writing prose; but it expresses the daily bread of his life while he lived.

'I like what I see,' said W. J. Ibbett on his deathbed. This old poet and scholar, of whom I shall write something more one day, uttered these words when he was lying bedridden, past writing and reading, facing a window filled with the branches of a tree. Birds came and went in it, weather moved in it, it changed with the seasons.

'Keep your senses fresh,' was Professor John Earle's first advice to his children in the nursery of his Somerset rectory. One of them took, remembered, and lived by it for seventy-nine years.

Edward lived thirty-nine years. In all of them he kept his senses fresh, and liked what he saw. He saw more than anybody I ever knew, and he saw it day and night. The seasons and the weather never failed him. It made him wonderful to walk with, and to talk with, and not to talk with. And when he was alone—as I think he loved best to be, except when Robert Frost increased what he saw and smelt and heard and felt and tasted—he walked with *himself*, with his eyes and his ears and his nostrils, and his long legs, and his big hands, in shape so strong, in touch so sensitive. These things were the continuous life of his thirty-nine years. The years might have numbered more, but soldiering did not rob him of what he liked. He could not live a day in the open air without being given something to 'enjoy enormously'; clear weather, flat shingle, a line of trees, the tallness of a church tower on a marsh, even a row of huts—he liked what he saw. And knew that nobody else liked it as much as he did.

R.A. Mess,
Tintown,

11 xii 16   Lydd.

My dear Eleanor,   Not much news yet, except that Hooper had to clear out at short notice—to be ready for France by the 15th. Of which the only advantage is that it doesn't matter how badly he did in his exam. 5 men of my class suddenly went too today, before the end of the course. But it seems quite likely I shall go, with a man I have got on with quite well, to a Battery not yet fully trained. If I do I may stay on here with no leave or at most just Sunday, so that I can't promise to go to Bertie's on Sunday. If I do have leave I might see you for a moment on Saturday afternoon. But then I shall not know till the last moment whether I can come or by what train. So it is not much use. But if I do feel sure I will suggest something.

Of course TINTOWN means a town of tin, just tin huts and not nearly as ugly as you might think—in fact not at all.

I saw Conrad and in fact I stayed the night. Then he drove me back in the rain. The marsh is lovely in the rain. You can see so far to the hills and every tree is fine, but especially the Lydd trees and the church sticking up through the top. I had been inoculated again so I couldn't walk much.

I can imagine Clifford's party. I am so glad, though, that I never actually saw it. I am sure I am more at home at Tintown.

I must have been very crude if I left you a chance of thinking yourself $\frac{1}{1000000}$th responsible for the bag. But I don't believe you did. It is a nuisance though. It would have been worse if I had had to go overseas very suddenly.

No news. But I believe Bronwen's better—but have not heard for days now.

In every way one gets to feel nearer the real thing here. Not only the sound of the guns at the ranges either.

I wonder how Hooper will do. I believe he will make a good officer. Possibly even he will make a gunner when it comes to practice. He hates lectures and theory a great deal more than I do, which is very hard to do. I shan't see him for an age now.

Goodbye. You are seeing Mother soon aren't you? I don't know when I shall, but I shall try to on Saturday for a moment.

Yours ever
Edward Thomas.

I went to Balham to see Granny Thomas for two reasons. One was to see her. It is enough reason for seeing anyone you love. The other was to make a cake.

My passionate cooking days had not begun. My ignorance was abysmal, in spite of Helen's example. But at least I no longer tried to grind coffee-beans in the mincing machine, and whenever I hovered on the fringe of another cook's kitchen I was like a moth trying to get inside the lamp-glass. Granny

Thomas, like Helen, was a Cook. And she made, as all Grannies should, the perfect plum cake. I had been to tea with her and eaten it; and she volunteered to let me make one under her eye. I said it must be made for Edward at Christmas, and must have *everything* in it, almonds and cherries as well as all the usual fruits; and though she must tell me how, and watch and warn me at every step of the way, I must be able to say it was entirely the work of my hands (as Rose, in Miss Alcott's *Eight Cousins*, made the loaf of bread for her uncle). When baking-day came I went early to Balham, so that the cake could have full time to cool on the sieve after it came out of the oven. Then I carried it home, and next day packed it for Edward.

Postcard postmark 15 December 1916
Friday   Lydd

This is only to say it is pretty certain I shall not have leave this week end or at Xmas. I don't know yet what is going to happen. I have just had my examination and been inoculated, and neither quite agrees with me. In fact I only write to ask you not to expect me yet. I hope the cake is all right, that is as good as it smells. I feel almost ———— enough to write. But solitude is a little too cold here.

                                                                E. T.

A letter followed which seemed to kill all hope of Christmas at home for him and Helen, of my getting a glimpse of him coming or going. What were the childish things he had put away? What were the fifteen lines he wrote, but did not send?

                                        244th Siege Battery
                                            R.A. Mess,
                                            Tintown,
16 xii 16   Lydd

My dear Eleanor, This address tells you something. We hung about all this morning waiting for our fates. It was 2 before we heard. I and two others of the Trowbridge squad are posted to this battery which is now I believe about half way through its training here at Lydd. It may go out within a month: and may meantime shift to Salisbury Plain. Ultimately it will have four 9.2 inch howitzers which is just what I wanted. We are seven officers—a Captain, a full lieut., and 5 2nd lieuts. There are about 150 men, and we are to start straight away taking charge of them and on some subjects instructing them. Under the new rule only 15 or 16 can be away at Xmas, and it can hardly include me. But I should have 6 days leave before going over. I did wish to be home—when I was certain to be in England—for Christmas.

Give my love to your mother and Bertie and Clifford.

This is only just a word to tell you I really have at last put away childish things. Last night by the way, after I wrote that card to you, I was very much alone for a time (till a dog began to kill a cat outside the hut) and wrote 15 lines. But I doubt if I shall do anything with them.

Yours ever
Edward Thomas.

And two days later, on a postcard marked December 18th, this:

After all, I believe I may get away and see you on Friday. Isn't it—or won't it—be luck?

E. T.

But still there seemed no certainty of Christmas leave, and Helen's heart was aching in High Beech, with the saddest Christmas in prospect of her life.

Then the small miracle happened, the unexpectedly radiant Christmas which Helen describes in *World Without End*. Within a few days of the 25th I saw Viola Meynell, between whom and myself nothing remained unspoken. Before I left her Wilfrid Meynell came to me, and said in his kindest voice, 'A friend who prefers to remain anonymous allows me at this time of year to administer a little fund for writers to whom it may be useful. I believe Mrs. Thomas has special expenses just now, and I would like you to undertake to send her this, if you think she will not mind.' 'This' was a cheque for twenty pounds. I sent it joyfully, with Wilfrid's message, and had from her a doubly joyful reply, for by the same post she had the news that Edward would, after all, be given leave to spend Christmas with his family at High Beech. She rushed into town to spend her cheque on everything that could make the day glorious: good fare of all sorts, presents all round, everything Edward might still require for France, and a little secret tree to surprise Baba. She asked me to convey her joy to Wilfrid Meynell, who had delicately made me the go-between. For a long time I suspected that this delicacy concealed his identity as the anonymous friend. One of Wilfrid's habits was to walk about London after dark with a pocketful of half-crowns, which were bestowed quietly and without question on the poor people he met. It was easy to think that the cheque was his own gift, but Viola has told me since that the anonymous donor existed, and knew he could not leave his fund in better hands than her father's.

I had sent to High Beech my own budget of presents to add to the gaiety, and with Edward's I enclosed as a Christmas card a new London-Town Nursery Rhyme:

ST MARY AXE

Saint Mary, ax, Saint Mary, ax,
  Saint Mary, ax your fill,
Saint Mary, ax whatever you lacks
  And you shall have your will.—
O bring me a Rose, a Christmas Rose
  To climb my window-sill.—
You shall have your Rose when Heaven snows,
  Saint Mary, sleep until.

Postmark 27 December 1916
Christmas   High Beech

My dear Eleanor,   I am bloated with your presents. But that is not their fault. The apples were and are delicious, and the poem is I think one of your very happiest. Why do I like the last line so much? What does the 'Until' remind me of? Or is it just that it reminds me of something else that is good? It has been an entirely lovely day of sun on melting snow, and we have been out in it half the time in batches, I in each batch. If you had been here we should have been more Christmassy, but I thought it was absurd to ask. I am going to see Mother tomorrow and then—'home' I was going to say.

Nothing, not a word, from the Frosts. Did you hear?

There is nothing wrong with the handkerchief either that I should leave it to the end. It must be the end. The Christmas tree is afoot. It is 5.30, and Baba has no suspicions. Goodbye. I hope we shall meet next Christmas time.

Yours ever
Edward Thomas

I should think Maeterlinck or somebody lived in this palace. I thought I was writing on notepaper.

He had picked up a sheet of what did indeed look like super cream-laid paper, but on the other side was a picture of a building, half Abbey, half dwelling, which might have been Ste. Wandrille.

This letter must have been written on Boxing Day, and posted next day on his way back to Lydd. From there he wrote again on the same evening, after finding the parcel I had sent to Lydd when I thought he would be spending his Christmas in Tintown—so sudden was the blessed leave which took him home.

R.A. Mess,
Tintown,
Lydd

27 xii 16

My dear Eleanor,   I only found your cake this morning. It is very good. If you and a cup of tea would appear it would be excellent—only of course I shouldn't mind whether it was or not. I am going to send you in exchange some verses I made on Sunday. It is really Baba who speaks, not I. Something she felt put me on to it. But I am afraid I am meddling now. A real poem would include and imply all these things I am writing, or so I fancy.

I have been both drilling and lecturing today. I am glad they are going to try me as an instructor. But I had to use a greasy door instead of a blackboard.

It is curious how I feel no anxiety or trouble as soon as I am back here, though I was so very glad to be at home.

I will just copy out the verses and send this off. Goodbye. Oh, the Christmas tree was a great success. Baba went pale with surprise as she came into the room and found it. Thank *you*.

Yours ever
Edward Thomas

Out in the dark, over the snow
The fallow fawns invisible go
With the fallow doe;
And the winds blow
Fast as the stars are slow.

Stealthily the dark haunts round
And, when a lamp goes, without sound
At a swifter bound
Than swiftest hound,
Arrives, and all else is drowned;

And I and star and wind and deer
Are in the dark together,—near,
Yet far,—and fear
Drums on my ear
In that sage company drear.

How weak and little is the light,
All the universe of sight,
Love and delight,
Before the might,
If you love it not, of night.

1917

SOMETHING new appears in the letters Edward wrote from France, when he began the experience of danger shared in common with men for whom he was responsible. He gives no hint of the trust these men had in him and the affection they felt for him (plain in the things they wrote and said after his death), but he must have been aware of it, and it must have satisfied him. It makes the 1917 letters a little different from the rest.

The letters that cover so closely the last four years of Edward's life are a continuity. I have not tried to choose among them. Something would go if they were pruned and edited. They run like a clue through his complicated nature—the Cretan Labyrinth was not more tortuous—and though the thread is often knotted and ravelled, it is always true in fibre, twisted with nothing that is second-rate.

As for the man in the centre of the maze, how can he be conveyed? To speak of Edward's qualities of mind, his extreme sensitivity, his humours, his power to hurt, his scorn of humbug, his love of natural things, his personal beauty, tells nothing at all to those who had not 'the blessing and illumination of knowing him'. Bottomley's words have full meaning only for those in whose lives he had lived. His death broke James Guthrie's heart. 'Even to think of him makes him as present as if he were entering the room,' Walter de la Mare wrote in 1953; adding, like a sigh, 'How I wish he were.'

But even these words, left by men who loved him, tell nothing of the man they loved—Edward Thomas who *knew*

239

that Hamlet was written for him—except that he drew the un-
qualified hearts of his friends, as Hamlet drew Horatio's.

                                        R.A. Mess
                                TIN   Hut   Town
                                              Lydd

                                           3   i   17
My dear Eleanor

        I can't write much now. We are shooting every day and
sometimes twice a day (16 rounds each time), the reason is we
mobilize on the 13th and go to Codford on Salisbury Plain and
thence the end of the month overseas.

        I owe you a card and a letter, but I can't repay you. I just don't
feel inclined to say anything but goodbye. If I get leave—as I may
do on Saturday—I will surely see you. I wish I could see Bertie
too. But I shall have very little time. Perhaps you and I could go
and see him. I will suggest it when I know.

        I did hear from Frost with a poem, but no other news. He was
thinking somewhat imperially.

        We leave here on the 13th after that 244 Siege By

                                Codford
                                nr Warminster
will find me I suppose.

        By the way, the noise of the guns doesn't trouble me at all, at
20 yards distance. Also I have a very good pair of field glasses and
it is a pleasure to observe with them. Next week we shall do some
revolver shooting.

        Goodbye. My love to your Mother.

                                        Yours ever
                                        Edward Thomas.

P.S.   Your letter came while I was waiting to hear about leave.
(I have heard nothing yet). Thank you so much for typing those
lines and I wish you could have liked the 3rd verse, because, do
you know, I like it best. And I do care two pins, too, though now
it looks more than ever as if I shall not begin writing again for
some time. All my evenings now are spent in measuring angles
and distances on the map, and preparing for the next day's shoot.
It is late now and I have almost a headache with the finicking work.
Goodbye.

The date for Edward's last leave was fixed immediately after this letter, and on January 4th he wrote again.

My dear Eleanor   I expect to be tomorrow night at 13 Rusham Rd and go home on Saturday. Could I see Bertie and Joan also if I came over on Saturday at lunch time? If so send me a word to Rusham Rd and I will try to do whatever you suggest. I must stay at Rusham Rd till about noon on Saturday and must get home not long after dark.

Goodbye. Yours ever
Edward Thomas

I would go straight to Bertie's if you liked.

This was the last time Bertie and Joan saw him. But I was to go on Monday the 6th to High Beech, for one day and night of his leave. That evening and the next morning passed almost like any other evening and morning I had so often spent with him and Helen and the children. The Christmas tree and decorations were still about, I was shown the presents, and while Helen made supper, Edward, as so often, bathed Baba in front of the fire, singing Welsh songs while he dried her. 'The Bells of Aberdovey' lives in my ears in his grave hummed tones. After supper, when the children were in bed, we sat and talked as usual, of poetry, and persons, and Edward's forthcoming book of poems, which I and John Freeman were to see through the press for him. One of the persons we spoke of was Kenneth Hooper. Edward was hoping that they would go to France together, as they were being drafted about the same time. While we chatted, there was no sense of this being the last night; Helen kept her bravely smiling face, and it was still a continuation, not an ending. Presently she went upstairs to see to the bedrooms. I said good night to Edward and followed her, leaving him to do the last things in the house. But in my room at the head of the stairs, I knew it was an ending. I wished I had managed to break through the wave of shyness which had kept me from kissing him good night downstairs. Strong as it was, and for me so very deep, our friendship had remained undemonstrative from beginning to end. Now, as he came up the stairs, I opened my door, and said again 'Good night, Edward,' and lifted my face. We kissed, he said 'Good night', and went on, and that was the real goodbye.

Next morning after breakfast he went part of the way to Loughton Station with me, walking down the hill through Epping Forest to the foot, where we shook hands as usual. He was returning that night to Lydd, but would shortly be passing through town for the last time on his way back to Codford. 'I might see you in London in three days', he said as we parted. We turned once to wave to each other.

> 244 Siege Battery
> 15 Camp
> Codford Salisbury
> 13 i 17

My dear Eleanor   I could not see you in town. Now I have to hang on here till Monday simply as a matter of form—to hand over our premises and stores to a new battery. Then I go to Codford and this is the address. I have plenty of time, but I must walk when I am not wanted. It is cold and everybody has gone that I know. Perhaps I can write later. Goodbye and will you give my love to Clifford. His address always eludes me when I have a chance of paying a flying visit.

> Yours ever
> Edward Thomas.

> 244 Siege Battery
> 15 Camp
> Codford, Salisbury
> 17 i 17

My dear Eleanor,   You will have heard from me by this. Perhaps I could have seen you again, as I could have seen my Mother again. But I thought I would not.

I shan't take Shelley. Some Shakespeare, the Prayer Book, and 'The Sentimental Journey' is what I have with me. It will probably be all I want.

I have had some beautiful walks here. There is little to do. I have also taken the man 2 fine marches. Tonight we came back slap over the plain in the dark and only went astray 200 yards, which would not have happened had I been alone.

To judge by other batteries we shall leave next week.

I can do anything but write now. I could enjoy a ballet but I couldn't write about it. We found such a nice inn at Chilmark tonight and Smith suddenly played something rapid and clever that was quite suitable in the dark.

Goodbye.

Yours ever
Edward Thomas.

P.S. If John Freeman sends you the proofs of my verses will you revise them after him? He is at

29, Weighton Rd
Anerley
S.E.

Edward did not live to see his poems in print, or read their praises by some of the very men who had rejected them when they were sent out under the name of Eastaway. John Freeman and I became friends over the production of the book, and I understood why Edward felt affection for this quiet poet, this 'sort of angel, you know'.

Between Edward's last two letters, when all chance was gone of seeing him I stayed for a week at Elsa and Arnold Bax's house in Marlow. It was a week of very thick snow, weather that in England and France held back the spring till April. We walked in the snow between the snowfalls, and at home in the comfortable house sat round the fire and talked, breaking off for music. Elsa sang in her fine voice, and Arnold improvised gloriously—no other musician has ever given me so much pleasure on a piano played in a room.

Very early one morning I slipped away while the house was still asleep and set out in the snow for Penn. With my stick and map, in my thickest boots and warmest woollens, I disappeared into a heavenly solitude. I walked in woods where no one seemed ever to have walked before, only the claw-prints of birds traced hieroglyphics on the surface of the snow into which my boots sank ankle-deep. The day was restorative. Only Edward's company could have made it better. I sent him an account of it, and of the inn I had lunch at in Penn.

243

On January 20th word came of the birth of Bertie's and Joan's first child, and I went back to London to share the family joy.

> *Postmark* 26 Jan 17
> Codford

My dear Eleanor,   I am glad Joan and the baby are all right.   But this is only to say we are all leaving on Monday.   I might go before but probably not.   The address will be simply

> 244 Siege Battery
> B.E.F.
> France

We are packing to send off most things tomorrow.   The guns and advance party leave on Saturday.

Frost and I walked to Penn once and had a drink in a little inn there when he lived at Beaconsfield.   He doesn't write, but I have had a copy of his new poems from Haines, and they are very good, though never better or different from 'North of Boston'.

I have asked Freeman to send you the proofs.

Goodbye.   We have lost our captain.   He is in hospital and I don't know quite what will happen.   The 2nd in Command is taking us out anyhow.

It is cold.   But I suppose we may be getting towards the end of Winter rather quickly.   It won't be possible to be warm now.

> Yours ever
> Edward Thomas.

There was only one more letter from England, written from Arthur Ransome's house in Tisbury, where Ivy Ransome was taking care of Baba for Helen, and Edward, being so near, was able to spend his last night in England with the smallest of his family.

> *Postmark* 29 i 17
> Manor Farm
> Hatch
> Near Tisbury
> Wiltshire

My dear Eleanor,   I did write to you the night before last but had the sense to destroy it because it was doleful.   The dirty east wind, I being lame and unable to get about, had brought me down rather.

But yesterday I walked over here to see Baba and the Downs in the cold sun were so beautiful that I didn't worry till I got here about the blisters that somebody else's shoes gave me. Now I have got somehow to get back. Probably I shall hire a bicycle. We start tomorrow morning. It seems certain we are for the Somme, but how directly we don't know yet of course. I have my hands full as I not only have to manage the mess and the cook but have to keep the accounts and pay the bills. How much better to be digging at High Beech or Billingshurst than paying 2d a lb for potatoes.

I was glad to hear Raymond Jeremy was safe, as I suppose he and his Mother desire it. I should like to send my love to him through Harry. I hope Harry is better and your elder niece—the younger can't be better, I conclude.

It is nice here and a fine day but I am chiefly occupied (though quite unconsciously I assure you) in being quite patient and not really thinking of tomorrow though it will just flit through my head.

Are you well? God bless you and your Mother.

Yours ever
Edward Thomas.

Mrs. Ransome admires your London Rhymes extremely, I mean very much indeed.

The reference to Billingshurst marks a new turn in my life. My brother Joe and his wife wanted to live in the country and Fan had discovered Gillman's Cottage in the middle of farmland in Billingshurst, set adorably in its own apple-orchard among cornfields. I paid part of their rent of twenty pounds a year for one of the bedrooms, to which I was to come and go as I pleased. The cottage was not ready yet, but the rooms were being newly whitewashed, furniture collected and bought for a song locally, and seed potatoes ordered. The garden and orchard were in going order, kept so by the tenant who had just moved out to enjoy the conveniences of a new and ugly cottage on the road. Edward and Helen had taught me all I knew of cottage life, and I had much to tell him of the beginnings of my own adventure, in my letters to France. All his were addressed to Fellows Road, but many of them were read by candlelight within the wattle-and-daub and under the grey oak beams of Gillman's Cottage.

The first letter from France, written in pencil.

Wednesday 31. i. 17

My dear Eleanor   I have time to write now, but if I had less time I should have more to write about. There is little to do and still less I can do, because of my ankles. Practically all I do is censoring letters. I try to rest my feet, but the place is extraordinarily uncomfortable and crowded. If I were able to get about I shouldn't notice it, as there is a big town and harbour close by.

We await orders to go up country. The place is just a clearing house or junction, and all there is to do (besides completing our stores) is to go route marches. If we stay more than a day or 2 I am sure to run into somebody. Yesterday I met one old Artist I had known moderately well.

The worst of this hanging about is that everybody gets on ones nerves, or my nerves. They all worry me and I imagine I worry them, as they spend all the time possible out in the town and leave me to my own mercies.

So far all I have done when I have been alone in this little crowded room, is censoring letters and writing them, and sometimes looking at last month's Sketch or so. I can't read, I doubt even if I can write—I am practically certain I can't, except a brief diary. I was interrupted by a boy going through a list of games and asking if I played any of them, which I didn't.

I had better not go on with this negative news. Tea in —— cost me 2 frs; for I did take the train in yesterday and did my ankle no good by it.

The crossing was easy, and the departure and arrival beautiful and unforgettable. There were some cold slow hours to be passed and still are. I daresay what makes me not very cheerful is all the things to be seen and noticed and commented on and just undergone. I shall know more what I am seeing and feeling later on.

We may move soon or late. We do not know. And I may not receive any letters till we have moved up into position. There is a notion that that position will be midway between the two I thought of. I can't say more.

Tears doesn't rhyme with care, does it? So I shan't make it—but let me know when the verses begin to arrive. It would be a relief to have them here to correct, but nothing reaches me at present. I wonder would you make sure that the dedication

TO ROBERT FROST

doesn't get left out.

I had your Goodbye just before I left. No more goodbyes now. I shall begin to look ahead perhaps, if I ever do look ahead again. Long it is since I did so. Yours ever

Edward Thomas.

'Tears doesn't rhyme with care, does it?' Camouflaged by the reference to his own verses, he had wrapped up the troops' movements beyond decoding by the enemy, should his letter go astray. At the same time he had written to Helen, 'What do you think of "Armed Men in Tears" as the title of my next book?' When we compared our letters Helen said, 'I think it's a very *bad* title, don't you, Eleanor?' I said I did—but that he was telling each of us, in a different way, that he was going to Armentières.

Feb 10

My dear Eleanor, Will you send me a village almanac and a portrait of Queen Victoria to hang on the walls of our billet and a Family Bible for the window table? Otherwise we lack nothing here. We have crept slowly, uncomfortably, but to me amusingly up to our fighting position, often cold, never certain of the next 24 hours, picknicking, pigging it, and arrived at last yesterday afternoon. We officers are in a farmhouse alongside a main road leading to a cathedral town 2 miles off. We are warm but have no other luxuries. We are part of the target of the German artillery 3 miles or so to the east of us; their shellholes are common behind us and the shells rattle our windows frequently, while friendly batteries shoot over our heads. We have become a fairly jolly party.

The weather is continually very cold but clear and not windy and the nights are glorious.

My work has been odd jobs of selecting billets for the men

(mostly barns) and putting the men in, superintending jobs, signing orders etc. till today we had to go into the trenches to examine some observation posts and see what could be seen from them. I was with an officer from another battery and did some interesting work with maps. We got disturbed by trench mortars, but were not sniped at. I am fairly pleased at not being made at all uncomfortable sitting in a ruin within easy range of the Huns. I could not see a living thing, only snow, posts and barbed wire, a dark shadowline marking the enemy trench, a line of trees and houses along a road behind. The only men we saw were around corners of the trenches as we passed, and there was one dead man lying like a monument covered with sacking. I enjoyed the exercise, the work with map and fieldglass, the scene, the weather, and the sense of being able to do a new job. I am going again tomorrow and then I shall have to take our own officers round. I foresee I shall be let in for a good deal of this kind of work.

Altogether I have never seen or done anything out of doors more exciting or interesting and not much more pleasant.

But   Nobody has had a letter or parcel since leaving England and I believe I am trying harder than I know not to be impatient.

Give my love to your Mother and Bertie and Joan and Maitland.

> Yours ever
> Edward Thomas

I think this letter shows clearly why Edward was so excellent and so contented and so greatly liked a soldier. Not that any aspect of war itself made him so, but that he was completely suited to the job required of him among men of all sorts for whom he was responsible: fitted for it by years spent in the open air on all roads in all weathers, of field-work and observation, of mixing naturally with uncomplicated people, of doing practical things in the elements he was at home in: knowing that he was doing all this well, and more than 'fairly pleased' that, without too much fear, he could enjoy in war-time France the sort of things he had enjoyed in peace-time England.

Feb 13

My dear Eleanor,   This is my idlest morning. It is sunny and mild, but I have got the chill that everyone has had in turn and I shall not go out till I must, which will probably be this afternoon, for

we have a shoot on then. My servant is a gem. He is a carpenter
from Oxford named Taylor, rather slow but extraordinarily good-
humoured, and thoughtful and ingenious. He washes and darns
for me and pillages wood to keep our stove going and in between
he keeps up a slow stream of nice rustic remarks. He wont lose
anything if he can help it. He is the most devoted thing I have met
since we lost our dog. He mutters 'They put upon good nature,
dont they, Sir' but though I tell him not to listen to anyone but me
he goes on being put upon without complaint. This is a fine hilly
country with trees only on the roads and in a few woods. The
villages lie along the slopes above the streams, with tiled roofs and
mud in brick walls, and churches with towers and short spires
something like Sussex, but often shell-bitten. There are hardly any
hedges. You see nothing yet but snow and field telephone posts
and barbed wire entanglements. No cattle out, no sheep. Then the
straight main road lined with young trees leads past our window to
the town and cathedral. There we are to be in an orchard on the
outskirts. Looking out of the window we see our dug-outs just
across the road, beyond that a short slope of snow and posts and the
trees lining a road on another hill a mile off. It is a somewhat
dangerous position, but all the shells fall fairly well behind us,
being aimed at a battery some hundreds of yards away. They
had one of their guns hit yesterday, but the men were all in cover
and no one was hurt. You could bury several horses in the shell
holes. But I don't think anybody is seriously troubled when the
firing rattles our windows, though whether we shall be less or more
troubled as time goes on remains to be seen. It is not what is called
a healthy spot, but as these buildings are isolated they are hardly
worth making a target of and only an accident will demolish them.
It is nice to have sun without rain, but it would not matter which
the weather was if I had no chill and my boots were a good old pair
that didn't make me feel as if my feet were artificial wood. There is
not much traffic on the road, but small parties do use it and despatch
riders and a farm cart or two go along. I haven't had the curiosity
to go into the town yet and have only seen the cathedral with
fieldglasses. Partly it is the lack of perfectly comfortable boots.
Partly, of course, one does not stroll here, but only moves with an
object. Do you know I have not had a letter—nor has anyone—
since leaving England, so that I am even more egotistic than usual,
as I am the only person that I really know exists, apart from these
strangers round me. We are strangers who just talk insincerely

and humorously when we are not talking shop. But we have come
to a modus vivendi. T—— and I get on when it is pure talk
between us two, but he is intolerable to live with, being dismal,
timid and clumsy. I should like to know you were well and what
you were doing. I suppose letters will begin some day. And how
are your nieces, and do you ever see Maitland? I have to admit I
have joined the majority against T——. He is the most unpleasant presence imaginable in our midst. He was born with the
most dismal face and voice as ever was, and no doubt he is not happy
in this frivolous coarse crowd. I think perhaps we are not too cruel
to forgive him for that. But then he has never mixed with men and
never learns day by day and is never helpful except with a horrible
suffering sad look and manner as if this were the last day. We can
perhaps forgive it but we can't forget it. He hurts us and we hurt
him—only his hurting us is no satisfaction to him as our hurting
him is to us. I used to think I was dismal till now.—And perhaps I
sound like it still, so I will be off. In fact I have just found it is
12 and not 11, I have to take a party along at 12.30.

> Yours ever
> Edward Thomas.

This letter had been written on my birthday. For his on
March 3rd I ordered a boxful of tuck from Fortnum and
Mason, including a good supply of ginger, one of his weak-
nesses. He did not know this was on the way when he wrote
his next.

Feb 21

My dear Eleanor,   Your letter has just found me out in —— I
am right in the town now, temporarily (I hope) on the headquarters
staff of the Group which our battery is under. I don't know why I
am transferred except the little Adjutant here is away and an officer
was wanted in his place. I hate office work, but so far I have avoided
most of it and just go about with the Colonel on supervise jobs such as
the present one of moving into a new billet—a fine modern mansion
in the new quarter. We could have a room apiece if we liked. Our
own guns all round us are the chief annoyance at present.

Well, you are unlucky to have influenza again. How do you do
it? I only hope you will have forgotten you had it by the time this
arrives. Perhaps you are at High Beech.

My proofs sound as if they would be perfect. Thank you ever so much for reinstating that line in 'Lob' and separating 'When he should laugh' from its neighbour. I shall begin reading again when the book arrives. For a week I haven't read a Sonnet a day. I couldn't think of writing, or so it seems. Except letters, that is, and a very brief diary.

Do you remember one PERTWEE who compiled anthologies? An officer was boasting of having a literary man under him and that is who it was. My Colonel insists on calling me Beach Thomas. By the way he thinks because I am a writer that I might be able to write a diplomatic letter to a Town Mayor. He seems to think the chief thing in writing is to make grammatical sentences.

Now I am left alone at dusk in the old billet, now empty, to hang on to the telephone till they can get through to the new billet. It would be annoying to have to hang on all night. You will chuckle cruelly at the idea of me at the telephone.—I believe you are going to bring out a book of parodies now. The line 'The greyness of the twilight and myself' is, I believe, very just although impossible.

Oh, how I wish I could hear Raymond Jeremy. I am glad he is C3 if he doesn't mind. I remember now that one of his ears is wrong. That April with Bronwen and Mervyn at his house by the sea and then going on to Ledington was—something I am not going to talk about. But here's the telephone. They are through. And now we are in the new place with about 4 candles between us to light a score of big rooms and corridors, one of which is about 100 ft by 20 ft. It is amusing.

The Colonel is largely concerned about the cellar in case we are strafed. I say we, but I don't like to think I am staying here away from the battery for good. It would mean a new address. As it is I am dependent on 244's charity for sending my letters over.

Goodbye in case I cannot add to this before tomorrow's post.

Yours ever
Edward Thomas

I had to miss the post because I had not an envelope left. There isn't anything to say. It is another dull wet day and so cold in this chilly decent house that is only fit for the sun. Nothing can be done by artillery on such a day. If we get many more such it will be some time before anything happens. I got off for the afternoon to warm

my feet by walking up to 244. They are 2½ miles off. They are
everyone out. But here comes Horton, I think. I wish you were
well again.   Yours ever   Edward Thomas.

Two Pertwee anthologies had come to Edward in consecutive years among the heterogeneous volumes of verse and
poetry sent to him for review. The first, he informed me with
great gravity, was called 'The Humorous Reciter'. The
second, he announced with still greater gravity, was 'The
Very Humorous Reciter'.

Feb 25

My dear Eleanor,   While I was dining with 244 last night your
letter of the 10th arrived. Thank you. But no parcels at all have
reached me yet. By the way, never send tobacco, I get so much in
rations that I hardly need what I brought out. But I get no ginger.

My ills have disappeared except cold feet in this cold great house.
I am cold indoors all day. But out of doors I get too warm, especially today which has been mild and languid. So I think I was tired
with walking 2¾ miles up to 244 to tea this afternoon. They had
been playing 'Peer Gynt' ('Anitra's Dance' etc) on the gramophone,
and I was feeling almost as if I was what I once was. No I am not a
bit dismal. It is very unlikely I shall succeed in getting back for a
week or two.

I am quite all right in my mathematics and most of the practical
work—except that in my present indoor work I am getting stale.
I never speak a word of French now, even to get pears from a
village shop—I go without them.

I've only once heard from Mother. I fear she can't write. I
know. But I hope she is not worrying steadily.

My address is quite all right. You could only do harm by adding
letters or figures.

I wonder what you are having in Thorp's compilation? Shall I
see it? I read Frost's 'Snow' in 'Mountain Interval' lately but that
is all, and a Sonnet or two as I go to sleep.

Yours ever
Edward Thomas

March 1   St David's Day

My dear Eleanor,   The ginger came. All of 244 had a good dip
into it and there was still some left in the tin. It was very good and

it was still more good of you to send it. Thank you. Next day Helen wrote to say you really were coming to High Beech at last. I am expecting to hear now that you did. Well, I expect to return to 244 in a day or two. They know I don't want to stay here and a successor is being interviewed today, so that I shall soon cease to be a glorified lacky or humble adjutant to an old Indian colonel perplexed in the extreme. It has been a useful experience. I have got used to the telephone and I have seen how things are done and not done at Headquarters. Incidentally too I have been in the midst of quite a noisy artillery give and take. You can't imagine the noise this makes in a city. I don't pretend I liked it. Sometimes I found myself fancying that if only the enemy pointed the gun like this ———— instead of like this _____ he would land a shell on the dinner table and send us to a quieter place. However he didn't. 244 is just going into action with its own guns and I wish I were there. Soon I believe I shall be. I haven't heard of your R.F.C. man Haslam yet. The R.F.C. was unlucky here 2 days ago. They had 4 planes brought down and officers killed. I saw 2 of them, one with the tank burning white as it flopped down. The 'old Hun' as the Colonel always calls him is 'confoundedly cheeky' with his planes in these parts. We are wondering now if the enemy is going to retire from this front. It will be strange walking about in the ghastly village which was the first I saw of the enemy's ground, a silent still village of ruined houses and closegrown tall trees stark and dark lining a road above the trenches. It was worse than any deserted brickworks or mine. It looked in another world from ours, even from the scarred world in which I stood. In a curious way its very name now always calls up the thing I saw and the way I felt as I saw it. The name resembles a name in Malory, especially in its English pronunciation and this also gives a certain tone to the effect it had. I see it lining the brow of a gradual hill halfway up which is the English line with the German above it. The houses and trees dense and then to right and left only trees growing thinner till at last the ridge sweeping away is bare for some miles. But this is E. T.'s vein. Goodbye. Keep well and write soon.

Yours ever
Edward Thomas

Victor Haslam was the friend to whom three years later I dedicated *Martin Pippin in the Apple-Orchard*. He had written to me from the Front to thank me for keeping his spirits up by my nonsense rhymes of London Town in *Punch*, and on one of his leaves had come to tea with us in Fellows Road. Before the war he was a schoolmaster in Horsham. A household of his best friends lived near Billingshurst in Adversane, where I went to see them. The lovely name wove itself into *Martin Pippin* when, later in the year, I began to write its medley of love-stories and interludes, which I sent one by one to Victor Haslam in France. In 1920 J. D. Beresford read for Collins this fantasy written to amuse a soldier of thirty and the book was accepted and published at that level. It has always surprised me that, over forty years, *Martin Pippin in the Apple-Orchard* has come to be regarded as a book for young children. The book was not even begun at the time I mentioned Victor Haslam's name in one of my letters, in case he and Edward came across each other. They would have been congenial.

March 8

My dear Eleanor, Another letter from you today. I think I already owed you one, but was waiting for the Fortnum and Mason to arrive. It hasn't done so yet, so I won't wait any longer, though I doubt if I can do much tonight. I have become rather fed up by this job. It has meant a lot of idle cold hours indoors, a lot of dissatisfaction with myself and some with other people. The Colonel here, though a charming and often entertaining man, is very tyrannical and I have done many trivial things that annoyed me to have to do. Also the nights have been disturbing. I must expect that, but of course artillery in a city is exceptionally noisy. As a matter of fact though I fall asleep very quickly both on putting out my candle and after being wakened up by the fear of God. You mustn't joke about leave. There is no leave for anyone in this army, neither for men who have been out 9 months nor for men whose wives are dying. If I come back it will be wounded or at the end of the war, I don't mind which. However I am leaving here today (March 9) to return to 244 and am as pleased with that as with anything at this moment. I had to sit up late last night for despatches and have had a rotten sort of morning and am fretting to pack and go. It was wretched here last night too, as the Colonel lost his temper with the Interpreter whom he despises as a Frenchman and said 'We'll change the subject, you rather annoy me.' The silence, the

looking at the plate, and then the trickling attempts at renewing conversation, and the Colonel looking at us each in turn to see what we
were thinking—it was amusing but it doesn't really help, this sort of
thing. This is a poor letter for you. I hope it will find you in fine
weather in your cottage garden and able to imagine me much better
off than in this belated frost.

Maitland ——

Hooper is still in England, so I suppose he got my letter and
may write again. Goodbye.

Yours ever
Edward Thomas

I have heard from Frost—or Helen did, saying he had found a
pushbike, but too late, I suspect.

Kenneth Hooper, still in England, never in fact left it.
His story is an odd one. Edward was the first to go, and
Kenneth was to follow. The day before his Company sailed he
was knocked down by a motor-bus and carried unconscious to
hospital. By the time he came to and remembered who he was
his draft was in France; and when he was fit enough to present
himself to the authorities, they informed him that he too was in
France. His absence from the Company had not been noted;
the records confirmed that he was now serving his country
overseas. Protest was useless; military regulations cannot be
knocked down by a single motor-bus. Kenneth walked out of
Headquarters as free as if he were dead, and went back to
farming and dog-breeding for the rest of the war.

My next letter is missing from an empty envelope post-
marked March 14th. Perhaps the to-and-fro between Fellows
Road and Gillman's Cottage accounted for some mislayings.
Letters and parcels had also been straying in France.

March 18

My dear Eleanor,   Your parcel has come and the Hun has retired.
Those are the latest things. The stupid F and M directed the parcel
to me as R.F.A. so of course the Army wouldn't hear of it, but
apparently G for F did the trick. And it brought a letter too,
which of course was what I liked best, even tho I had one the day
before yesterday. Oh, and I found the one I thought I had lost.
The Hun has gone back though, which of course is not really good

or bad news, but pleases me because we shan't fight the battle in a city. I dreaded that. And now I shall be in a dug-out near that ghastly village over there that I told you of. I don't mind what happens just now. It was a lovely day yesterday and today is determined to be so I am only wondering how the pioneers will be suffering as they bridge the trenches with roads obliterated by them. I was in the O.P. yesterday I suppose for the last time as it is now useless, only showing us our own country. We shall be shifting any moment onwards and out of this place. But as I say it's a lovely day—I have at last got my old artist boots and am perfectly comfortable for the first time out here—and I have done 2 shoots and am due for a few idle hours. Now the larks shall have No Man's Land and the pairs of magpies no longer run any risk—they didn't know they did before. And the bat can go to sleep again in his shed till it is settled spring. I am so glad about your cottage and garden. They sound just the perfection of what I am keeping entirely out of my mind now. It is easier to imagine our orchard restored to its orchardliness; for we shall certainly leave it and go up closer. To imagine England is as impossible as to eat your parcel on March 3. Now I must write and tell Helen about this move. She will be glad also that the battle is likely to be postponed. Goodbye. I forgot to say I am glad you liked the Shepherd's Life. I agree with you about it. It is more a book than any of his other English country volumes. And the poaching over the snow is perfect. It is equal to the best of Jefferies in that vein.

Yours ever
Edward Thomas

I ordered another parcel from Fortnum and Mason, to be in time for Easter Sunday which fell on April 8th. It contained nothing but Cox's Pippins, which Edward liked above all other apples, and apples above all other fruit; but as in my Easter parcels Edward had always had a chocolate egg for himself, I asked for one in silver-paper to be placed among the apples near the top of the case.

March 22
My dear Eleanor, I am glad you get my letters quickly, tho yours still take nearly a week. I found one yesterday when I got back from 24 hours in the new front line. I read your letter, washed, etc., and slept for 16 hours. It was most interesting and amusing as well as

infinitely tiring—I had to stand up in mud, wet and cold all night watching hostile flashes and listening to shells which I have learnt not to worry about when they are going over and not coming to me or near. The time hasn't come for field postcards yet. We are still at the edge of the town and have no definite news when or where we move. So I am still in the orchard. The old Frenchwoman probably left it to live in a safe cellar at the edge of the town. This place hasn't a safe cellar. Also I suppose a battery coming here made it unfit for her to stay. You have heard now that I collared that F and M parcel. I did not get any stomach-ache from it. The muscatels and almonds are just the things for my 24 hours in an observation post. I hope Hooper gets his paper. He is lucky to be there and not here. At least I am sure he thinks so. It would be fun to have somebody like him—I mean him, because there is nobody like him—out here. You know that village I told you about, the ghastly place, well it is just near there that I observe. I shall be sleeping in it soon, I expect. The Hun fires into it all night. When I was in the front trench, all night long his shell came whistling over to roost in ——, like flights of birds. You have often heard of the mud out here, haven't you? Well, I have been in it. It is what you have heard. You nearly pull your leg off, and often your boot off, at each step in the worst places—the stiff soft clay sucks round the boot at each step. The telephone wires are deep in this and have to be repaired in the dark. Imagine it. Now I have to go. Goodbye.

> Yours ever,
> Edward Thomas

The next letter is the last but one I received during his lifetime, and it means more to me than any he ever wrote.

March 27

My dear Eleanor

As everybody is sleepier than I and I am alone I am going to drink hot brandy and water with you for a quarter of an hour. The gramophone (and Raymond Jeremy) is silent, and the guns are mostly half a mile off or more, and nothing is coming over. But these are busy times. Again the battle is promised us and we long to be into it, I suppose because then it will be nearer over. We are up late and down early. We do all kinds of things. Today I solemnly took 10 men and an N.C.O. and a trench cart to steal a small truck for carrying shells on rails. I had to guide them and stand by officially as if it were an official act while they loaded the cart and marched off. The other things I did were more technical, and in doing them I dashed about over copse and made extra paths that the Hun will photograph. Just for 5 minutes Thorburn and I looked for primroses—in vain among the moss and ashtrees. We have to cut off 10 feet from the tops of the prettiest birchtrees, because they are dangerously in our way. Not one shell—touch wood—has fallen into the copse yet, though a quarter of a mile off they crack every day.

Yet we have pleasant and even merry hours and moments. We are kind to one another often. And we do eat well, in spite of the loss of that parcel, for the one that came from F. & M. was certainly not the one you spoke of. It contained sweets and muscatels and almonds and tinned paste and soup tablets. It contained also the wrapper of the originally misdirected parcel to explain the delay. You send what you like. Muscatels and almonds are what I like best, and fruit fresh or dried of any kind. Best of all is to have my pockets fat with your letters as they are now. I was nearly forgetting to thank you for more ginger and several kinds of sweets. They were very good. I ate some of them in the sun at lunch in the O.P. the other day, sitting on some wooden steps till I suppose the Hun got envious and shelled me away. It is walking up to or among ruined houses—gable ends all big holes and piles of masonry round and splintered walnut—that I dislike most, with a lowering sky like this evening's. I keep feeling that I should enjoy it more if I knew I would survive it. I can't help allowing it to trouble me, but it doesn't prey on me and I have no real foreboding, only occasional trepidation and anxiety. The men are better but then they are comrades and I am usually alone or with them. I wish that what is coming would be more than an incident—the battle of —— Still I can't wait a great while, though of course what is coming is to be worse than anything I know so far. It is worse for you and for Helen and Mother, I know. I wish I could keep back more of what I feel, but you mustn't think it is often fear or ever dread for more than a moment.

You will be in your cottage by the time this arrives with all your pretty things. I wish I could like more pretty things—the only one I like is that gavotte from Ambrose Thomas's 'Mignon'. I shall get it played now and go to bed. Good night.   Yours ever
                                                   Edward Thomas.

In those two words 'for you', Edward laid by his reserve for the only time in our friendship, and allowed me to know that he knew how much I loved him.

March 30

My dear Eleanor, Another penultimate letter before I shall be unable to write from press of work. And first I must thank you for sending the apples and also for the apples themselves, which arrove today.

It was a good post, a parcel also from Mother and letters from Helen and Mother—there was one from you yesterday which I believe I must have answered. I have just looked at your letter again and I see you ask if I prefer things that can't be pooled. Perhaps I do, but perhaps I had better not. Everything is useful, and will be especially in the time to come when I have to take up food for perhaps considerably over 24 hours and pig it in noise and darkness and worse. Subalterns are told nothing but I happen to know what is intended, only not what difference this rain may make. I say this rain, but a most lovely cold bright evening, clear and still, has just passed, with many blackbirds singing. I fancy though that the Easter weather is not really beginning yet. I wish it was. I should welcome a warm night. Tomorrow I rather fear I shall have nowhere at all to shelter in, and no fire.

But nothing is so hard as the days of hanging about seeing that the men work like one I had 2 days ago.

You will hear soon enough about what is doing, before I can tell you.

We have got a stray dog here, a big hairy bundled old thing, who likes us all and the fire too and stays in most of the time. Horton gives him bars of chocolate and often remarks that he's a lovely creature.

The town is catching it badly now and we are well away—touch wood—though we aren't in a paradise or the bagpipes wouldn't have played what they did last night. The crossings and corners are dirty places. But the Hun must be confounded with our numbers, though you might think he couldn't fire without hurting more than the open fields. Luckily he often does. He bangs away at one part [of ?] the beautiful grass and we can feel safe in another not far off. It isn't nice, though, going up in the cold dawn. If only one could keep warm without being burdened with clothes and all sorts of ornaments—glasses, maps, waterbottles, haversacks, gas-helmets, periscopes etc., so that a trenchcoat isn't wide enough, and if you have to throw yourself down you feel like an old woman home from marketing and still more so when you get up—while you on shore and a great many more are sleeping warm and dry— oh. Don't forget your old houseboat mate, Fol-de-rol-de-riddle-fol-de-rol-de-ri-do. Who is ever yours

Edward Thomas

This sudden throw-back to the summer of 1913 and our house-boat party with Stacy and Gertrude Aumonier, this out-break into a sea-shanty we had often sung together, is too un-like him to be a spontaneous bubbling, as he made it seem. I think, as the day of the battle drew nearer, and with it the possibility of his death, something loosened the strict guard he kept on himself in his letters. Some men when they write to their friends give their full harvest; Edward harvested himself only in his poems. But to those who knew and loved him best, the gleanings dropped on the surface of his letters tell almost as much. The rollicking mood, induced to lift a shadow from the last words he might write or I might read—induced deliberately at a moment when he could not have felt rollicking, is sharply revealing because it was so uncustomary. They *were* the last words I read during his lifetime, though not the last he wrote me.

On April the 9th I was alone in Gillman's Cottage. Joe and Fan and little Joan had gone back to London; I was to follow in a day or two. Spring had come at last, and once the snows went it came all together in one glorious burst of flowers, from the earliest whose season had been checked by the long winter to those whose season was barely due—celandine, wind-flowers, primroses, blue and white violets, cowslips, bluebells, bee-orchis, and cow-parsley flooded the orchard under the low-branched apple-trees whose foam of blossom met the tide of blossom from the grass. I never remembered such another spring, such flowers, such birds, such stars in such warm clear skies, come together so late and so soon in the year. At night in the cottage, among my 'pretty things', I wrote to Edward once more before I left; and when I posted my letter at Billingshurst Station I did not know that another was on its way to Gillman's from Helen in High Beech, where she had received the news that broke her heart. I went blithely in ignorance to London, and in Fellows Road found an envelope addressed in Viola Meynell's delicate hand. The family was sitting at the supper-table; still standing, I opened the letter.

'My darling Eleanor, I can hardly bear this for you . . .'

I made some sort of cry as I dropped the note. Somebody said, 'What is it?' I said, 'Edward', and went upstairs to my room where I went on standing in a state beyond feeling. The door opened and my mother came to me, and stood there with her mouth trembling and her eyes full of tears. I heard myself saying to her very clearly, 'Mother, it was never as you feared with Edward and me'. I say *I heard myself*, for I seemed sepa-rated from my body's movements and words and actions. I remember her saying, 'Nellie——' pleadingly. After a little while we went back to the dining-room, and I sat down with the others. I never forgot Harry's quiet injunction the day our Father died: 'We've got to eat, you know': at times when I've known I mustn't break down. When I had eaten I said I was going to see Viola, whom I expected to find at the Meynell flat over Burns and Oates at the corner of Orchard Street. I climbed the many stairs and rang the bell at the door which closed in the top floor. It was opened by Olivia, whose face when she saw me filled with a look of compassion I have never forgotten. She said that Viola had gone to Greatham. I asked what they had heard. 'We don't know anything, Eleanor, only that Edward Thomas's death is reported in the papers.' I went back home, to wait for the next news. It came in the morning, in Helen's letter forwarded from the Billingshurst post-office. She did not say much, only that she had had the telegram, was coming to her sister Mary's in Chiswick, and would be returning almost at once to High Beech, and wanted me to go with her. I got in touch with Mary and was told the train Helen would take to Loughton next day. We were to meet at the Liverpool Street ticket-barrier.

I was waiting for her there when she arrived, not with the laughing face and hurrying steps with which she always ran a little to a meeting. She was very pale, said 'Eleanor' in a faint voice as we passed through, and found a corner seat in a carriage. She sat in it, and I by her, between her pale face and the incoming travellers. We held each other's hands. Suddenly in a great burst came her sobs and tears. 'Don't let me cry, don't let me cry,' she sobbed. I put my arms round her and held her while she wept, and nobody looked. Presently she whispered, 'I asked you to come because I thought I could comfort you—oh Eleanor, you'll have to comfort me.'

I stayed in High Beech, for the next two weeks. I slept with her. Grief like hers was shattering thousands of homes all over the world, but I had never before been identified with such grief. My own seemed to be obliterated in it. I took responsibility, as best I could, for the house and children; the meals and shopping, and whatever has to be thought of in a home. After a fortnight Irene, Helen's elder sister came, and I went back to Fellows Road.

A strange thing happened. Mary, talking one day to a neighbour in Chiswick, mentioned by chance that her sister was Edward Thomas's widow. The woman, astonished, exclaimed, 'Why, the Sergeant of his Company is staying with us now, on leave.' Helen came immediately to town and asked me to meet her at Mary's, so that we could hear together all he had to tell us. We sat on a sofa, the man on a chair near us, speaking simply, answering her questions in a grave respectful voice. He spoke of the perfect trust Edward's men had in him, and how, when it was his duty as an officer to instruct them on matters of conduct and morals he did so as a man like one of themselves; they brought their letters to him to be censored confident that their secrets were safe with him. And then the Sergeant spoke of the Battle of Arras.

'At the end of the day when the battle was over we had the Huns on the run, and the plain was full of our men shouting and singing and dancing. We thought we had won the war! Mr. Thomas came up from the dug-out behind his gun and leaned in the opening filling his clay pipe. One of the Huns turned as he was running and shot a stray shot, and Mr. Thomas fell. It was all over in an instant. I went out to the men and called, "Men, we've lost our best officer." The cry went up—"Not Mr. Thomas?" and there was no more shouting that day.'

When Edward fell he was still holding his half-filled clay. It did not break, and came back to Helen with his other things. She gave it to Mervyn.

This was the story as nearly as I remember it in the Sergeant's own words. But my memory had misled me about the stray shot, it was a stray shell. When Helen came to know Edward's Captain, Franklin Lushington, he told her that as Edward stood by his dugout lighting his pipe all the Germans had retreated, but a last shell they sent over passed so close to him that the blast of air stopped his heart. 'He told me,' Helen writes, 'there was no wound and his beloved body was not injured. This was borne out by the fact that when the contents of his pockets were returned to me—a bundle of letters, a note-book and the Shakespeare Sonnets I had given him, they were all strangely creased as though subject to some terrible pressure, most strange to see. There was no wound or disfigurement at all. He just died standing there in the early morning after the battle.' Captain Lushington told Helen that Edward could have had a job 'back and safe, but he chose the dangerous front observation post.'

Here is the letter which Captain Lushington wrote to Helen on April 10th when Edward was buried.

April 10th, 1917.

Dear Mrs. Thomas,

    You will have heard by now from Mr. Thorburn of the death in action of your husband. I asked him to write immediately we knew about it yesterday, but delayed writing myself until the funeral, from which I have just returned.

I cannot express to you adequately in words how deep our sympathy is for you and your children in your great loss. These things go too deep for mere words. We, officers and men, all mourn our own loss. Your husband was very greatly loved in this battery, and his going has been a personal loss to each of us. He was rather older than most of the officers and we all looked up to him as the kind of father of our happy family.

He was always the same, quietly cheerful, and ready to do any job that was going with the same steadfast unassuming spirit. The day before his death we were rather heavily shelled and he had a very narrow shave. But he went about his work quite quietly and ordinarily as if nothing was happening. I wish I could convey to you the picture of him, a picture we had all learnt to love, of the old clay pipe, gum boots, oilskin coat, and steel helmet.

With regard to his actual death you have probably heard the details. It should be of some comfort to you to know that he died at a moment of victory from a direct hit by a shell, which must have killed him outright without giving him a chance to realise anything, —a gallant death for a very true and gallant gentleman.

We buried him in a little military cemetery a few hundred yards from the battery: the exact spot will be notified to you by the parson. As we stood by his grave the sun came and the guns round seemed to stop firing for a short time. This typified to me what stood out most in your husband's character—the spirit of quiet, sunny, unassuming cheerfulness.

When I get to England again I shall be happy to come and tell you anything more you'd like to know. My address is The White House, Heath End, Farnham, Surrey, and I will write you in case you would like to see me.

Yours very sincerely,
Franklin Lushington
(Major Comdg. 244 Siege Battery, R.G.A.)

Please do not bother to answer this as I know how busy you will be. I shall understand.

*

Edward's last letter of all came after his death. It was begun in ink, six days before the battle, and finished in pencil five days later.

April 3

My dear Eleanor I didn't discover the Egg till Easter Monday, because I was taking apples out one by one from a corner I had nibbled out. So now I must write again to thank you for an Easter Egg. It was such a lovely morning Easter Monday, though I

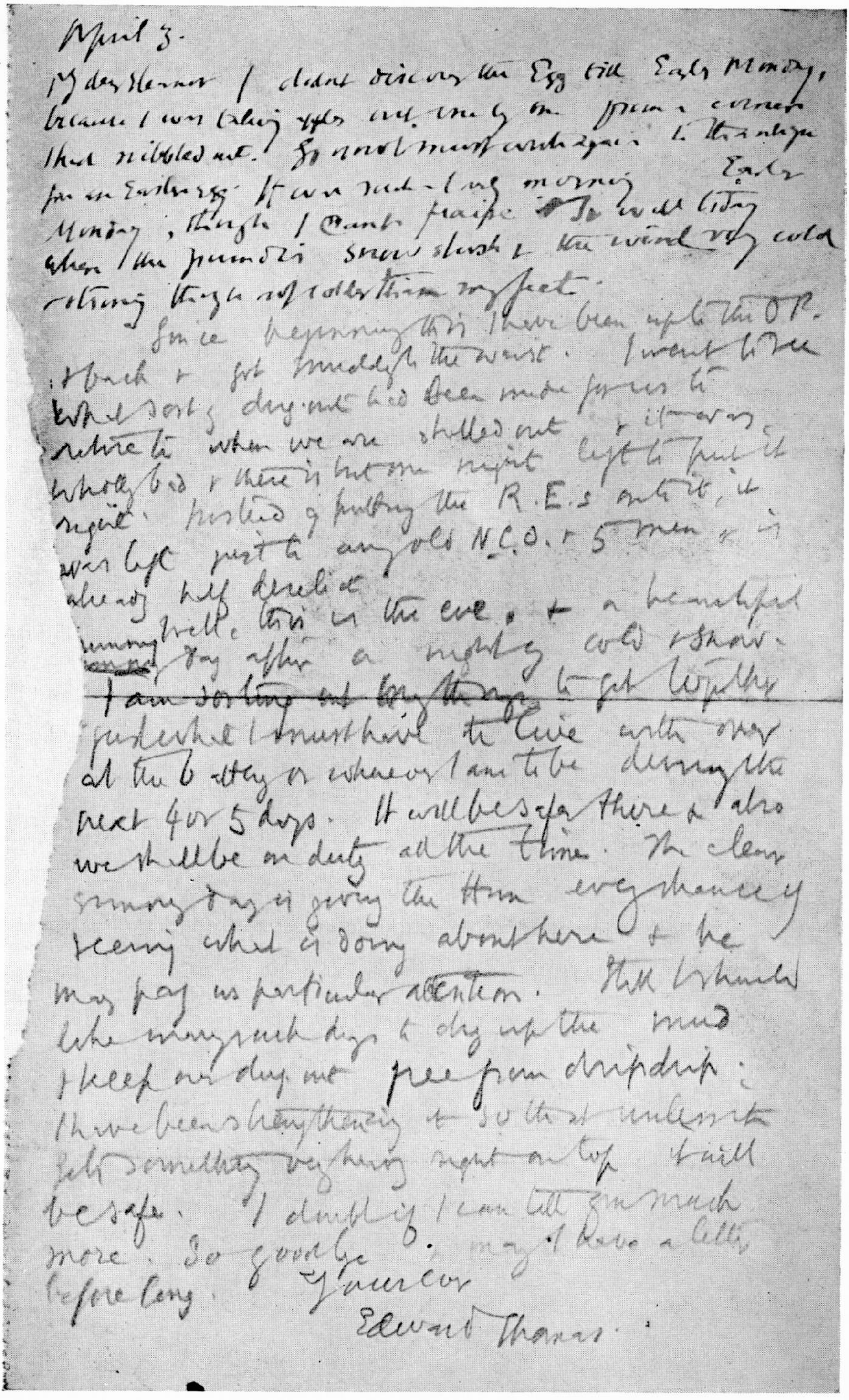

April 3.

My dear Eleanor I didn't discover the Egg till Early Monday, because I was taking off all the wrappings on the paper corner that nibbled out. So now I must write again to thank you for an Easter egg. It was such a long morning Early Monday, though I can't praise it so well today when the ground is snow slush & the wind very cold & strong through softer collar than my feet.

Since beginning this I have been up to the O.P. & back & got muddy to the waist. I went to see what sort of dug-out had been made for us to retire to when we are shelled out & it was wholly bad & there is but one night left to put it right. Instead of putting the R.E.s onto it, it was left just to an old N.C.O. & 5 men & is already half derelict.

Well, this is the eve, & a beautiful ~~sunny~~ day after a mighty cold & snow. ~~I am sorting out my things~~ to get together just what I must have to live with over at the battery or wherever I am to be during the next 4 or 5 days. It will be safer there & also we shall be on duty all the time. The clear sunny day is giving the Hun every chance of seeing what is doing about here & he may pay us particular attention. Still I should like many such days to dry up the mud & keep our dug-out free from drip drip: I have been strengthening it so that unless it gets something very heavy right on top it will be safe. I doubt if I can tell you much more. So goodbye & may I have a letter before long.

Yours ever

Edward Thomas

THE LAST LETTER FROM FRANCE

can't praise it so well today when the ground is snow slush and the wind very cold though not colder than my feet.

(So far in ink; then pencil to the end)

Since beginning this I have been up to the O.P. and back and got muddy to the waist. I went to see what sort of dug-out had been made for us to retire to when we are shelled out, and it was wholly bad, and there is but one night left to put it right. Instead of putting the R.E.'s on to it, it was left just to any old N.C.O. and 5 men and is already half derelict.

Well, this is the eve, and a beautiful sunny day after a night of cold and snow. I am sorting out my things to get together just what I must have to live with over at the battery or wherever I am to be during the next 4 or 5 days. It will be safer there and also we shall be on duty all the time. The clear sunny day is giving the Hun every chance of seeing what is doing about here and he may pay us particular attention. Still I should like many such days to dry up the mud and keep our dug-out free from dripdrip. I have been strengthening it so that unless it gets something very heavy right on top it will be safe. I doubt if I can tell you much more. So goodbye. May I have a letter before long.

Yours ever
Edward Thomas.

The eve of the Battle of Arras was April 8th, so the pencilled lines, with 'but one night left to put it right', were written on Easter Sunday. I read with bewilderment those odd sentences the letter begins with. 'I didn't discover the Egg till Easter Monday'—(but Easter Monday was still a week away). 'It was such a lovely morning, Easter Monday'—(but this is still Easter Sunday, this is the eve). I don't try to understand them. Two of my letters were on the way to him. The third he did not get was written from Gillman's Cottage the night he died.

Ten years afterwards Bertie said to me, 'I wake in the night and cry for Edward still'.

Index